He is willing. He is able. He restores.

U-TURN

Find Rest in God's Grace
Through a U-Turn Back to God

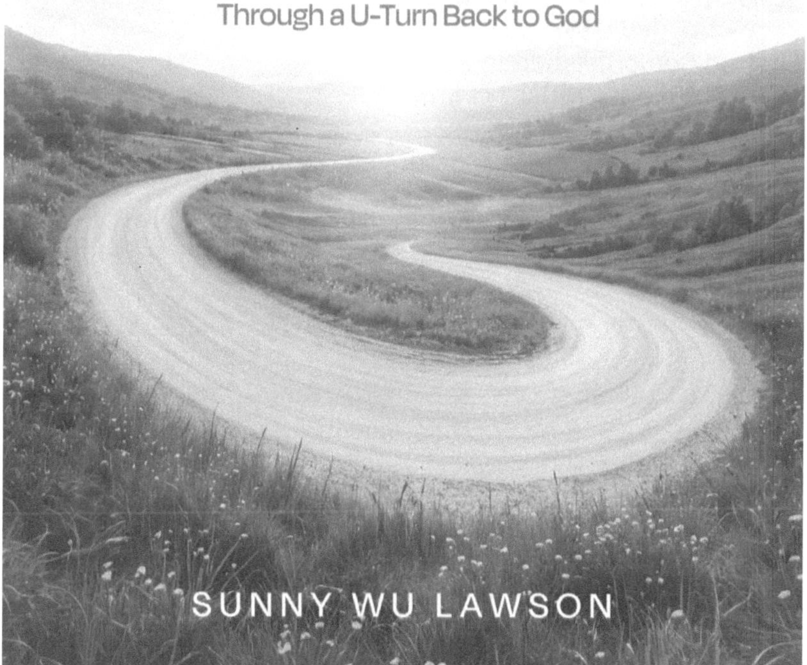

SUNNY WU LAWSON

Because of the dynamic nature of the Internet, any web addresses or links contained in this book may have changed since publication and may no longer be valid.

Paperback ISBN-13: 979-8-9868682-6-4

eBook ISBN: 979-8-9868682-7-1

First edition published in 2026.
Published in the United States.

Published by 415 Leadership Inc.
100 Mall Parkway, Suite 500
Wentzville, Missouri 63385

Visit the author's website at: https://www.sunnylawson.com

"I have had the privilege of watching Sunny live the U-Turn long before she ever wrote it. What you hold in your hands is not a theory. It is a testimony. I have seen this framework reshape her inner life, and I have watched her walk many others through the same journey with grace, precision, and the kind of authority that only comes from having made the turn yourself. This message is not just for a Sunday morning. It is for every person who has ever felt the gap between the life they are living and the life they were created for. As her husband, I can say with confidence: this is the real thing."

— Erik Lawson

U-Turn

Find Rest in God's Grace
Through a U-Turn Back to God

By Sunny Wu Lawson

Table of Contents

Foreword

In a world that accelerates with each passing year, it is easy to drift from the life God designed us for, life in relationship with Him, without even realizing it. Our bodies keep moving. Our calendars remain full. Yet our hearts quietly run empty. Scripture interrupts this pattern with a sacred command: "Be still, and know that I *am* God." (Psalm 46:10 New King James Version NKJV).

This is not merely an invitation for quiet moments; it is a rescue call for the overwhelmed soul. Many of us live in constant motion, carrying the weight of responsibility, leadership, family, ministry, and expectation. Somewhere along the way, we learn to function without truly listening. We adapt. We cope. We survive. And slowly, almost imperceptibly, we begin to drift. Fear begins to crowd the space where faith once led. Self-reliance replaces trust. Old patterns attempt to return to places where the Spirit has already begun His healing work. Often, a U-Turn does not begin with a crisis, but with an awakening, the quiet realization that something within us has become misaligned. I know this drift personally. I have lived it.

This is where this book begins.

A U-Turn is not driven by shame; it is led by the Spirit. It is repentance in its truest form, a Spirit-led return of the heart to God. It is the courage to stop striving in our own strength and to allow Him to restore us to alignment with His voice, His truth, and the way He created us to live in Him. God did not design us to live continually hurried, reactive, or spiritually fragmented lives. He created us for communion, clarity, and continual return.

For many years, I grieved what I believed I had lost. But God, in His kindness, reframed my story. He revealed this unshakable truth: in His hands, nothing is wasted (Romans

8:28 NKJV), not our pain, not our detours, not even the seasons we thought were lost. Every U-Turn, whether dramatic or quiet, becomes a doorway to restoration when it is surrendered to Him.

This journey often unfolds in seasons—**awakening, alignment, transformation, and multiplication**. Each season invites us deeper into communion with God and into the life He has always intended for us. The U-Turn Open Network is not a program; it is a sacred space. A place to slow down, reflect, and intentionally apply truth. At its core, this book is an invitation to create unhurried space with God. While God can move in a moment, transformation is often formed over time, in stillness, surrender, and the simple prayer: *"Lord, speak. I am listening."*

Sometimes all it takes is one quiet moment, one open Bible, one honest heart, and one small U-Turn at a time.

My prayer is that as you journey through these pages, you will hear the gentle voice of the Father saying, *"This is who I created you to be. Walk with Me, and you will become* who I created you to be in Me.*"* This book is not a map to perfection. It is an invitation back to the Father.

Sunny Wu Lawson

Acknowledgments

This book did not emerge from my efforts alone. It was formed through love, prayer, and the faithful presence of those God placed in my life. To each person who walked beside me on this journey, thank you.

To my husband, thank you for being woven into every layer of this book. From the earliest ideas to the final pages, your wisdom, spiritual support, and unwavering love have been a constant source of strength. You carried confidence when mine felt unsteady and saw purpose when I could only see process. I thank God for you, deeply and continually.

To my parents, my sister, and in loving memory of my brother, as well as our extended family, thank you for the story we share and the foundation you have given me. Even the difficult places became soil where God, in His faithfulness, brought healing and redemption.

To Coach Duke Matlock and Pastor Jae Chung, as well as those who helped bring this book to life, thank you for your guidance, encouragement, and faithful support throughout this journey.

To my editor, Betty Norlin, thank you for your excellence, patience, and care in refining this work while preserving its heart.

To my church family, ministry team, and the friends, mentors, and brothers and sisters in Christ who have prayed, encouraged, and walked with me through seasons of growth, thank you.

And above all, to my Heavenly Father, thank You for graciously redeeming and restoring my story, for leading me with gentleness, and for turning broken places into a testimony of Your grace.

Dedication

To my parents,

Thank you for the countless sacrifices, the quiet endurance, and the love that helped shape the foundation of my life. Your strength has shaped me more than you know, and your courage is woven through every chapter of my story.

To my husband,

Your steady love has been a place of deep safety for my heart. Thank you for seeing me, believing in me, and standing with me through valleys and victories.

To my late brother,

Your memory lives gently within me. Your life and memory remain part of every chapter of my story.

Introduction

There are seasons when God speaks gently, and seasons when He allows what is unsteady in our lives to be shaken so that it can no longer remain hidden. I have lived through both. Over time, I have learned that whether His leading feels quiet or disruptive, His motive is the same: love—a faithful love that calls us back to truth, restores our hearts to Him, and steadies us when everything familiar feels uncertain.

This book was born out of that faithful love.

It did not begin as a finished message, but as an awakening. What felt like disruption was an invitation. God was not bringing disruption to punish me; He was making space so something truer could take root. The systems I relied on for stability and identity no longer held, and He began revealing a deeper reality. I believed in Him, yet many of my decisions were shaped more by fear, performance, and survival than by my identity in Christ. Fear, I discovered, can be subtle. At times, it disguises itself as wisdom, responsibility, or even strength. It hides in habits, reactions, and the need for control. God brought these patterns into the light not to condemn me, but to restore me.

Scripture echoes this clearly:

> "Nevertheless I have *this* against you, that you have left your first love. Remember therefore from where you have fallen; repent and do the first works." (Revelation 2:4–5a NKJV).

This is not condemnation; it is an invitation to return.

As my roles shifted, deeper questions surfaced. When familiar identifiers fell away, I had to ask who I was, apart from them. God was not only redirecting my assignment but realigning my heart. Through prayer, Scripture, and intimacy with Jesus, fear gradually lost its influence. I learned that surrender is not weakness; it restores our surrender to the Lord who leads with perfect love. Jesus said, "without Me you can do nothing." (John 15:5 NKJV). Apart from Him, even our best efforts can lead to striving. In Him, we are invited into a life that is led, sustained, and transformed by His presence.

We are living in a time of acceleration and distraction. Many sincere believers are spiritually weary and disconnected from rest and intimacy with God. What we ultimately need is not merely another strategy, but a return, a U-Turn of the heart rooted in Scripture, shaped by our identity in Christ, and guided by the Holy Spirit.

The U-Turn journey often unfolds through four movements: Repent, Receive, Renew, and Reproduce. Each one restores our hearts layer by layer until love for God once again becomes central in how we live and respond. This book is not a self-improvement plan. It is an invitation to slow down, listen deeply, and allow God to realign what has quietly drifted. Writing it has been an act of obedience. Living it has been an act of surrender.

Every true U-Turn begins with His invitation and our response. Every lasting transformation is sustained by His love and empowered by His Spirit.

Part I — AWAKENING

Realizing We Need a U-Turn

> "The LORD *is* near to those who have a broken heart, And saves such as have a contrite spirit." — (Psalm 34:18 NKJV).

Every U-Turn begins with awakening, a growing awareness that leads us toward repentance. Before direction can change, awareness must come first. We cannot turn back to God in areas when we refuse to see or hear what remains hidden. Awakening is the moment God begins to open our eyes, inviting us to see with compassion and clarity what has been shaping our lives.

Often, this begins in seasons of difficulty or disruption. What feels like loss or disruption can become a doorway to clarity. In God's hands, pain is not wasted, but redeemed for His purposes, awakening a deeper hunger for truth. These chapters invite you to slow down and reflect.

Awakening is not about self-criticism, but about holy awareness. It reveals where fear, striving, or distraction may have begun to take the place of intimacy with God. By the end, you will begin to sense where God is inviting you to turn, as your heart is softened and prepared to turn back to Him.

Chapter 1 — The Breaking That Became the Beginning

"Awakening is not always about finding God for the first time. It is about realizing He has been near all along."

Awakening: When the Old Life No Longer Holds

I did not expect a new beginning in my life to come through loss. I believed growth would come through effort, clarity, and doing the right things well. For a time, that belief seemed to work. My life was marked by stability, ambition, and visible progress. I trusted that if I prepared well, stayed disciplined, and made wise choices, the future would remain secure.

Then the life I understood began to fall apart. It did not unravel all at once, but fractured quietly and persistently, leaving me disoriented and exhausted. What broke was not only my circumstances, but the identity I had built around strength, competence, and control. The things I relied on to define my worth no longer held, and without them, I did not know who I was. This is often how awakening begins. Not always with clarity, but often through disruption, sometimes through collapse. God often awakens us not by strengthening the systems we depend on, but by exposing the ones that cannot carry us forward. What once felt stable loses its grip, and what once defined us stops working. In that space, something deeper begins to surface.

What followed was not a strong season. I was tired, confused, and unsure of God's nearness. Stillness did not begin through discipline alone, but through reaching the end of myself. I questioned what I believed, resisted what I could not understand, and carried a longing I could not quiet. Yet even there, God was present.

Awakening is not always about finding God for the first time. It is about realizing He has been near all along.

In the silence of unanswered questions, God reveals Himself not as distant or demanding, but as patient, attentive, and faithful. He does not rush the process of healing. He invites. He creates space where performance ends and honesty begins.

This chapter is an honest beginning. It is not about having answers, but about allowing collapse to create space and longing to lead us toward truth. What feels like breaking becomes the place where God begins rebuilding us from the inside out. Awakening teaches us that breaking is not failure; it is exposure. It reveals what can no longer sustain us and prepares the heart to return. Before direction is restored and transformation takes root, the soul must awaken to its need for God.

The U-Turn begins here, not with strength, but with surrender; not with movement, but with awareness; not with answers, but with the quiet realization that the life we were created for cannot be built without Him.

Country Childhood

I grew up in the countryside of central China, surrounded by farmland, animals, and a quiet that allowed childhood to unfold slowly. The sky felt endless, and the world felt safe and predictable. My older brother led by example: steady, disciplined, and kind. My sister and younger brother were my closest companions, sharing work, play, and ordinary moments that later became lifelong treasures.

We did not have much materially, but we were rich in love, stability, and what mattered most. Our home was steady. Love was consistent. Belonging was not something to earn; it was simply given. Life followed a simple rhythm of shared meals and laughter, creating a deep sense of security. I never questioned whether I was valued. I knew I was loved.

My father led with strength, discipline, and sacrifice. To him, leadership was responsibility, not position. My mother balanced him with quiet strength. She was gentle yet firm, nurturing peace within the structure my father built. Together, they shaped my understanding of work, love, respect, and resilience. Even then, I can now see that God was forming values in me that would guide every season of my life.

School Life

As I grew older, education widened my world beyond the familiar fields of home. I developed a deep love for learning, especially English. I studied it out of curiosity, not requirement. The language became a doorway to cultures, ideas, and possibilities far beyond my own experience.

During university, that curiosity deepened. I read American books on leadership, management, and personal development. Those ideas stirred vision in me and awakened a hunger for purpose. At the time, I never imagined I would live in America. Looking back, I can see that God was already preparing me, guiding me along paths I could not yet recognize.

I earned a degree in English literature and later completed a master's degree in business administration. Education played a significant role in shaping my character as well as my mind. It taught me discipline, perseverance, and confidence. Those years laid a foundation for dreams I could not yet fully name, and I trusted that preparation mattered.

Corporate Ambition

My education led me into the corporate world, where my passion for leadership and organizational growth came alive.

I was drawn to how vision becomes structure and how leadership shapes people and culture. My academic research focused on international culture and global communication, and even then, God was, in ways I could not yet see, equipping me with skills I would one day need.

I got married after completing my master's degree. At that time, life felt secure and promising. My career was advancing, leadership opportunities were opening, and I believed I understood what success looked like. I worked in international corporations, serving in Human Resources and leadership development across countries. These roles immersed me in global leadership, strategy, and human development, shaping teams and organizational culture during seasons of growth and change.

My work and travel took me across countries and cultures. I loved collaborating with people from different backgrounds and learning how culture influences leadership and communication. Each experience expanded my worldview and deepened my appreciation for diversity and innovation. Over time, I received promotions that reflected growing responsibility and influence. Corporate life taught me excellence, humility, and the complexity of leading people well. It showed me that growth is not linear and that true leadership requires continual learning.

Looking back, I can now see God's hand. Every role, every challenge, every conversation, and every season became part of God's preparation in my life. Long before I understood His purpose, God was shaping my character, strengthening my discernment, and preparing me for what He was leading me into.

Looking back, I can clearly see God's hand. Every role, every challenge, every conversation, and every season was preparation. Long before I understood His purpose, God was shaping my character, strengthening my discernment, and preparing me for the calling ahead.

When Everything Fell Apart and Purpose Began to Awaken

In 2014, at thirty-three years old, my confidence did not slowly erode. It shattered. One day I believed I understood who I was and where my life was going. The next, it felt as though everything I had built my identity upon collapsed. Life did not unravel gently. It fell apart, leaving me standing in ruins I no longer recognized.

The deepest grief lived quietly beneath everything else. During my first marriage, I experienced multiple pregnancy losses, each one beginning with hope and ending in sorrow. They were silent goodbyes to dreams I had already begun to love. With each loss, something inside me fractured. It was not only the loss of life, but the loss of the future I had imagined. In the hidden places of my heart, a painful question echoed: *What if something is wrong with me?* My marriage eventually ended for reasons that remain tender—not because they are hidden, but because some stories are sacred. Its ending dismantled more than a relationship. It dismantled my sense of security and the belief that love, if tended carefully enough, would always remain.

While my heart was still reeling, my corporate career also came to an abrupt end. The place where I had invested ambition and much of my worth disappeared almost overnight. Titles vanished. Structure fell away. The measures I once used to define value were stripped from my hands. Everything that had reinforced who I thought I was suddenly vanished.

As these losses converged, I felt myself fading. Nights were the hardest. Sleep came in fragments, if at all. Anxiety filled the silence. I questioned my worth, my choices, my future, and even God. Shame followed close behind, and isolation settled in. This was more than sadness. It was identity undone. Yet in that darkness, when I had nothing polished or spiritual to offer, something unexpected began to awaken: a prayer.

Not one shaped by habit or performance but born from desperation. Sometimes whispered. Sometimes angry. Sometimes only tears. But it returned again and again to one honest cry: "How long, O Lord?" (Psalm 13:1 NKJV).

In the breaking, God had not left me. Even there, He was present. In the midst of the breaking, He was gently revealing and loosening what I had used to define myself so He could reveal who I truly was in Him.

The Turning Point

Looking back, my U-Turn did not begin with strength or clarity. It began with exhaustion, not the kind sleep can fix, but the kind that settles deep and makes everything feel heavier than it should.

It began the moment I admitted I could no longer hold myself together. I had reached the end of my capacity. My strategies were depleted. My confidence was gone. For years, I had worked to appear steady and composed, managing emotions and controlling outcomes while quietly unraveling inside. The harder I tried to maintain order, the clearer it became that something essential had broken, and I did not know how to repair it. During that fragile season, Scripture began to meet me, not as correction, but as invitation. One verse surfaced again and again:

"Be still, and know that I *am* God." (Psalm 46:10 NKJV).

I was not still because I felt peaceful. I was still because I could not strive any longer. Stillness did not begin as discipline; it became surrender. The performing ended. The composure fell away. What I first saw as failure slowly became space, and in that space, God met me. During this time, God, in His kindness, brought someone unexpected into my life. Her name was Cathy. She did not rush me or try to fix what was broken. She listened. She was comfortable with silence. Her steady presence helped me breathe again.

She prayed with a sincerity that felt safe. She opened Scripture with tenderness, making it personal rather than distant. Faith was no longer something I performed; it became something I received. Over time, we began attending church and gathering with other believers in simple, unpolished spaces that felt healing. Some days worship brought tears. Other days I stood unsure. Even in that uncertainty, something was shifting. The walls built from self-protection began to soften.

Through Cathy's presence, Jesus no longer felt distant or reserved for the spiritually strong. He felt near, gentle, and present in my collapse rather than disappointed by it. That is why I believe so deeply in the power of Life Groups. God often meets us through people who listen, pray, and walk with us in our most vulnerable seasons. That quiet, vulnerable season became the true beginning of my U-Turn. It was not dramatic or loud, but it was real—and it changed everything.

When Longing Led Me to Truth

At the deepest point of my breaking, before anything began to heal, something unexpected surfaced within me. It was not strength, clarity, or hope. It was longing, a quiet, persistent ache that refused to leave, no matter how much I tried to distract myself or move forward.

For most of my life, I relied on answers that helped me function. I knew how to manage pressure, meet expectations, and appear steady even when things were falling apart inside. But when everything I depended on collapsed, those answers stopped working. I began to see how much of my identity and sense of worth had been shaped by performance and external stability. Those things carried me through success, but they could not carry me through loss. In that season, I did not want reassurance. I wanted truth, even if it unsettled me. Beneath the grief and exhaustion, a deeper hunger began to emerge.

I was no longer searching for solutions to fix my life. I was searching for God Himself.

I did not yet know how to trust Him. I questioned Him, resisted Him, and at times doubted His nearness. Still, I could not escape the quiet pull toward Him. I was tired of pretending I was fine and exhausted from holding myself together. I wanted a truth strong enough to hold me when everything else fell apart, and a God who would not turn away from my pain. Scripture began to meet me there, not as something I mastered, but as something that began to search my heart. Where I expected judgment, I found invitation. Where I assumed distance, I encountered patience.

"As the deer pants for the water brooks, so pants my soul for You, O God." (Psalm 42:1 NKJV).

That verse gave language to what my heart could not yet name. My soul was thirsty, not for the restoration of my old life, but for God Himself. I longed for His presence more than answers, and His truth more than certainty. Slowly, I began to understand that this longing was not weakness, but evidence that God was already at work, drawing me toward Himself. My questions turned toward God instead of inward against myself. The defenses I had built through years of self-protection began to soften.

That longing did not remove my pain, but it redirected it. Without realizing it, my hunger for truth was part of how God was preparing my heart for the transformation still to come.

The Long Slow Rebuild

Healing did not come quickly or primarily through a single powerful encounter with God. It came slowly, unfolding in layers over time. There were seasons when it felt as though He was restoring parts of my heart I did not even realize were broken. What I once expected to happen in a moment, God chose to form over time, with patience and intention.

Over the past eleven years, God has been rebuilding me from the inside out, reshaping not only what I believe about Him, but how I see myself, how I respond, and even the quiet words I speak within. Much of that inner language had been formed by fear, striving, and wounds I had never learned to name. My husband, Erik, has been a gift in this journey, walking beside me with patience and steadiness, never rushing what God was doing in me. Gradually, truth began to replace lies I did not know I carried. Peace began to take root where anxiety once ruled, and the inner chaos that had shaped me for years began to settle.

I did not change because I was strong, nor did I heal by trying harder. Most days, I felt weak and uncertain. What transformed me was God Himself, His steady presence and His patience with the process. Only later did I begin to understand that God had not destroyed my life. He allowed what had been built apart from Him to be shaken and exposed so that something truer could stand. Today, my life is no longer sustained by fear, control, or performance. It is held together by Him.

The Meaning of the Ashes

Eleven years later, I no longer say, "That was the year I lost everything." It was the year much of what was false and fragile was stripped away so that something truer, rooted in God, could begin. What felt like breaking became invitation, and what felt like silence became the place where God taught me to listen. The ashes I once thought marked the end of my story became the soil where new life quietly began to grow.

"To give them beauty for ashes..." (Isaiah 61:3 NKJV).

It was not the ending I feared, but the beginning I did not yet recognize. Only later did I understand that God had always been with me, even when I was not looking for Him. I lived for years striving in my own strength, unaware that I was already being held. There were moments when I felt completely lost, yet He protected me and, in His faithfulness, brought people into my life at the right times. Even when I did not recognize His hand, it never withdrew.

For a season, regret tried to follow me. I wondered if I had awakened too late. But God did not rush or condemn me. He remained patient and faithful. My story is not about delay. It is about being pursued by a God who does not leave. The breaking did not restore what was lost, but it awakened me. It exposed how much of my life had been built on control and self-reliance, and how fragile those foundations were. What I once called failure became clarity. This was not yet transformation, but awareness, a holy interruption that revealed my need for God as the source of life itself.

Awakening is only the beginning. Pain does not automatically produce growth, and suffering alone does not guarantee wisdom. The question that follows every breaking is this: What will we do with what has hurt us? The U-Turn does not begin by escaping pain, but by allowing God to redeem it.

In Chapter 2, *Do Not Waste Your Pain*, we turn to this question and explore how God uses suffering not as punishment, but as a teacher, and how what feels unbearable can become the ground where humility, truth, and redemption take root.

Reflection Questions

1. What past losses or failures might God be redeeming or working through to begin something new in you?
2. Where have you built your identity on success, stability, or performance, and how has that been tested?
3. What honest questions or longings have surfaced in your hardest seasons, and how might God be using them as invitations to draw you closer to Him?

4. Who has God brought into your life during times of breaking, and what has their presence revealed about His care?
5. What feels like ashes in your life right now, and what would it look like to entrust them to God?

Prayer

Lord,

You see every season of my life, including the ones I tried to walk through alone. Thank You for staying with me when things fell apart and for meeting me in exhaustion and grief. Teach me to be still and to trust You where I no longer have strength.

Take what feels broken or lost, and in Your way and timing, bring forth something true and lasting in me. Help me trust that this season is not the end, but a beginning shaped by Your love. Form in me a heart that turns toward You, even in uncertainty, and rests in Your faithful presence.

In the name of Jesus, Amen.

Chapter 2 — Do Not Waste Your Pain

> ***"Pain can become a place where God's mercy meets us, interrupting our drift and calling us back to Him."***

Chapter 2 deepens the awakening that began in the breaking. If Chapter 1 reveals what collapsed, this chapter asks a more personal and pressing question: What will we do with what has hurt us? Pain is no longer something to escape, but a meaningful signal that exposes misalignment and invites surrender. Through Scripture and lived experience, suffering is reframed as formative rather than disqualifying. Loss does not create our hidden patterns of control, performance, or self-reliance. It reveals them.

This chapter distinguishes between wasted pain and formed pain. Pain alone does not transform us. Our response does. When avoided or managed apart from God, pain can keep us stuck. When surrendered to Him, it becomes a place where humility, repentance, wisdom, and deeper intimacy begin to grow. God is able to redeem suffering that is placed in His hands. Pain is not merely punishment; in God's hands, it can become preparation in the life of a believer.

God can use seasons of loss, waiting, and unanswered questions to expose false foundations and prepare us for lasting transformation. By the end of this chapter, the question shifts from what went wrong to what God has been inviting all along, setting the stage to rediscover who we were created to be and to continue the U-Turn toward His design.

Pain as the Awakening Signal

"Before I was afflicted I went astray, But now I keep Your word." (Psalm 119:67 NKJV).

Scripture shows that pain often precedes awakening, and God, in His mercy, meets us there. David did not say affliction destroyed him; he said it redirected him. Pain revealed where his heart had drifted and realigned him with truth. The same was true for me. Pain marked the moment I could no longer pretend I was fine. Sleep grew restless, anxiety surfaced, and the strength I relied on felt fragile. In the quiet, questions I had long avoided demanded answers. Who am I without the roles I built my life around? Who am I if the future I imagined never unfolds? Pain stripped away what once stabilized me and brought me face to face with my need for God.

Throughout Scripture, awakening often begins with disruption. Jacob wrestled through the night, Joseph endured betrayal and imprisonment, and the prodigal son came to himself only after everything was gone. Pain did not disqualify them. It positioned them to see clearly. It interrupts our momentum and exposes the gap between who we appear to be and who we truly are. Like an alarm we cannot silence, pain calls us back to what is true.

Pain can become a place where God's mercy meets us, interrupting our drift and calling us back to Him.

For many of us, pain becomes the first honest invitation to return. It confronts our trust in control and self-sufficiency and slows us enough to listen. Awakening begins when life becomes unsustainable without God. Yet awareness alone is not healing. Pain gets our attention, but it does not give direction. The deeper question remains. What will we do with it? When brought to God, the same pain that awakens us becomes the place where wisdom forms and purpose begins to emerge. Awakening opens our eyes, but surrender teaches us how to walk forward.

What Pain Reveals Beneath the Surface

Pain does more than wound us. It reveals us, bringing to the surface what has been quietly shaping our inner life long before anything visibly collapses. The psalmist prayed, "Search me, O God, and know my heart; Try me, and know my anxieties" (Psalm 139:23 NKJV). When my life began to unravel, pain answered that prayer in ways I would not have chosen. What had remained hidden beneath momentum and success became impossible to ignore.

As my first marriage ended and my career unraveled, pain stripped away the image I had carefully maintained. I believed I was strong and composed, trusting discipline to guard me from uncertainty. Yet loss revealed how much of my identity rested on performance, control, and outcomes. I did not realize how tightly I had been holding everything together until I no longer could. In the quiet, questions surfaced that I had long avoided: Who am I without success? Who am I if the future I planned never arrives? Pain did not offer quick answers, but it brought honesty, and that honesty became a doorway.

Jesus describes the prodigal son coming to clarity only after everything he depended on was gone: "When he came to himself" (Luke 15:17 NKJV). Loss stripped away illusion and brought him face to face with truth. In the same way, pain returned me to the place where my need for God could no longer be minimized, and where dependence on Him could finally begin to grow.

Pain does not create what is within us; it reveals what we have been relying on.

Pain exposes what we trust when life feels unstable. It reveals where we turn for comfort and what we try to control. In my story, it uncovered self-sufficiency where surrender was needed and control where trust was lacking. That exposure felt unsettling, but it was merciful. God does not reveal our weaknesses to shame us, but to heal us. Pain did not destroy my life; it revealed where my life needed God.

The Difference Between Wasted Pain and Formed Pain

Not all pain transforms us. The apostle Paul writes, "For godly sorrow produces repentance *leading* to salvation, not to be regretted; but the sorrow of the world produces death." (2 Corinthians 7:10 NKJV). Pain itself is not the turning point; our response is. The same suffering that softens one heart can harden another, drawing us either toward self-protection or toward surrender.

I did not learn this quickly. At first, I wanted relief more than revelation. I asked God to change my circumstances without allowing Him to expose what was forming beneath them. I remained busy and outwardly composed, while grief and fear went unaddressed beneath the surface. Yet avoided pain does not disappear. It continues to shape us quietly, influencing our decisions, relationships, and inner life without ever being brought into healing.

Formed pain is different. It is pain brought honestly before God and entrusted to His redemptive work. It is acknowledged, named, and surrendered. Formation begins when we stop resisting and start yielding. Joseph's life offers a clear picture. Betrayed, enslaved, and imprisoned, he had every reason to grow bitter. Yet he later declared, "You meant evil against me; *but* God meant it for good" (Genesis 50:20 NKJV). He did not deny the injustice; he allowed God to work through it. In doing so, his suffering produced humility, wisdom, and leadership that comfort alone could never form.

In my own journey, formation began when I stopped asking God to simply fix my life and started asking Him to search my heart. Pain exposed my dependence on control and performance, and what once felt like punishment gradually began to be reframed as preparation in God's hands. Wasted pain keeps us bound to unresolved wounds, but formed pain becomes the pathway through which God leads us into transformation. It deepens our dependence on Him and reshapes us with humility, wisdom, and spiritual clarity. Pain will come to every life, but the question remains whether it is avoided and wasted or surrendered and redeemed as the turning point of a true U-Turn.

Pain as Preparation for a Life Transformation

Pain is rarely the end of the story, though its timeline and outcome may unfold differently than we expect. More often, it is where God begins a holy redirection. What feels like collapse becomes preparation in His hands. My own turning did not happen in a single breakthrough but unfolded over many years of unraveling and rebuilding. Scripture reveals this pattern repeatedly. Moses was formed in the wilderness before leading a nation. Elijah encountered God's whisper after exhaustion and despair. Peter wept bitterly before he was restored to lead. In each of these lives, pain was not wasted or outside of God's purpose but became a training ground in His hands.

It dismantles what once defined us and exposes what cannot sustain us, creating space for something truer to take root. Over time, I began to see how much of my identity had been anchored in strength, certainty, and forward momentum. What I once called confidence was often control, and what I thought was faith was sometimes familiarity. Pain stripped these layers away and invited me into deeper dependence on God and a clearer understanding of my identity in Christ.

"The LORD *is* near to those who have a broken heart" (Psalm 34:18 NKJV). I learned that His nearness does not always appear as immediate relief; more often, it is revealed through His sustaining presence. God did not rush me out of the breaking but met me within it. There were nights when my prayers were reduced to breath and honesty, echoing the cry, "How long, O LORD?" (Psalm 13:1 NKJV). That question did not distance me from Him; it anchored me in relationship with Him. In that place, I discovered that God is not absent in our pain but attentive, patient, and faithful to complete what He begins in us.

Transformation did not appear dramatic from the outside, but it formed steadily within. Pain reoriented my heart, clarified my desires, and reshaped my understanding of who God is and who I am in Him. It did not define my future, but it prepared me to receive it. When surrendered rather than avoided, pain becomes sacred ground where God restores order to the inner life and renews the heart according to His truth. Pain is not condemnation; in God's hands, it becomes preparation for transformation and even loving discipline that draws us back to Him. It awakens us to misalignment, exposes what comfort once concealed, and invites us into a deeper life of obedience and trust.

As we move into Part II, Alignment, the journey shifts from awakening to recalibration. We begin to explore God's original design, the internal patterns that shape our choices, and the daily crossroads where direction is either restored or lost. Alignment steadies the heart and prepares us to move forward with clarity, trust, and faith, ready to respond to God's leading rather than resist it.

Reflection Questions

1. Where has pain entered your life in a way you did not plan, expect, or feel prepared for, and how has that experience shaped your perspective?
2. What has this pain revealed, with God's help, about where you have placed your identity, security, or sense of worth?
3. When pain surfaced, did you find yourself moving toward God, drawing back from Him, or trying to manage it on

your own? What patterns do you notice in your response, and how have they affected your relationship with Him?

4. Are there places where pain has kept you stuck, and other places where God has begun to use it to shape your heart? What do you sense He is gently inviting you to surrender to Him?
5. If God is using this season not as condemnation but as preparation, and even as loving discipline, what transformation might He be forming in you right now?

Prayer

Lord,

You see my pain and are near to me in it. I bring You my broken places and the parts of my heart I do not fully understand. Search me and reveal what needs to be healed, surrendered, and brought into Your truth. Teach me to trust You with what I cannot control and to rest in Your presence even when I do not see the outcome.

Help me to believe that You are working in me even here, shaping my heart according to Your purposes and drawing me closer to You. Your truth and Your grace.

In the name of Jesus, I surrender this season to You and trust Your faithful hand.

Amen.

Part II — ALIGNMENT

Understanding What Must Change

> "And do not conform to this world, but be transformed by the renewing of your mind, that you may prove what *is* that good and acceptable and perfect will of God." — (Romans 12:2 NKJV).

Awakening reveals misalignment, but it is God who restores what must be reordered within us. Once our eyes are opened, He begins to renew and realign our inner life according to His design and truth. This is not self-improvement, but a Spirit-led return to truth, where our lives are reshaped through obedience and dependence on Him. Alignment is not something we achieve on our own, but the gracious work of God restoring the heart to Himself.

This section brings clarity to the gap between God's design and our lived reality. It uncovers the patterns of the heart that influence our thoughts and decisions and reveal how our daily choices shape our direction. As we grow in awareness, we begin to recognize both the ways God faithfully leads us back and the subtle ways we drift away from Him. Alignment steadies the heart, brings the soul under the authority of God's truth, and sharpens spiritual discernment so we can walk in step with Him. It prepares us to move forward with clarity and to respond to God's leading with confidence rooted in trust in Him.

Chapter 3 — The Gap Between God's Design and Our Reality

"Alignment is not achieved by effort; it is received through restored relationship and lived out through ongoing surrender and obedience."

This chapter has returned us to God's original design, where identity flowed from belonging and life was rooted in relationship rather than performance. Before striving and shame shaped human behavior, humanity was created for alignment with God, secure, known, and at rest in His presence.

Misalignment began not because God withdrew, but through sin, where truth was rejected and trust fractured. As trust weakened, identity became unstable, and as sin took root, fear replaced freedom and self-reliance replaced intimacy with God. What began as distortion in belief extended into behaviors, relationships, and generations. Humanity began living in the space between God's design and lived reality. Effort could not close this gap. Discipline may adjust behavior, but it cannot restore broken trust. Religious activity can structure outward behavior, but apart from God's transforming work, it cannot reconcile the heart. The divide required more than human striving. It required divine intervention.

In Jesus, God stepped into the separation humanity could not bridge. Where trust had been distorted, He revealed truth. Where identity had fractured, He restored belonging. Through His life, death, and resurrection, reconciliation was made possible. What we could not restore through effort, Christ accomplished through His grace on the cross. Alignment is not achieved by effort; it is received through restored relationship and lived out through ongoing surrender and obedience.

God's Original Design: Life in Alignment

Before there was striving, shame, or separation, there was alignment. Humanity began not in pressure, but in peace. God's original design was not built on performance for worth, but on relationship expressed through trust and obedience. From the beginning, men and women were created to live in unhindered fellowship with Him, surrounded by His goodness, provision, and delight.

In the garden, Adam and Eve walked with God in the cool of the day. This was not a distant ritual or formal encounter, but shared life with Him. They were fully known and fully loved before they had accomplished anything. Their identity flowed from belonging, not earning. Their security came from proximity, not achievement. Life was whole because it was rooted in His presence. This pattern of relational alignment continues throughout Scripture. When God called Abraham, He began with a promise, not a demand. He invited Abraham into trust before responsibility, into blessing before instruction. The relationship was marked by covenant love, not control. Faith, not fear, shaped the journey.

We see this intimacy again in the life of Moses. Scripture tells us that the Lord spoke to Moses face to face, as a man speaks to his friend. Before Moses led a nation, he learned to dwell in God's presence. Direction flowed from communion, and leadership emerged from intimacy. Assignment followed relationship. In this original alignment, the inner life was undivided. What humanity believed about God shaped how they saw themselves, and how they saw themselves shaped how they lived. There was no hiding, no self-protection, and no fragmentation of the heart. Love had not yet been questioned, so trust remained whole. God's intention was never righteousness achieved through human effort, but wholeness formed through relationship with Him.

Throughout Scripture, God is consistently the One who moves toward His people. He walked with Enoch. He extended grace to Noah. He chose to dwell among Israel. The initiative has always been His. From the beginning, His heart has been relational.

"Then God saw everything that He had made, and indeed *it was* very good." (Genesis 1:31 NKJV).

In God's original design, life flourished because it was rooted in His love. Alignment was not restrictive; it was freeing. It was not burdensome; it was life-giving. To live aligned with God was to live secure, purposeful, and at rest in Him. Though sin introduced fracture, God's design and invitation has never changed. He still calls us back into alignment through repentance, restored trust, and relationship with Him. The U-Turn is not a new idea. It is a return to what was always meant to be, a life lived near Him.

The Truth: God Has a Great Plan for Me

Many believers confidently declare that God has a great plan for their lives. We speak it in seasons of hope and cling to it in seasons of uncertainty. This belief is not rooted in wishful thinking, but in the character of God Himself. Scripture affirms His intentional care and sovereign design:

> "For I know the thoughts that I think toward you, says the Lord, thoughts of peace and not of evil, to give you a future and a hope." (Jeremiah 29:11 NKJV).

This promise, first spoken to God's people in exile, reflects His faithful character toward all who belong to Him. The truth is steady. God is purposeful and sovereign. He is not random with our lives, nor is He distant from our story.

Yet, while the truth itself remains secure, our understanding of it can quietly drift. When we say God has a great plan for me, we often interpret greatness through the lens of personal fulfillment, visible impact, stability, influence, or success. We assume His plan will align with our preferences and unfold according to our timelines. Without realizing it, we begin measuring His faithfulness by outcomes rather than by His presence. Subtly, expectation replaces surrender, and our perspective begins to shape what we believe about God's plan more than His Word does.

Throughout Scripture, God's great plan has always been relational at its core, shaping the person before revealing the direction. Before Abraham received land, he was invited into trust. Before Moses led a nation, he encountered God in obscurity and learned to dwell in His presence. Before David wore a crown, he cultivated worship and courage in hidden fields. In each case, God formed the person before fulfilling the assignment. His plan was never centered first on platform, productivity, or prominence, but on alignment with Himself. The shaping of the heart preceded the unfolding of purpose.

Misalignment can begin when we unintentionally love the idea of God's plan more than we love God Himself. We pursue purpose without prioritizing presence, and we desire calling without cultivating communion. When circumstances unfold differently than expected, disappointment surfaces. Not because God has failed, but because we have defined greatness differently than He has. We expected elevation, while He was forming humility. We anticipated clarity, while He was building trust. We looked for acceleration, while He was deepening dependence.

The truth is not that God's plan guarantees ease, recognition, or comfort. The truth is deeper and more enduring. God's great plan, fulfilled in Christ, is to restore us to Himself, to shape Christ within us, and to align our lives with His eternal purposes. What He builds in us often carries more weight than what He builds through us. Greatness in His kingdom is measured by faithfulness, not visibility, by obedience, not achievement, and by surrendered trust rather than controlled outcomes.

When alignment is restored, we begin to see that the greatest promise was never a particular destination, but His abiding presence. His nearness is not merely a means to the plan; it is the foundation from which His purposes unfold in our lives. His forming work is not a delay, but preparation. As we walk with Him, purpose unfolds from relationship, and direction flows from intimacy. The truth remains steady even when expectations shift. God has a great plan for me, and that plan is anchored in relationship, shaped by truth, and sustained by trust.

The Gap: Where Misalignment Began

The gap did not begin with God withdrawing from humanity. It began when humanity, through deception and choice, turned away from trusting God. Misalignment was not merely a matter of behavior but began in belief and resulted in disobedience. When truth was questioned, trust was fractured, and when trust was fractured, alignment gave way. Separation was not created by physical distance from God's presence, but by sin, which distorted perception and fractured relationship.

The serpent did not begin with open rebellion, but with a question that led to it. Doubt entered quietly, and the goodness of God was subtly challenged. "Has God indeed said, 'You shall not eat of every tree of the garden'?" (Genesis 3:1 NKJV). The question seemed small, but its implication was profound. It suggested that God might not be fully trustworthy and planted suspicion where there had once been confidence. When that suspicion was embraced, the human story shifted, and in that moment, the gap between God's design and human experience was formed.

The first fracture formed within the human heart. Before sin, there was no tension between identity and action. Humanity knew who they were because they knew God, and their sense of self flowed naturally from relationship with Him. But once trust was broken, the relationship with self began to unravel. Innocence gave way to shame, and confidence dissolved into comparison. Instead of living from a secure identity, humanity began striving to establish it. Fear replaced freedom, and self-protection replaced openness. The inner life became divided, creating a quiet struggle between who we were created to be and who we now felt compelled to become.

This internal fracture quickly affected the relationship with God. The One who had once been approached with joy was now approached with hiding. The lie suggested that God was restrictive, controlling, or unsafe. The divide was not only about how near God was, but about how He was now perceived through the lens of sin. Intimacy weakened as suspicion grew. Relationship was gradually replaced with either religious effort to earn approval or avoidance to escape perceived judgment. From there, the gap expanded outward.

When trust with God weakened and identity became unstable, trust with others grew fragile. Scripture reveals this almost immediately in the story of Cain and Abel. Comparison opened the door to resentment, insecurity gave way to jealousy, and fear distorted relationship. Brothers became rivals, and partnership gave way to competition. Humanity began relating through control and protection rather than shared dignity and love.

As generations unfolded, the same fracture shaped societies. Communities organized around survival instead of stewardship. Nations pursued domination rather than care. Systems were constructed to preserve power rather than protect people. War, injustice, oppression, and division all echo the same original distortion. When trust in God erodes, humanity attempts to secure itself through strength, ideology, or superiority. The gap that began in the heart extends into families, communities, and cultures.

In modern life, the gap remains, though often less visible. Individuals wrestle with identity, anxiety, and isolation. Families experience emotional distance, and communities become polarized. Even within the Church, unity can be strained by performance, fear, or misplaced allegiance. Information is abundant, yet intimacy is scarce, and activity is constant while peace feels distant. The symptoms vary, but the origin remains the same, misalignment rooted in fractured trust. Understanding where misalignment began helps us see why transformation must reach deeper than behavior. The issue was never merely external conduct, but the condition of the heart.

God's redemptive work has always moved in this direction. He restores identity as He calls His people into renewed responsibility and obedience. He reconciles relationships and begins to reform what has been broken. He heals the heart and reshapes lives according to His truth. The gap may be real, but it is not final, because God Himself has moved toward us in redemption. From the moment misalignment began, He initiated restoration, pursuing His people across generations and revealing His character.

What began with distortion is answered by truth, and what fractured through suspicion is healed through the love of God revealed in Christ. As trust is restored, alignment becomes possible again. The gap began in the questioning of God's goodness, and healing begins in rediscovering His goodness as revealed through His Word and fulfilled in Christ.

Living in the Gap — the Cost of Misalignment

When trust in God is disrupted through sin and self-reliance, life begins to be lived in the space between God's design and human experience. This gap is rarely sudden or obvious. More often, it forms quietly, shaping emotions, relationships, and decisions long before it is recognized as a spiritual issue. I have learned this personally. For me, drifting does not always begin with obvious disobedience, but often with subtle self-reliance that eventually leads away from God's will. I remain faithful in responsibility, consistent in service, and sincere in intention, yet slowly begin carrying what God never asked me to hold alone. Outwardly, life still appears aligned, but inwardly strain begins to grow. I do not stop believing in God, but I stop resting in Him.

Life in the gap produces striving where there was once Spirit-led dependence. What once flowed from trust now requires effort rooted in self. Peace slowly gives way to pressure, and rest is replaced by endurance. Instead of living from love and security, I find myself living for approval, control, or outcomes. The heart grows weary not because God's ways are burdensome, but because life is being lived outside the alignment it was created for. Scripture reveals this pattern again and again. After the fall, fear replaced freedom and hiding replaced intimacy. Cain, disconnected from trust in God's goodness, allowed comparison and resentment to grow until it led to destruction. Israel, though chosen and continually provided for, struggled with anxiety, complaint, and division whenever trust in God's presence and provision weakened. The issue was never God's faithfulness, but the gradual erosion of trust and the persistence of the human tendency toward self-reliance.

I see this same pattern in my own relationships when misalignment begins to take root. When connection with God weakens, I notice myself becoming more guarded, more controlling, and less patient. Love becomes cautious and trust becomes conditional. What was meant to be shared freely in relationship begins to feel heavy and complicated. In today's culture, this gap often shows up as exhaustion, confusion, and emotional disconnection. Many of us are faithful, informed, and outwardly fruitful, yet inwardly tired. Faith remains, but intimacy feels distant. We know about God, yet struggle to live with Him moment by moment.

Jesus spoke directly to this condition. He warned of honoring God with words while the heart remains far from Him. This is not always open rebellion. More often, it is a quiet drift, not rejection, and becomes gradual disconnection that touches every area of life. "These people...honor Me with *their* lips, But their heart is far from Me." (Matthew 15:8 NKJV).

Living in the gap was never God's intention. The weariness and tension we experience are not only signs of struggle, but also gracious invitations to return. God does not withdraw when we drift. He remains present, patient, and faithful, continually drawing us back into alignment with Him. Again and again, He calls us to return, not to performance, but to relationship; not to striving, but to trust.

When Knowing Truth Is Not the Same as Walking with God

Many believers know a great deal about the Bible. They have heard sermons, attended studies, memorized verses, and learned sound doctrine. Truth is familiar to them. Yet knowing truth and walking with God through the ongoing work of the Holy Spirit are not always the same.

It is possible for truth to remain in the mind, while daily life continues to be shaped by old habits, emotions, and self-directed choices. A person may sincerely believe God's Word, yet still respond to pressure with fear, react to conflict with defensiveness, or make decisions based on personal understanding rather than seeking the Lord's guidance. In those moments, knowledge alone does not produce transformation.

When Jesus went to the cross and declared, "It is finished," He completed the work necessary for our salvation and restoration. Through His sacrifice, the way was opened for us to live in relationship with God, receive forgiveness, and walk in the new life He prepared for us. The blessings of God are not withheld, though they are experienced in part now and more fully as we walk in alignment with His will. The challenge is not simply a lack of information. In many cases, believers already know what Scripture says. The deeper challenge is learning how to walk with God, how to align our thoughts, decisions, and direction with His will through daily surrender.

Scripture reminds us that relationship with God is not merely agreement with truth, but alignment with Him. "Can two walk together, unless they are agreed?" (Amos 3:3 NKJV). Walking with God requires more than understanding His Word. It requires surrender, attentiveness, and a willingness to allow His truth to shape how we live.

Transformation begins when truth moves from something we understand to Someone we follow. As our hearts become aligned with His will, truth no longer remains information but becomes direction. The journey with God is not about collecting more knowledge, but about learning to walk with Him step by step. Through repentance, renewed thinking, and restored sensitivity to His voice, we leave behind the patterns that once guided us and begin walking in the life God originally intended.

When Humans Try to Close the Gap

When humans become aware of the distance between their lives and God's design, the instinct is almost immediate to try to close the gap. We assume alignment can be restored through effort. We try harder, discipline ourselves more strictly, increase activity, refine our habits, and manage our behavior. The desire is often sincere. We want to please God and remain faithful. But effort, no matter how disciplined, cannot restore what was broken through sin and fractured trust before God.

Throughout history, when humans try to close the gap, the first response is often self-initiated action. In Eden, Adam and Eve covered themselves with fig leaves, attempting to manage shame without restoring relationship. At Babel, humanity built upward, striving to reach heaven through ambition rather than dependence. Even Israel, entrusted with the law, often relied on external obedience while the heart drifted from intimacy. The pattern is consistent. Activity can begin to replace trust, and performance can substitute for genuine dependence on God's presence.

This pattern is not only ancient, it is deeply personal. I recognize it because I lived it. For many years, I equated faithfulness with endurance. I knew how to remain committed, carry responsibility, and press on through discomfort. When something felt misaligned in my relationship with God, my response was not to slow down and listen, but to increase effort. I prayed more, served more, and tightened my standards — believing discipline would restore closeness. Instead, I grew weary. What I called maturity was often self-reliance shaped by survival rather than surrender. It is possible to appear faithful externally while experiencing strain internally. Effort can maintain appearance, but it cannot restore intimacy. When devotion becomes duty, love quietly gives way to pressure, and trust is replaced by performance. What begins in the Spirit can drift into striving in the flesh when dependence on Him is replaced with self-effort.

The apostle Paul addressed this tension directly: "Having begun in the Spirit, are you now being made perfect by the flesh?" (Galatians 3:3 NKJV). The question remains just as relevant today. What begins as grace cannot be sustained through self-effort. The gap was never meant to be closed by human strength. It cannot be bridged through striving, improved performance, or accumulated knowledge. When humans try to close the gap on their own, exhaustion eventually reveals the limitation of effort. The divide does not require more striving. It requires surrender expressed through repentance, faith, and renewed dependence on God.

Jesus: The Only Way to Close the Gap We Could Not Close

For generations, humanity has attempted to cross the divide through effort, morality, knowledge, discipline, and religion. Yet every attempt, no matter how sincere, reveals the same limitation. The gap between God's design and our reality cannot be closed from the human side. The fracture began with sin and broken trust, and no amount of striving can restore what only reconciliation can heal. The divide is not merely behavioral; it is relational and spiritual. Therefore, the solution cannot be self-improvement. It must be restoration initiated by God Himself.

Jesus did not come to offer better strategies for moral living, but to accomplish salvation and reconciliation through His life, death, and resurrection. Where trust was distorted, He revealed truth. Where identity was fractured, He restored our place as sons and daughters through adoption into God's family. Where shame caused hiding, He invited us into restored intimacy. In Him, God did not withdraw from the divide. He stepped directly into it. The incarnation declares that God was never content to leave humanity separated but moved toward us in love.

Scripture affirms this clearly: "For *there is* one God and one Mediator between God and men, *the* Man Christ Jesus" (1 Timothy 2:5 NKJV). A mediator stands in the space between two estranged parties. Jesus does not simply point toward reconciliation, He embodies it. Through His life, He revealed the Father accurately. Through His death, He bore the weight of sin and its consequences. Through His resurrection, He opened the way for restored relationship. The cross was not merely an act of sacrifice, but the decisive act that addressed the root of separation. This is why Jesus is not presented as one option among many, but as the way. "I am the way, the truth, and the life. No one comes to the Father except through Me" (John 14:6 NKJV). These words are not restrictive in spirit, but redemptive in intention, revealing that the way back to God is personal, relational, and found in Him alone.

What we could not restore through effort, Christ accomplished through His finished work on the cross, which we receive through repentance and faith. Where human effort exhausted itself, grace made a way. Where striving could not restore trust, love did. Through Christ, the inner fracture can heal, and identity is no longer rooted in performance but in belonging. Relationship with God is no longer sustained by fear or pressure, but by reconciliation and grace.

The gap was real and the divide ran deep through the human heart, relationships, and societies. But it was never stronger than God's desire to restore. In Jesus, the distance was crossed from heaven to earth so that earth could be reconciled to heaven. He did not merely show the way across the gap, He became the way, and in Him the distance is truly overcome. The invitation now is not to strive harder, but to trust fully and walk in the reconciliation already made available.

Though the divide has been bridged in Christ, its effects can linger in the patterns of our thinking, emotions, and responses. Realignment requires more than understanding truth. It requires allowing truth to reshape how we think, choose, and live. As we move forward, the focus shifts from the origin of misalignment to the internal patterns that sustain it. If the gap began with distorted belief, then healing must address the beliefs, habits, and responses that shape daily life. Lasting transformation is not merely theological understanding, but the steady reordering of the inner life so that obedience flows from relationship and intimacy becomes a natural way of living.

Reflection Questions

1. Where has my trust in God quietly shifted toward self-reliance and the pull of my own understanding, even while my faith practices remain intact?
2. What beliefs about God, myself, or life have most shaped my identity and decisions, and how do they compare with God's original design revealed in Scripture and fulfilled in Christ?
3. In what areas of my inner life or relationships do I see evidence of living in the gap and misalignment between God's design and my daily experience?
4. How has effort, endurance, or performance replaced intimacy and trust in my relationship with God, and what has that produced in me?
5. What would it look like for me, through surrender, repentance, and obedience, to allow God to realign my inner life so that obedience flows from love rather than striving?

Prayer

Father God,

Thank You for Your faithfulness and for drawing me back when I drift. Forgive me for the lies I have believed and the ways I have relied on myself instead of trusting You.

Restore what has been broken within me and reestablish my heart in Your truth. Teach me to trust You fully and to surrender what I have been holding onto. Lead me to walk closely with You, so that my life is shaped by Your love and aligned with Your will.

In Jesus' name, Amen.

Chapter 4 — The Believer's Life Operating System

> ***"What God forms within is faithfully expressed through the life we live."***

Chapter 3 revealed the gap between God's design and our lived experience, reminding us that restoration begins not with greater effort, but with restored trust. Now we move deeper into a question many sincere believers quietly carry. If Christ has reconciled us to the Father, why does misalignment still appear in lives that genuinely love Him and desire to walk faithfully with Him?

The answer often lies beneath conscious belief — which Scripture describes as the heart and mind. Many believers affirm biblical truth yet still operate from internal patterns formed long before spiritual maturity took root. These patterns shape how we interpret pressure, respond to challenges, and make decisions. In this sense, they function like a life operating system, not replacing truth, but influencing how truth is applied in daily life. Scripture points to this inner reality: "As he thinks in his heart, so *is* he" (Proverbs 23:7 NKJV). A believer may be devoted to God, yet still default to self-reliance, control, or fear under pressure. This does not reflect a lack of love for God but reveals areas where old patterns remain influential in practice. Christ is Lord, yet transformation unfolds as every area of life increasingly comes into alignment with His truth. Salvation restores relationship with God, and transformation flows from that restored relationship as the life of Christ is formed within us. "Be transformed by the renewing of your mind" (Romans 12:2 NKJV). reveals that this renewal is not a one-time moment, but an ongoing work of the Spirit.

The Believer's Life Operating System can be understood as the inner framework through which we process reality and respond to it. When this framework is shaped more by past experiences than by present truth, misalignment can persist even in a sincere walk with God. Lasting change begins as these hidden patterns are brought into the light and surrendered to the Holy Spirit. This is not an invitation to self-criticism, but to honest openness before God. "Search me, O God, and know my heart" (Psalm 139:23 NKJV). becomes a prayer of trust, allowing Him to reveal and restore what has been shaped outside of His truth. Alignment is not produced through human striving, but through Spirit-empowered surrender expressed in daily obedience.

This chapter marks a shift from managing outward behavior to understanding inward formation. As the Spirit reshapes how we think and respond, Christ is not only confessed in belief but increasingly trusted in the realities of everyday life. What was once instinctively driven by old patterns becomes steadily transformed under His truth. Alignment is no longer sustained by effort alone, but formed through a deepening submission to His rule, as the believer learns to walk in step with the Spirit and live from a renewed heart.

What Is the Life Operating System of the Believer

Alignment with God rarely breaks in a single moment. More often, it drifts quietly over time. Even when truth is sincerely believed, the inner life may still operate from patterns formed long before surrender took root. This is why sincere believers can experience recurring misalignment. The issue is not devotion, but what we continue to yield to in daily life.

To help make this inner dynamic more visible and understandable, we use the term *Life Operating System of the Believer*. This is not a replacement for biblical language, but a simple illustration to describe what Scripture consistently reveals about the inner life. The Bible speaks of the *heart* (Proverbs 4:23 NKJV), the *mind* (Romans 12:2 NKJV), the *inner man* (Ephesians 3:16 NKJV), and the call to *walk in the Spirit* (Galatians 5:16 NKJV). Together, these passages show that there is an unseen inner life that governs how we live outwardly.

This illustration is simply a tool to help us observe and understand the inner life more clearly; Scripture alone remains the authority for truth, transformation, and how we are to live.

In this sense, the phrase *Life Operating System* describes the functional reality of the heart and mind as Scripture presents them. Just as something unseen directs how a system functions, the inner life directs how we think, respond, and live. Jesus made this clear: "For out of the abundance of the heart the mouth speaks." (Matthew 12:34 NKJV). What is formed within will shape what is expressed outwardly. The Life Operating System of the Believer can therefore be understood as the inner framework of the heart and mind through which we interpret reality, form responses, and live out what we believe, often beneath conscious awareness. Scripture reminds us, "Keep your heart with all diligence, For out of it *spring* the issues of life." (Proverbs 4:23 NKJV). The heart functions as the center of inner life, directing how we respond under pressure, make decisions, and seek security.

This language is used not to introduce something new, but to help us recognize what Scripture already teaches: that life flows from within, and that transformation must take place at that level. Without this clarity, it is easy to focus only on outward behavior while overlooking the deeper patterns shaping it. The intention is to bring awareness to the inner life so it can be brought fully under the authority of Christ.

Over time, this inner framework is shaped either by the truth of God's Word or by past experiences and learned responses that have not yet been brought fully under His truth. This internal formation includes areas such as:

- Core beliefs about God, self, and others
- Identity beliefs about who we are in relation to God, ourselves, and others
- Desires and affections that shape what we pursue and prioritize
- Emotional and thought patterns formed over time
- Protective responses developed in seasons of pain or difficulty
- Thought habits that activate under stress
- Traditions, cultural influences, and inherited expectations
- Assumptions about safety, control, approval, identity, and worth

What once helped navigate pain can continue guiding reactions beneath awareness, even after coming to faith. The mind may agree with truth, yet the lived experience of identity may not fully reflect what is already secure in Christ, and desires may still pull toward self-reliance or control. This often appears in subtle ways. We pray, yet carry the outcome. We obey, yet feel inward pressure. We affirm trust in God, yet struggle to rest in that trust in daily life.

Scripture calls us beyond agreement into transformation: "Be transformed by the renewing of your mind" (Romans 12:2 NKJV). Truth is not only meant to be believed, but to reshape the inner life from which our thoughts, desires, and responses flow. "Bringing every thought into captivity to the obedience of Christ" (2 Corinthians 10:5 NKJV) reveals that this inner life is meant to come under His lordship. Transformation is the Spirit-led process by which what is already true in Christ becomes increasingly formed within us in daily life. It is not achieved through human effort alone, but through yielding to the Holy Spirit, who applies God's truth within.

Alignment is restored as these hidden patterns are brought into the light and yielded to God through His Word and the work of the Holy Spirit. "Search me, O God, and know my heart" (Psalm 139:23 NKJV) reflects a posture of trust that allows Him to reveal and realign what has been shaped outside of His truth. As we submit to His Word and walk in step with the Spirit, our thinking is renewed, our desires are reordered, and peace begins to replace inward striving.

Transformation is not merely behavioral change, but the renewal of the heart from which life flows, bringing every area increasingly into alignment with Christ. What God forms within is faithfully expressed through the life we live.

The Inner Architecture of a Spirit-Led Life

Before understanding how alignment functions, it is important to see how God has designed the believer's life to operate. Scripture reveals that our lives are not meant to function randomly or reactively, but according to the design and purpose established by God Himself.

> "Now may the God of peace Himself sanctify you completely; and may your whole spirit, soul, and body be preserved blameless" (1 Thessalonians 5:23 NKJV).

This passage shows that the believer's life is whole, while also speaking of spirit, soul, and body. These distinctions help us understand how God's work within us is received and expressed in daily life, without dividing the person into separate or independent parts. Within this design, the Holy Spirit reveals, leads, and empowers the life of God within us. Scripture speaks of the inner and outer life of the believer, helping us understand how we relate to God and live in the world. Together, they reveal the full picture of what it means to walk with Him. This can be understood as follows:

- **The spirit** is the innermost aspect of our being, where we are made alive in Christ and brought into relationship with God.
- **The soul** reflects the inner life of thoughts, decisions, and emotions, and is progressively shaped through the renewing of the mind.
- **The body** is the outward expression, where what is formed within becomes visible in daily living through actions, choices, and conduct.

When this is understood, it brings clarity to how transformation takes place. Life is no longer lived primarily from the outside in, reacting to circumstances, but from the inside out, as God works within us. Understanding alone does not produce transformation, but it positions us to yield more fully to the work of the Holy Spirit. Transformation is the work of God within us, as we respond in faith and obedience. Alignment is not sustained by human effort alone, but by grace, as we depend on the Holy Spirit and walk in obedience to God's Word. Transformation is not the creation of a new identity, but the outworking of the new life already given in Christ.

This is not meant to complicate the Christian life, but to bring clarity. It helps us recognize where alignment begins, how it grows, and how it is expressed in daily living. As our lives come under the influence of God's truth, we move from striving to steadiness, from confusion to clarity, and from reaction to a life increasingly led by the Spirit.

What God forms within is faithfully expressed through the life we live each day.

1. The Holy Spirit (Source of Life and Truth)

The Starting Point of the Believer's Life Operating System

As we have seen, the believer's life does not function randomly, but according to the design established by God. At the center of this lived experience is the Holy Spirit, who applies and sustains the life of God within us. Without His active work, the inner life tends to default to past patterns, personal reasoning, or external pressure. When we respond to His leading, life begins to function more fully as it was intended — not driven by reaction, but shaped by truth.

Because of this, everything in the believer's daily life begins with the Holy Spirit, who makes known and applies the finished work of Christ within us. He is not one part of the process, but the One through whom truth becomes living and active in the heart. Truth is not created in us but revealed and established by Him as He brings us into alignment with what is already true in Christ. A Spirit-led life does not begin with human reasoning, emotion, or circumstance, but with God at work within. "For the law of the Spirit of life in Christ Jesus has made me free from the law of sin and death" (Romans 8:2 NKJV). The Holy Spirit is the One who makes the life of Christ real and active within the believer, forming alignment from the inside out.

Who He Is and How He Works

The Holy Spirit is the third Person of the Trinity, fully God, not an influence or an impersonal force. He is sent by the Father and the Son and dwells within every believer. He is the Spirit of life who gives life in Christ, the Spirit of truth who reveals what is true, and the Spirit of God who works within to accomplish His purposes. His presence is not symbolic, but living and active, not distant or occasional, but abiding and continual. The Christian life is not lived for God at a distance, but with God through the presence of His Spirit within.

The Holy Spirit reveals, leads, empowers, and convicts — shaping how the inner life is formed and guided.

- He reveals truth, guiding the believer into what is true according to the Word of God, as Jesus said, "when He, the Spirit of truth, has come, He will guide you into all truth" (John 16:13 NKJV).
- He leads the believer in how truth is to be lived, "For as many as are led by the Spirit of God, these are sons of God" (Romans 8:14 NKJV).
- He empowers what God calls us to do, enabling a life that reflects Christ, "But you shall receive power when the Holy Spirit has come upon you" (Acts 1:8 NKJV).
- He convicts to restore alignment in light of the finished work of Christ, not through condemnation, but through clarity and grace, bringing awareness of what does not align with God's truth and leading the believer into repentance, restoration, and renewed fellowship with God (John 16:8 NKJV).

Living from the Source

To live from the Holy Spirit is to allow Him to shape how we think, respond, and live through His Word and His indwelling presence. The natural tendency is to begin with what feels urgent or visible, but a Spirit-led life begins by turning to Him before responding. This often requires a deliberate pause, especially in moments of pressure, not to withdraw, but to align the heart with God's truth. Instead of reacting immediately, the believer learns to be attentive, to listen, and to discern His leading in light of Scripture. Over time, what begins as intentional dependence becomes a steady rhythm, and life is no longer shaped by reaction, but by alignment with the Spirit's leading.

What the Holy Spirit reveals is meant to be received and established within, forming the foundation from which life flows. When the Holy Spirit is the starting point in daily life, the inner life is no longer governed by past patterns, but increasingly shaped by the truth of God at work within. As the Spirit forms the inner life, alignment with God is not forced from the outside, but expressed from within as a life yielded to Him.

2. The Spirit (Foundation)

The Foundation of the Believer's Life

As alignment begins with the Holy Spirit, what He reveals is meant to be received and established within. Within the believer's life, this becomes the foundation from which everything else flows. The human spirit is the innermost aspect of our being where the work of Christ is received through faith and where union with Him is established. What God makes known by His Spirit is not meant to remain external, but to take root within, shaping identity and relationship with Him.

The spirit is not the place where identity is achieved through striving, but where it is received based on what God has already accomplished in Christ. It is where the believer is joined to the Lord, and where life in Him becomes the unchanging basis for identity and relationship with God. Union with Christ establishes the foundation from which all true alignment flows. "But he who is joined to the Lord is one spirit *with Him*." (1 Corinthians 6:17 NKJV). The stability of the Christian life is not found in changing conditions, but in what God has already established in Christ. When this foundation is understood, the believer is able to remain steady even when circumstances are not.

What Is Established Within

The spirit is the innermost dimension of the believer where relationship with God is made real through Christ. It is where the Holy Spirit dwells and where the life of Christ is received and made active within. It is not defined by changing experiences or external pressures, but by what God has accomplished through Christ. From this place, the believer learns to live by faith in what is true, rather than striving to become what has already been given.

In this foundation, several realities are established.

- The believer is made new through Christ, not by gradual improvement, but by the new life He gives: "Therefore, if anyone *is* in Christ, *he is* a new creation" (2 Corinthians 5:17 NKJV).
- The believer is made right with God through Christ, justified by faith and not by works, receiving righteousness as a gift of grace, as revealed in Romans 5 NKJV.
- The Holy Spirit dwells within, making God's presence real and active in daily life.

These truths do not change with circumstance but remain the foundation from which the believer lives. What God has established in Christ becomes the unchanging reference point for the believer's life.

Living from a Secure Foundation

To live from this foundation is to return continually, by faith, to what God has already made true in Christ, especially when it is challenged by circumstances, emotions, or external pressure. These influences may attempt to shape how we think and respond, but what is established in Christ remains unchanged. Instead of striving to become something, the believer learns to stand in what has already been given, trusting the Word of God and yielding to the Holy Spirit who makes it real within. Alignment is not restored by achieving more, but by abiding in and living from what God has already done in Christ.

As this foundation becomes more firmly established in the heart, life begins to stabilize. The inner life no longer strives to secure what has already been given, and responses begin to flow from truth rather than insecurity or pressure. From this foundation, what is established within begins to shape how life is lived outwardly, forming a steady and consistent expression of faith.

3. The Soul (Alignment)

Where Alignment Is Worked Out in the Believer's Life

As alignment flows from the Holy Spirit and is established within, it is worked out through the soul. The soul is not the source of truth, but the place where truth is received, responded to, and lived out in daily life. Here, what God has made known begins to shape how life is experienced and expressed. As the soul comes into increasing alignment with truth, life reflects growing clarity, consistency, and peace. When it is not yet aligned, even what is true in Christ may feel unsettled in daily experience.

The soul is where the inner life becomes active. It interprets, chooses, and responds. While what is true is fully given through Christ, the soul reflects how that truth is being embraced and worked out over time. Because of this, transformation is closely connected to the renewal and alignment of the soul. Transformation becomes evident as the mind is renewed and life increasingly aligns with God's truth. "And do not be conformed to this world, but be transformed by the renewing of your mind" (Romans 12:2 NKJV). Transformation is not the creation of a new truth, but the aligning of the inner life with what is already true in Christ.

What the Soul Is

The soul is the inner working place of the believer, consisting of the mind, the will, and the emotions. It is where life is processed, decisions are made, and responses are formed. It does not originate truth but responds to what God has made known through His Word and by His Spirit. "For As he thinks in his heart, so *is* he" (Proverbs 23:7 NKJV). It is not meant to function independently from God, but to come into alignment with His truth. As it is brought under His truth, the soul becomes the place where what is received from God is increasingly expressed in daily life.

How the Soul Functions

The soul functions through the mind, the will, and the emotions. These are not separate parts, but integrated expressions of how the inner life responds to truth.

- The mind interprets reality. It forms thoughts, beliefs, values, and perspective, shaping how situations are understood. What the mind holds to be true influences how life is perceived and how decisions are approached. When the mind is not yet renewed, it often reflects past experience or fear. As it is renewed in truth, clarity replaces distortion, and perspective becomes increasingly steady rather than reactive. "Set your mind on things above, not on things on the earth." (Colossians 3:2 NKJV).

- The will chooses direction. It determines the course of life through decisions and continues in that direction over time. The will reflects what is being trusted, especially under pressure. Alignment is not formed by intention alone, but through choices that follow truth. A surrendered will responds in obedience, even when it is difficult, allowing truth to move from understanding into action. "Choose for yourselves this day whom you will serve" (Joshua 24:15 NKJV).

- The emotions respond to interpretation. Emotions are a God-given part of the inner life and reflect what is being believed and understood. They are not meant to lead independently, but to come into alignment with truth. When ordered rightly, emotions support what is true and deepen our experience of it. When not aligned, they can intensify reaction and shape perception in unhelpful ways. Emotional alignment is not achieved by suppression, but by bringing emotions before God and allowing them to be shaped by truth so they settle into peace rather than direct decisions. "You will keep *him* in perfect peace, *Whose* mind *is* stayed on *You*" (Isaiah 26:3 NKJV).

Living in Aligned Response

The alignment of the soul involves intentional, Spirit-dependent response. While truth is given, it must be received and applied in daily life through faith and obedience. This often requires slowing down in moments of pressure, not merely for self-reflection, but to turn the heart toward God and His Word. Instead of reacting immediately, the believer learns to discern what is being thought and believed in light of truth. Misalignment is often revealed first within, before it is seen outwardly. "Bringing every thought into captivity to the obedience of Christ" (2 Corinthians 10:5 NKJV) describes this ongoing, Spirit-empowered process.

As the mind is renewed, the will is yielded, and emotions are brought under truth, the soul increasingly reflects what God has already made known. Over time, this alignment becomes more consistent, and life carries greater clarity, stability, and peace. Alignment grows as truth is not only understood but trusted and consistently chosen in daily life.

From Alignment to Expression

What is aligned within the soul does not remain internal but is expressed in daily living. Through choices, actions, and responses, what has been received and embraced becomes visible. In this way, the believer's life increasingly reflects God's truth, with alignment flowing from the inside out.

4. The Body (Expression)

Where the Life of God Becomes Visible

Within the believer's life, what begins with the Holy Spirit as He applies the finished work of Christ, and is worked out in the inner life, is ultimately expressed through the body. The body is not the source of life or direction, but the place where what God is doing within becomes visible in daily living. It does not initiate alignment, but it participates in expressing it through obedience and action. What is formed within, will, over time, be expressed outwardly through words, choices, and patterns of life. Because of this, the body becomes the visible expression of what is shaping the inner life. What is established within will be made evident through how life is lived.

What the Body Is

The body is the physical aspect of the believer through which life is expressed in the natural world. It includes actions, speech, and conduct, the outward expression of what has been received and embraced within. It is not separate from the inner life, but the means through which it is made visible. Scripture calls the believer to present the body to God as an act of worship and surrender. "I beseech you therefore, brethren, by the mercies of God, that you present your bodies a living sacrifice, holy, acceptable to God, *which* is your reasonable service" (Romans 12:1 NKJV). In this way, the body is offered to God and made available for His purposes.

How the Body Functions

The body expresses alignment through a life that is surrendered to God, responsive to His Word, lived in obedience, and sustained in a consistent walk with Him.

- Surrender establishes posture. The body is presented to God in response to His mercy. This is not only a single act, but an ongoing posture of offering one's life to Him. It flows from understanding what Christ has done, not from pressure or obligation, and is sustained by dependence on the Holy Spirit.

- Yielding establishes daily response. Surrender is lived out through daily yielding. This is the willingness to respond to God in practical situations, allowing His Word to shape actions and decisions. Yielding is not passive, but a conscious, Spirit-dependent choice to respond in alignment with God rather than reacting to circumstances.
- Obedience establishes visible expression. Obedience is where what is known inwardly is lived outwardly. "But be doers of the word, and not hearers only, deceiving yourselves." (James 1:22 NKJV). Through obedience, faith is expressed in practical ways, as the believer actively responds to what God has made known.
- Walk establishes consistency. Scripture describes the Christian life as a walk. "Walk in the Spirit, and you shall not fulfill the lust of the flesh." (Galatians 5:16 NKJV). This speaks of a steady pattern of living over time, where daily choices increasingly reflect God's truth as we remain in step with the Spirit.

Living as an Expression of Alignment

The body reflects what has been received within and embraced in daily life. Because of this, transformation does not begin with outward behavior, but behavior will reveal what is taking place within. When the body is not yielded to God, life can be shaped by impulse, habit, or external pressure. When it is presented to Him, it becomes an instrument through which His will is expressed.

> "And do not present your members as instruments of unrighteousness to sin, but present yourselves to God... and your members *as* instruments of righteousness to God." (Romans 6:13 NKJV).

The body does not produce transformation but actively participates in expressing what God is forming within through obedient response. What is formed by the Spirit within is faithfully expressed through the life we live outwardly.

This is not sustained by striving alone, but through ongoing surrender and Spirit-empowered obedience. As surrender becomes the posture, yielding the practice, being obedient to the response, and walking the pattern, the body increasingly reflects the work God is doing within.

The Full Flow of the Believer's Life

When the body is rightly ordered, it reflects the full flow of the believer's life. Life begins with the Holy Spirit, who applies the work of Christ. The Holy Spirit is received and established within, is worked out in the inner life, and is expressed through the body in daily living. When this is understood and lived, life becomes steady and consistent, shaped not by reaction, but by alignment with God. Alignment is not merely inward reality, but a visible life that reflects the truth of Christ in everyday living.

The Distorted Architecture of a Misaligned Life

A Shift in Source and Governance

The believer's life was never designed to be governed by pressure, reaction, or the weight of circumstances. It was meant to function from alignment with God, anchored in His truth and led by His presence. Yet when alignment with God's design is displaced in daily experience, a distorted pattern begins to form. This shift often develops quietly within sincere faith. Instead of life flowing from within under God's leading, it becomes increasingly shaped by external pressures and internal reactions. When alignment shifts, life does not stop functioning, but it begins to function from the wrong source.

This shift is not always the result of intentional rebellion, but often the effect of subtle deception, along with the influence of the flesh and the pressures of the world. Scripture reveals that the enemy works through distortion of truth, influencing how we perceive God, ourselves, and our circumstances. When what is untrue is believed, even sincerely, it begins to shape how the inner life functions. In this way, misalignment can develop quietly, not because God has withdrawn, but because the inner life has begun to respond to self-reliance, fear, or misperception rather than to His truth. This is why discernment is essential. Alignment is not only about devotion, but about recognizing what is truly from God and what is not.

Many believers love God and remain committed to His truth yet still experience cycles of striving and instability. This is not a failure of devotion, but a shift in reliance in daily living. When the inner life depends more on personal understanding than on God's direction, what was meant to be sustained by grace begins to feel carried by effort. Scripture calls us back to the right foundation:

> "Trust in the LORD with all your heart. And lean not on your own understanding; in all your ways acknowledge Him, and He shall direct your paths." (Proverbs 3:5–6 NKJV).

Misalignment is not the absence of faith, but the misplacement of trust in how life is lived.

Life Shaped by Urgency Rather Than Truth

As this shift deepens, life becomes shaped more by urgency than by truth. Instead of being guided by God's peace, the believer begins reacting to pressure, managing outcomes, and trying to hold everything together. The Holy Spirit may still be acknowledged, but His leading is no longer consistently followed, and other influences begin to shape responses.

When the source shifts, stability is affected, and the life formed from it begins to lose its steadiness.

"For to be carnally minded *is* death, but to be spiritually minded *is* life and peace" (Romans 8:6 NKJV). Where God leads, there is life and peace within, even in the midst of external pressure. When life is shaped by other influences, even sincere ones, that inner peace begins to diminish.

Inner Misalignment Revealed in Outer Living

When truth is no longer steadily guiding the inner life, instability begins to surface. Identity can become shaped by performance or comparison rather than by being rooted in God. Thoughts become crowded, decisions inconsistent, and emotions begin to influence perception rather than respond to truth. Even when truth is known, it is not consistently lived. "Can two walk together, unless they are agreed?" (Amos 3:3 NKJV). Walking with God requires alignment with Him.

What takes place internally will, over time, be reflected externally. Actions become reactive, consistency gives way to fluctuation, and strength becomes difficult to sustain. The outward life may still appear active, but it lacks the steadiness and peace that come from alignment with God. The outward life will reflect, over time, the condition of the inner life.

Yet even here, God's invitation remains. He does not reveal misalignment to condemn, but to restore. The call is not to strive harder, but to return, to trust Him again, and to allow Him to reestablish a life that flows from His truth, marked by clarity, peace, and enduring strength. God's exposure of misalignment is not rejection, but an invitation to restoration and renewed alignment with Him.

Restoring the Rightful Authority Within

Within the believer's life, restoration does not begin with correcting outward behavior — it begins with bringing the inner life into renewed alignment with what governs it. At salvation, the believer is united with Christ, the penalty of sin is removed, and the Holy Spirit dwells within. This establishes a complete and unchanging reality grounded in Him. Yet the outworking of that reality within the inner life unfolds over time. Christ is confessed as Lord, but patterns of thinking and response may still reflect earlier influences. Restoration begins not by striving harder, but by bringing the inner life into alignment with Christ's lordship so that what is already true in Him is increasingly lived.

Scripture speaks to this ongoing work: "And do not be conformed to this world, but be transformed by the renewing of your mind" (Romans 12:2 NKJV). What God has accomplished in Christ is complete, yet the renewal of the inner life is progressive. Before coming under Christ's leadership, the inner life was shaped by past experiences, learned responses, and natural understanding. These patterns do not disappear automatically. When they continue to shape decisions or disrupt the peace that flows from alignment with God's truth, they influence how life is lived. Restoration requires more than agreeing with truth; it involves yielding these patterns so that Christ's lordship is not only confessed but increasingly expressed in daily life. Transformation is not the establishment of something new, but the realignment of the inner life with what is already true in Christ.

This process begins by bringing hidden patterns into the light. Many believers continue to operate from internal responses formed over time, such as striving to control outcomes, seeking approval, or avoiding vulnerability. These patterns can quietly shape behavior beneath awareness. As they are brought before God, they are not merely replaced but surrendered and renewed by the truth through the work of the Holy Spirit. What once felt necessary is released, and what once provided a sense of security is entrusted to Him.

The expression of Christ's lordship in the inner life is worked out through the will as it responds to God in faith. It is not driven by emotion, but by a Spirit-enabled surrender in response to truth. Feelings may resist and fear may surface, but alignment is strengthened as the believer chooses to trust God above those responses. The Holy Spirit faithfully reveals where realignment is needed and leads the believer into truth. As the will yields in response to His leading, Christ's lordship becomes increasingly evident in daily life.

As this alignment deepens, divine order begins to take shape within. The Holy Spirit leads, truth becomes established, and the inner life begins to align in thought, decision, and response. What was once driven by pressure settles into peace, and what was sustained by effort begins to flow from grace. Transformation is not the result of managing behavior, but of restoring alignment within the inner life under Christ's rule.

Clarity replaces confusion, and stability replaces striving. Life is no longer shaped by reaction or circumstance, but by the steady leadership of Christ within. This restoration is not a one-time moment, but a daily returning. As these choices accumulate, Christ's lordship is not only affirmed, but increasingly expressed in how life is lived. What is already established in Christ becomes progressively evident in the life of the believer.

Yet even as alignment deepens within, the believer may still encounter unseen limitations in how truth is believed, expected, and lived. At times, these limitations are not rooted in resistance, but in incomplete understanding or unexamined assumptions about God's nature and ways. Where these remain, they can quietly limit what is experienced and expressed in the believer's life, not because God's power is lacking, but because trust has not yet fully aligned with His truth.

It is here that the next step becomes necessary. A life restored in order must also be free from the limitations that hinder its full expression. In the next chapter, we will explore how subtle limitations in belief, expectation, and trust can affect how God's work is experienced, and how renewed alignment allows His work to be lived out more fully and freely.

Believer's Life Operating System Assessment

Living in alignment with Christ's authority involves both revelation and response. Alignment is not only what you believe, but how your inner life functions under His lordship in daily living. This assessment is designed to help you discern where Christ is actively leading your thoughts, decisions, and actions, and where familiar patterns may still be shaping your responses. This is not about perfection, but about honest awareness before God. As these areas are brought into the light, they can be surrendered, allowing divine order to take root from the inside out.

Why This Assessment Matters

Transformation is not sustained by effort, but by alignment with God's design and dependence on His Spirit. Many believers desire change without clearly recognizing where misalignment still exists in daily life. What remains unseen is often difficult to surrender, and what is not brought before God is less likely to be transformed in experience.

This assessment is not a measure of your worth, but a reflection of your current alignment in practice. It helps you recognize where the Holy Spirit is leading and where old patterns may still be influencing how you live. Within the journey of a U-Turn, this becomes a practical step from understanding truth to living it. A U-Turn begins as the Holy

Spirit brings clarity and reveals what is currently shaping your life. Before direction can change, there must be a recognition of what is guiding your responses. As you walk through this process, you are not being asked to fix everything, but to respond to what God reveals. What God reveals, He invites you to surrender, and what is surrendered, He faithfully begins to transform.

How to Use This Assessment

Approach this time with honesty and openness before God, anchored in His Word and attentive to His Spirit. Pause, quiet your heart, and invite the Holy Spirit to guide your reflection and bring clarity according to truth. Respond based on what is consistently true in your life, not what you hope is true. This assessment follows the pattern of God's design, beginning with the Holy Spirit as the source, moving into what is established in Christ, worked out in the inner life, and expressed in daily living. As you move through each section, consider whether your life is flowing from alignment with Him or being shaped by external pressures and internal habits. The goal is not to correct everything at once, but to recognize where God is inviting your next step of surrender.

Move through each area thoughtfully, without overanalyzing or justifying your responses. Remain attentive to what the Holy Spirit is bringing to light. Where you see alignment, give thanks. Where you see misalignment, bring it before God in humility and trust. Transformation begins as the Holy Spirit reveals truth and the heart responds in surrender and faith.

Rating Scale

Score	Description
1	Rarely true
2	Occasionally true
3	Sometimes true
4	Often true
5	Consistently true

Believer's Life Operating System Assessment Questions (Appendix A)

#	Category	Subcategory	Statement	Score (1-5)
1	**Holy Spirit**	Revelation	I am attentive and responsive as the Holy Spirit reveals truth throughout my day	
2		Guidance	I am learning to seek the Lord first in decisions, allowing His Spirit to direct my steps rather than relying on my own understanding	
3		Empowering	I actively depend on the Holy Spirit's power to live out what God calls me to do, rather than relying on my own strength	
4		Conviction	When the Holy Spirit brings correction, I respond with humility and realign my life to God's truth	
5	**Spirit**	Identity in Christ	I live from my identity in Christ rather than being shaped by performance, approval, or comparison	
6		Identity in Christ	When challenged or unsettled, I return to what God has established as true about me in Christ	
7		Righteousness by Grace	I relate to God from the righteousness given through Christ, not from striving to earn His acceptance	

8		Indwelling Presence	I live with growing awareness that the Holy Spirit dwells within me, shaping how I think and respond	
9		Truth as Foundation	God's Word governs how I form beliefs, interpret situations, and make decisions	
10	**Soul**	Mind	I regularly examine my thoughts in light of God's truth rather than assumptions or past patterns	
11		Mind	My perspective is increasingly shaped by truth rather than by circumstances or emotional reactions	
12		Will	I choose obedience to God even when it is difficult or not fully understood	
13		Will	I follow through on what God leads me to do, not only what I intend to do	
14		Emotions	I acknowledge my emotions honestly without allowing them to govern my decisions	
15		Emotions	I bring my emotions under God's truth, allowing them to settle into peace over time	
16	**Body**	Surrender	I am learning to present my life to God, offering my actions and choices to Him	
17		Yielding	I yield my actions and decisions to God, allowing	

			my life to reflect His direction	
18		Obedience	I consistently act on what God reveals, allowing truth to be expressed through what I do	
19		Walk	My daily life reflects a growing pattern shaped by the Spirit rather than by impulse or pressure	
20		Stewardship of Life	I steward my time, energy, and responsibilities in a way that reflects God's priorities and leading	

Score Summary

Category	**Max Score**	**Your Score**
Holy Spirit (Source)	20	
Spirit (Foundation)	25	
Soul (Alignment)	30	
Body (Expression)	25	
Total	100	

Understanding Your Total Score

Score Range	Operating State	Summary	Next Step
80–100	**Steady Operating Alignment**	Your Believer's Life Operating System is functioning in a steady and aligned way, flowing from the Holy Spirit through to consistent daily expression.	Remain attentive and responsive, allowing God to deepen and strengthen this alignment.
60–79	**Forming Operating Alignment**	Your Believer's Life Operating System is functioning, but not consistently. Alignment is present, though sometimes shaped by pressure or habit.	Return intentionally to the Holy Spirit as your starting point and stand in what is established in Christ.
40–59	**Inconsistent Operating Flow**	Alignment is present, but the flow is often disrupted. Truth may be known but not consistently lived, leading to inner and outward inconsistency.	Restore order at the source by returning to the Holy Spirit and allowing truth to be reestablished within.
20–39	**Disrupted Operating Order**	Your Believer's Life Operating System is out of order. Life may feel reactive or unstable, shaped by other influences.	Begin again by restoring God as the source and allowing Him to rebuild alignment from the inside out.

Reflection Questions

1. What patterns or default responses is the Holy Spirit revealing that show where I may still be relying on myself rather than on Him?
2. Where has my starting point shifted from the Spirit to circumstances, pressure, or emotion in my daily life?
3. What beliefs or internal agreements might be shaping my reactions more than God's truth?
4. In which area is God inviting me to surrender control and trust His leadership more fully?
5. What would it look like, in practical terms, to return to the Holy Spirit as my starting point in this season?

Prayer

Father,

Thank You for Your grace and for revealing what has been shaping my inner life. I acknowledge Your rightful authority over my life, and I surrender every area where I have relied on myself instead of trusting You. Realign my thoughts, my decisions, and my responses according to Your truth. By Your Spirit, teach me to trust Your leading and walk in obedience with peace. Lead me by Your Spirit so my life reflects Your truth from the inside out.

In the name of Jesus, Amen.

Chapter 5 — When We Limit God

"We do not limit God in who He is, but we can live within limits in how we trust Him, expect from Him, and follow His leading."

Chapter 4 examined the believer's operating framework, revealing how unseen governance shapes visible direction. Alignment is not primarily about outward behavior, but about what governs the inner life, as whatever holds influence within the heart will shape every response. When the will remains influenced by fear, pride, control, or self-reliance, the path forward reflects that mixture. Transformation begins as these competing influences are surrendered and the inner life comes into alignment with Christ's lordship, so that what is already true in Him is increasingly lived.

Even when alignment deepens within, another issue can quietly remain: our perception of God. We may yield control in practice while still carrying a limited understanding of the One who leads us. How we see God shapes how we trust Him, respond to Him, and follow Him. If our understanding has been shaped by disappointment, assumption, or incomplete knowledge of His Word, our faith often adjusts to that smaller vision. Obedience can become cautious, and expectation begins to diminish. Without realizing it, we may begin to live within a reduced view of God, shaped more by experience than by the fullness of His revealed truth.

We do not limit God in who He is, but we can live within limits in how we trust Him, expect from Him, and follow His leading.

Because of this, we often struggle to follow beyond the boundaries our perception has formed. As our understanding of God's character is renewed according to His Word, trust deepens, faith strengthens, and obedience becomes steadier and more courageous. As our vision of God is restored by truth, our capacity to trust and follow Him expands.

This chapter is an invitation to examine where perception may have been reduced and to allow God to renew our understanding of Him. As He does, what has been shaped by experience is brought into alignment with truth, and faith begins to rise in response to who He truly is.

When We Limit God to Our Own Size

We rarely announce that we are limiting God. We do not consciously decide that He is incapable or unwilling. Instead, limitation forms quietly in the space between disappointment and understanding. When prayers seem delayed, outcomes differ from expectation, or obedience feels costly, the heart begins to adjust what it expects from Him. Without realizing it, we redraw the boundaries of what we believe God will do according to our understanding rather than according to His Word. This shift is often less about doctrine and more about self-protection.

When God does not move as we hoped, we may begin to conclude that He no longer moves in that way. When waiting stretches longer than expected, expectation can lower in an effort to guard against further disappointment. Yet Scripture reminds us that God's nature is not shaped by our seasons. His character remains constant even when circumstances fluctuate. The tension is not in His faithfulness, but in our perception and response to Him.

Throughout Scripture, we see this subtle drift. When circumstances grow large, our vision of God can quietly become small. What feels overwhelming begins to redefine what we believe is possible, not because God has changed, but because our understanding has shifted away from His truth. In practical ways, we begin to live within self-imposed limits when:

- We interpret delay as denial rather than trusting His timing
- We reduce our prayers to what feels reasonable instead of what aligns with His Word and promises
- We obey cautiously, calculating outcomes rather than surrendering them
- We allow past disappointment to shape future expectation
- We trust Him for salvation yet hesitate to trust Him with provision, restoration, or calling
- We rely on visible evidence more than on His Word

Scripture calls us back to a different posture:

> "Trust in the LORD with all your heart, And lean not on your own understanding; in all your ways acknowledge Him, And He shall direct your paths." (Proverbs 3:5–6 NKJV).

Direction flows from trust, and trust reveals how we truly see God. Fear often reinforces limitation. Hope can feel vulnerable, and bold faith can feel costly. To believe God again may feel like risking disappointment again. The heart may begin to negotiate, choosing to believe enough to remain faithful, yet not enough to feel exposed. Faith is not reckless optimism; it is settled confidence in the character of God as revealed in His Word.

We do not limit God in who He is, but we can limit how we trust Him, follow Him, and live in response to Him.

Limiting God does not protect us; it restrains how we trust, obey, and respond to Him. It narrows obedience and reduces vision. God is able to do far beyond what we ask or think, according to the power at work within us. When our expectations fall beneath what He has revealed, we may be mistaking restraint for humility while living beneath His invitation. Expanding our vision of God is not exaggeration; it is alignment with who He has revealed Himself to be. He does not require enlargement, but our understanding does.

As our perception is renewed by truth, courage begins to rise, prayer regains expectancy, and obedience becomes steady rather than cautious.

The question is not whether God is limited, but whether our view of Him has been shaped more by past disappointment than by present truth. Until that perception is renewed, we may continue to live within boundaries He has never placed on us.

The Small God I Saw Came from Us

It is not easy to admit, but the smallness we sometimes perceive in God does not begin with Him; it often develops within our own perception. God has not diminished. His authority has not weakened. His promises have not faded. Yet over time, our expectations can quietly narrow. What we once believed with bold confidence, we may begin to approach with caution. What we once prayed with expectancy, we may begin to temper. This shift is rarely dramatic. It forms gradually through unprocessed disappointment, prayers not answered as we expected, and seasons that stretch beyond understanding. In an effort to guard our hearts, expectation adjusts. We may call it wisdom or maturity, but beneath it, we may be protecting ourselves from pain and redefining what we believe God will do.

The small view of God we sometimes carry is not a reflection of His character, but often a reflection of our wounds, our fears, and our limited understanding.

"For I *am* the Lord, I do not change." (Malachi 3:6 NKJV).

Scripture shows how easily perception can shift. The spies saw the promise, yet fear shaped their response, and they viewed themselves as small in comparison. Israel, standing at the Red Sea, allowed present pressure to overshadow what God had already done, forgetting His faithfulness in the face of fear. In both moments, the issue was not God's ability, but how they responded to Him in light of what they saw. We see a similar pattern in the New Testament. Martha believed in Jesus, yet her expectation remained shaped by what she had previously seen Him do. Her faith was real, yet still growing in understanding. Jesus did not reject her faith; He expanded it.

Psalm 78:41 NKJV offers a sobering insight. God was not limited in His power, but His people limited what they experienced of Him. In the same way, we may hold sound theology while quietly lowering expectation in daily life. We trust Him for salvation, yet hesitate to trust Him with restoration, provision, or calling. We must also recognize a subtle distortion. What we sometimes call humility can, at times, reflect a diminished expectation of God. True humility acknowledges our limitations while exalting His sufficiency. Anything less risks lowering our expectation of what He has revealed Himself to do. The vessel is fragile, but the treasure within is not.

Often, this reduced view of God is rooted in fear. Hope can feel vulnerable, and faith can feel exposed. It may seem safer to expect less, pray cautiously, and remain within what we can manage. Yet this guarded posture does not protect us; it restrains how we trust and respond to God. What feels like delay may be divine patience. What feels like silence may be preparation. His ways may stretch beyond our understanding, but His character remains steady.

God has not been confined by our perception, but we can live confined by it until our understanding is renewed by His truth.

This is not an invitation to exaggeration, but to clarity. When perception is shaped by truth rather than experience, trust steadies, prayer regains expectancy, and obedience becomes courageous again. The issue has never been His capacity, but whether we will allow our vision to be formed by His Word rather than shaped by our experience.

Restoring a God-Sized Vision

Restoring a God-sized vision does not begin with striving; it begins with remembering. When perception has been shaped by disappointment, fear, or delay, the answer is not emotional intensity but renewed revelation. We do not need to enlarge God; we need to realign our sight according to His Word. He has not diminished; our view has. A God-sized vision grows where His character, as revealed in Scripture, speaks louder than our circumstances. Throughout Scripture, God calls His people to remember because memory recalibrates vision. When David stood before Goliath, he did not deny the size of the threat; he recalculated it in light of God's past faithfulness. The same God who delivered him before would remain faithful again. Remembrance restores proportion. The giant does not shrink; God's faithfulness becomes clearer in our sight.

At times, weariness quietly reshapes perception. When strength feels depleted, it is easy to assume that heaven is distant or disengaged. Yet Scripture restores clarity:

> "Have you not known? Have you not heard? The everlasting God, the Lord, The Creator of the ends of the earth, Neither faints nor is weary. His understanding is unsearchable." (Isaiah 40:28 NKJV).

Confidence is not restored through changed circumstances, but through renewed understanding of who God is. Restoring a God-sized vision also requires surrendering the quiet agreements formed in pain. Statements like "This will probably never change" or "It is better not to expect too much" may sound wise, but they begin to define the boundaries of our obedience. What feels like maturity can become limitation when it is shaped more by disappointment than by truth. Abraham faced this tension directly. Natural evidence pointed to impossibility, yet he anchored his confidence in God's promise rather than his circumstances. This is the restoration of right proportion, not denying difficulty, but refusing to let it define what God is able to do according to His will.

This restored vision reshapes prayer and daily living. When perception is limited, prayer becomes cautious and restrained. When vision is renewed, prayer aligns with God's character and His revealed will. We no longer pray from guarded expectation, but from confident trust in who He has made Himself known to be. Faith does not demand control over outcomes; it rests in the certainty of His nature and submits to His wisdom. Such restoration requires continual renewal of the mind. Scripture calls us to be transformed through renewed thinking. The world measures possibility by visible evidence, but Scripture trains us to measure by the unchanging character of God. As the mind is renewed, fear loosens, cynicism fades, and hope becomes steady, not because outcomes are guaranteed on our timetable, but because God is faithful.

We do not need a bigger God, but a clearer vision of the God who has already revealed Himself as faithful, powerful, and unchanging. Ultimately, restoring a God-sized vision brings peace rather than pressure. When we see Him rightly, we release the need to control outcomes. Obedience becomes freer because the weight of results rests in His hands. His sovereignty does not diminish our participation; it anchors it. We move forward not because every detail is known, but because He is trustworthy.

As our vision is renewed by truth, courage rises, faith steadies, and obedience strengthens. We begin to recognize that some boundaries we accepted were shaped more by perception than by God's revealed truth. As these are brought into the light, we rediscover what has always been true. He is faithful, powerful, sovereign, and near. And a heart that sees Him rightly will follow Him differently.

Stepping Into His Greater Path

A restored vision is not meant to remain internal. When we begin to see God rightly, our steps are invited to follow that revelation. Faith that enlarges perception also calls for deeper obedience. It is one thing to confess that nothing is too hard for the Lord; it is another to order our lives in a way that reflects that truth. Revelation invites response, and clarity calls for movement. Vision may open what is possible, but obedience brings us into alignment with what God is leading us into. Throughout Scripture, renewed vision consistently leads to faithful action.

When Peter saw Jesus walking on the water, revelation alone was not enough. He said, "Lord, if it is You, command me to come to You on the water." So He said, "Come." (Matthew 14:28–29 NKJV). And when Peter stepped out of the boat, he walked on the water toward Jesus. The invitation was simple, yet the step defied natural reasoning. The greater path was not found in the safety of the boat, but in responding to the voice of Christ. The miracle unfolded as Peter responded to the word he was given. In the same way, stepping into God's greater path often feels vulnerable because it loosens our grip on control and invites deeper trust.

Abraham faced this same tension when he was called to leave what was familiar. By faith he obeyed and went out, not knowing where he was going. The greater path did not begin with full clarity, but with trust. Obedience preceded understanding, and security was anchored not in a detailed plan, but in a faithful God. This pattern continues in our own lives. God often reveals direction without providing every detail, inviting us to trust Him before we fully understand. Hesitation may still arise, but the invitation remains the same: trust Him enough to take the next step.

"And when Peter had come down out of the boat, he walked on the water to go to Jesus." (Matthew 14:29 NKJV).

Walking the Path with Courage and Consistency

Obedience does not end with the first step; it is sustained through continual trust. What begins as a step of faith becomes a life shaped by faith. Vision may be restored in a moment, but it is established through consistent obedience over time. This is where many hesitate, not because they lack revelation, but because outcomes remain undefined. Yet God does not reveal the entire path at once. He gives light for the next step while forming deeper dependence within us.

Stepping forward requires courage, especially in the presence of resistance. When Joshua stood before the promise, the Lord commanded him to be strong and courageous, reminding him that His presence would go with him. The greater path is not free from challenge, but it is sustained by divine presence. Courage is not self-generated strength; it is confidence rooted in who walks with us. At times, this journey stretches identity as much as circumstance. Gideon saw himself as the least, yet the Lord called him a mighty man of valor. The greater path required him to receive God's perspective over his own. In the same way, God calls us according to who He is forming us to be in Christ, and obedience aligns us with that truth.

This path is not about personal ambition, but about alignment with God's will. As vision expands, desire is refined. We begin to pursue not what appears impressive, but what reflects His purpose. Faith matures through expression, and living faith moves. It obeys before certainty and trusts beyond comfort. When we refuse to confine God to past disappointment, we begin to walk with greater freedom from those limitations. What once felt restrictive begins to open, and cautious living gives way to courageous obedience.

"But the path of the just *is* like the shining sun, That shines ever brighter unto the perfect day." (Proverbs 4:18 NKJV).

A restored vision leads to a responsive life, where trust in God is not only believed, but consistently lived through obedience. When our perception of God is restored, something shifts at the core of our walk with Him. Fear loosens its grip, and hesitation loses its hold. The path ahead may not become fully clear, but it becomes steady because it is anchored in His character. A diminished vision produces guarded obedience, but a restored vision produces courageous trust. We begin to expect His faithfulness, lean into His promises, and move forward with confidence.

The greater path is not defined by full clarity, but by faithful obedience to the light God has given.

Yet every step forward ultimately leads to a decision point. Vision alone does not determine direction; response does. What we believe about God shapes how we respond when obedience requires action. In each moment, we are continually being formed either toward trust or back toward what feels familiar. The greater path is not walked in theory, but in daily decisions. This leads us into the next step in the U-Turn journey. If alignment restores authority within and vision restores clarity above, then it is at the crossroads where these realities are tested and revealed. In Chapter 6, we will explore how the choices we make in everyday moments determine whether restored vision becomes lived obedience – for it is at the crossroads that transformation takes visible form.

Reflection Questions

1. Where have I quietly lowered my expectations of God due to past disappointment, delay, or prayers that were answered differently than I expected?

2. Do my prayers reflect confidence in God's character, or have they become cautious and limited over time?
3. In what areas of my life am I confident in God for salvation, yet still learning to trust Him for provision, restoration, or calling?
4. Have I, at times, labeled guarded expectation as wisdom or humility, when it may actually be influenced by fear?
5. What step of obedience would I take today if I truly trusted that nothing is too hard for the Lord and that His will is both good and faithful?

Prayer

Father,

You are faithful, unchanging, and true. Forgive me for allowing disappointment or fear to shape my view of You. Renew my mind through Your Word and restore my vision so I may see You as You truly are. Teach me to trust Your character above what I see, to pray with confidence, and to walk in obedient faith. I surrender every limited expectation and choose to align my life with Your truth.

In Jesus' name, Amen.

Chapter 6 — Awakening to Choice at Every Crossroad

"Every moment carries the grace God provides to return to Him and realign with His truth."

Chapter 5 restored our vision. It revealed how disappointment, delay, and fear can quietly narrow our expectation of God, and reminded us that He does not change when circumstances do. His power is not diminished by waiting, nor is His faithfulness reduced by what we do not yet understand. As our vision is restored, we begin to see again not only who God is, but how faithfully and patiently He has been leading us, drawing us back to Himself with steadfast love.

Yet restored vision always invites a response. When we begin to see God rightly, all crossroads become more than a place of decision. They become a sacred invitation to trust Him more deeply and to walk with Him more closely. Alignment with God begins with the posture of the heart and is expressed through obedient living. Long before anything shifts outwardly, the heart has already leaned either toward trust or toward self-reliance. Vision shapes expectation, but choice determines direction. At every crossroad, fear may arise and faith is invited, control gives way to surrender, and resistance is met with the call to repentance. These moments are rarely dramatic, but are often tender and easily overlooked, revealed in a quiet prompting we respond to or dismiss, or a gentle invitation to surrender that we either embrace or delay.

In these small and often hidden moments, God is faithfully leading us step by step back to Himself. Scripture reminds us,

> "Trust in the LORD with all your heart, And lean not on your own understanding; In all your ways

acknowledge Him, And He shall direct your paths." (Proverbs 3:5–6 NKJV).

Transformation begins with an inward turning toward God and is then expressed through visible change in how we live. In that place of surrender, His grace meets us with both tenderness and strength, guiding us forward with clarity and peace. Every crossroad is not only a test to navigate, but an invitation to return to the love and leadership of God.

What Is a Crossroad?

A crossroad is not merely a moment of external decision, but an internal point of alignment where the heart chooses what it will agree with. It is the place where truth and perception meet, and where the will yields either to the Holy Spirit or to self. Long before direction changes outwardly, it has already been chosen inwardly at the crossroad.

What Is Happening Within You at the Crossroad?

At every crossroad, the decision we make is not random. It is shaped by what is quietly operating within us, often operating within the heart even when we are not fully attentive to it. These moments may seem small, yet they carry deep significance because they reveal not only what we believe, but what we are trusting in. In the journey of the U-Turn, God does not lead us through confusion or coercion but calls us to respond to Him with willing obedience. He faithfully meets us in these moments, gently leading us step by step back to Himself and into the life we were created to live.

Many believers sincerely love God and are familiar with Scripture yet still find themselves uncertain or conflicted in moments of decision. The struggle is often not a lack of truth, but a lack of clarity in how to walk in that truth when it matters most. There is a difference between knowing what God has said and yielding to His voice in real time. At the crossroads, this gap becomes visible, not as a place of failure, but as an invitation into deeper alignment with Him. The crossroads reveal not only what we know, but what we are yielding to.

The God-Designed Order Within

God, in His wisdom and love, has created us with an order that allows us to live in alignment with Him.

- The Holy Spirit reveals truth with clarity, bringing both conviction and peace as He guides us.
- Our spirit, made alive in Christ, anchors us in our identity as His children.
- The soul, which includes the mind, will, and emotions, processes what is being revealed and determines how we respond.
- The body then expresses that response in action.

This order is not mechanical, but deeply relational. God does not lead us from a distance, but from within, with patience and tenderness. He understands our weaknesses, our history, and our struggles, yet He remains faithful to guide us. When we begin to understand how He has designed us, the Christian life becomes less about striving and more about learning to walk in step with His Spirit.

The Influences Within

At every crossroad, there are different influences shaping our response.

- The Holy Spirit leads with truth, peace, and a quiet assurance that draws us toward trust.
- At the same time, the mind interprets through past experiences and patterns, and emotions respond to what is perceived in the moment.

- Sometimes those emotions align with truth, but at other times they are shaped by fear, uncertainty, or past wounds. The will then chooses direction, determining what we yield to.

This inner tension is something many believers experience but do not always understand. It is possible to know God's truth clearly yet feel pulled in another direction. This does not mean something is wrong with your faith. It simply reveals that there are different influences present within the heart. In the midst of this, God remains near, patient and kind, continuing to lead us back to truth. Scripture reminds us of His faithful guidance: "For as many as are led by the Spirit of God, these are sons of God." (Romans 8:14 NKJV).

The Choice of Yielding

At the crossroad, the deeper question is not simply what I should do, but what am I yielding to in this moment. Scripture describes two ways of responding, walking according to the flesh or walking according to the Spirit. The flesh is not merely the physical body, but a way of living shaped by self-reliance and independence from God. It reacts to circumstances based on what is seen and felt, often seeking control or protection.

In contrast, the Spirit leads us into dependence on God. His leading is marked by truth, conviction, and peace that invites trust. He draws us toward surrender, not through pressure, but through love. Even when His leading requires faith, it carries a steady assurance that anchors the heart. Scripture brings clarity to this reality: "For to be carnally minded *is* death, but to be spiritually minded *is* life and peace." (Romans 8:6 NKJV). God's leading will always draw us toward life, peace, and deeper trust in Him.

From Knowing to Walking

At every crossroad, truth revealed by God through His Word and Spirit is received within, the soul chooses alignment, and the body expresses the outcome. What begins as an inward yielding becomes a visible direction over time. This is where transformation quietly takes place, not only in significant moments, but in the steady rhythm of daily choices. Many believers live in the tension between knowing and walking, yet God in His grace does not leave us in that gap. He patiently teaches us, step by step, how to respond to Him. As we continue to yield to the Holy Spirit, even in small decisions, our lives begin to change, not because we are striving harder, but because we are learning to trust Him more deeply.

Scripture describes this journey beautifully: "But the path of the just *is* like the shining sun, That shines ever brighter unto the perfect day." (Proverbs 4:18 NKJV). Over time, as we continue to respond to His leading, the heart becomes more willing, and the life becomes more aligned with Him. This is the faithful work of God within us, leading us step by step, choice by choice, into the life we were created for.

Every Moment Is a Crossroad

We often imagine crossroads as dramatic life altering events, moments that are obvious and impossible to miss. Yet Scripture reveals that most turning points begin quietly, forming within the hidden places of the heart long before they are expressed outwardly. In the journey of the U-Turn, God does not only meet us in the major decisions of life, but in the small, everyday moments where direction is quietly shaped. Every moment carries the potential for alignment, and every response, no matter how small, participates in forming the path we walk. Long before our feet move, our hearts begin to lean, yet the Holy Spirit continues to call us back toward truth in every moment.

In the quiet moments of daily life, God is gently inviting us to turn toward Him again and again. Every moment carries the grace God provides to return to Him and realign with His truth. From the beginning, Scripture reveals this pattern with clarity. In the garden, the serpent did not force Eve into rebellion. He introduced a thought, subtly reframed truth, and questioned the goodness of God's word. The true crossroad was not only at the tree, but within the heart, where agreement with deception was first formed. By the time the outward action took place, a deeper decision had already been made. Even in this, we see both the seriousness of the moment and the tenderness of God, who, after the fall, came searching and calling, drawing humanity back toward Himself.

This same pattern continues throughout Scripture. Saul's failure was not merely the offering of an unauthorized sacrifice, but a decision shaped by fear and control rather than trust in God. David's fall did not begin in public exposure, but in a private moment where the heart drifted before the action followed. In both cases, the outward expression revealed an inward direction that had already been chosen. The distance between obedience and compromise is first crossed within, before it is expressed outwardly in action. Yet even here, God's heart toward us remains steadfast and full of mercy. He is not watching from a distance, waiting for failure, but walking with us patiently, inviting us to recognize His voice in these very moments. Each crossroad becomes an opportunity, not for condemnation, but for return.

Scripture speaks honestly about this inner tension:

> "For the flesh lusts against the Spirit, and the Spirit against the flesh; and these are contrary to one another, so that you do not do the things that you wish." (Galatians 5:17 NKJV).

This struggle does not mean we are abandoned. Rather, it reveals that there is a real and ongoing place of decision within us, where God continues to lead and invite.

Every moment is shaping us, and every moment holds an invitation to align again with God's Spirit and truth. This is the kindness of the Lord in the U-Turn. He does not require perfection but invites response. With each small decision, each quiet yielding, and each return of the heart, He is faithfully guiding us step by step back to the life we were created for.

The Battle Behind the Decision

If every moment is a crossroad, then every decision carries influence, even when it feels small or unnoticed. Scripture reveals that our choices are not formed in isolation. Beneath what appears ordinary, there is often a deeper, unseen movement within the heart. In the journey of the U-Turn, God is not distant from this process. He is present within it, faithfully leading, gently inviting, and patiently guiding us toward truth.

At the center of this inner movement is the heart, expressed through the mind, where agreement is formed and direction begins to take shape. What we come into agreement with will influence the direction of our lives, even as God in His grace continues to pursue, correct, and guide us. He meets us even in our thoughts, inviting us to align with His truth rather than be led by shifting circumstances or internal reactions. Scripture speaks clearly to this reality: "For to be carnally minded *is* death, but to be spiritually minded *is* life and peace." (Romans 8:6 NKJV). This is not merely a warning, but an invitation. God is drawing us toward a way of thinking and living that leads to life and peace, a life that is anchored in Him rather than in ourselves. At every crossroad, there is a quiet invitation to come into agreement with truth.

Recognizing the Source of Your Response

At the crossroads, the challenge is not always the decision itself, but discerning what is shaping that decision. Different influences may feel strong in the moment, yet not all carry the same source or lead to the same outcome. Learning to recognize these influences is part of growing in spiritual maturity and alignment with God. When the Holy Spirit is leading, His voice often comes with a quiet clarity that does not demand attention yet remains steady and sure. Even when the path requires faith, there is a peace beneath the weight, a sense of assurance that aligns with Scripture and reflects the character of God. His leading invites rather than pressures, guiding the heart toward trust and obedience.

When the mind operates without renewal, reasoning can become self-justifying. Past experiences begin to shape interpretation more than present truth, and trust can slowly be replaced by analysis. What once appeared as wisdom may begin to drift into self-reliance, making it harder to respond in simple faith. When emotions take the lead, urgency often increases. Feelings can begin to seem authoritative, as though they must be acted upon immediately. Reaction feels necessary, and the space to pause, pray, and discern becomes smaller. While emotions are a gift from God and reveal what is happening within us, they are not meant to govern our decisions.

When the flesh, meaning the pattern of self-reliance apart from God, influences the will, control begins to feel safer than surrender. Immediate relief is prioritized, and obedience may be delayed, negotiated, or quietly resisted. In these moments, the heart may still desire God yet hesitate to fully trust His way.

The question is not whether something feels strong, but whether it is true according to God's Word. Intensity does not determine authority. God's voice is not always the loudest, but it is always faithful, always consistent with His Word, and always leading toward life. Scripture reminds us of the fruit of His leading: "But the fruit of the Spirit is love, joy, peace, longsuffering, kindness, goodness, faithfulness." (Galatians 5:22 NKJV). Where His Spirit leads, His nature is revealed. In the midst of every inner tension, God remains patient and near. He is not hurried, and He is not harsh. He gently teaches us to recognize His voice, to pause before reacting, and to yield rather than strive. Step by step, decision by decision, He leads us back to alignment, shaping a life that reflects His truth and is rooted in His love.

Decisions Rooted in Truth or Lies

At every crossroad, the deeper question is not simply what we will do, but what we believe. Beneath every outward decision lies an inward agreement, a quiet place where the heart chooses what it will trust. In the journey of the U-Turn, God is not merely adjusting behavior, but lovingly restoring belief, bringing us back into alignment with what is true about Him, about ourselves, and about the life He has prepared for us.

Behavior is the fruit, but belief is the root. What we consistently choose outwardly is shaped by what we have come to accept as true inwardly. Yet even when our beliefs have been shaped by fear, disappointment, or misunderstanding, God does not turn away. In His kindness, He patiently reveals truth again, inviting us to exchange what is false for what is life giving. Scripture lovingly reminds us, "He who trusts in his own heart is a fool, But whoever walks wisely will be delivered." (Proverbs 28:26 NKJV). This is not meant to condemn, but to remind us that our understanding, apart from God, is limited. True wisdom is found in trusting Him. What we believe in the hidden place will quietly shape the direction of our lives.

From the beginning, the enemy has not worked through force, but through distortion. In the garden, truth was not removed, but subtly reframed. Once a false belief was accepted, the direction of the heart began to shift. This pattern has not changed. Yet neither has God's response. He continues to come near, speaking truth, restoring clarity, and drawing us back into alignment with His Word.

The Hidden Divide at the Crossroad

At every crossroad, there is a hidden divide that shapes the direction of our lives:

	Truth-Based Decision	**Lie-Based Decision**
Core Belief	God is trustworthy. His Word defines reality.	I must secure or control outcomes rather than entrusting them to God.
Inner Dialogue	Even if this costs me, obedience brings life.	I cannot afford to wait. I need immediate resolution.
Emotional Driver	Faith, humility, reverence.	Fear, pride, impatience, insecurity.
Posture of the Heart	Surrender and trust.	Self-preservation and control.
Short-Term Effect	May feel stretching but steady.	May feel relieving at first but often leads to underlying restlessness over time.
Long-Term Fruit	Peace, maturity, deeper intimacy with God.	Drift, strain, spiritual dullness, instability.

At the crossroads, the decision is not merely between actions, but between trusting God or trusting ourselves. This contrast is not meant to condemn, but to awaken. Lies rarely present themselves as destructive. They often appear practical, urgent, or protective, subtly suggesting that control is safer than surrender and that delayed obedience carries little consequence. Yet over time, decisions rooted in deception can hinder our experience of intimacy with God and quietly reshape the direction of our lives.

Truth, by contrast, may confront before it comforts. It exposes what is misaligned and challenges our desire for control, yet when we align with truth, even when it stretches us, the fruit is freedom and peace. Every decision reinforces the belief beneath it, and over time, those beliefs establish the direction of our lives. Small agreements with what is false compound quietly, but the invitation to realign is always present. We are never permanently bound to deception, because God's grace continually invites us back into truth. When we recognize the root, we can choose again. At the crossroads, what matters most is not simply what we do, but what truth we stand on, because the root we choose will always determine the fruit that follows.

The Direction Hidden in Daily Choices

Most life altering moments do not arrive with drama. They come through ordinary decisions, small responses, and quiet agreements formed in the unseen places of the heart. The direction of a life is rarely shaped in a single event. It is formed through daily choices that seem insignificant at the time. What we tolerate, justify, entertain, resist, and surrender gradually establishes the path we walk. Scripture reminds us that trajectory is determined by accumulation: "Do not be deceived, God is not mocked; for whatever a man sows, that he will also reap." (Galatians 6:7 NKJV). Sowing is rarely dramatic, but the harvest is certain.

Scripture reveals that small acts of obedience or compromise carry more weight than we realize. David's fall began not in public failure, but in a private moment of misplaced attention. What seemed small set in motion far reaching consequences. In contrast, Daniel's quiet, daily faithfulness prepared him to stand firm under pressure. The direction of a life is not determined in moments of crisis, but in the daily choices that precede them.

Every decision carries a trajectory. A thought becomes a belief, a belief forms a pattern, and a pattern sets direction. The enemy often works through gradual drift, as small compromises, quiet justifications, and delayed obedience accumulate over time. These choices either sharpen our sensitivity to truth or dull our discernment. Yet the same principle works in our favor. Small acts of faithfulness strengthen the heart. Choosing forgiveness, integrity, and surrender in ordinary moments forms stability within. Wisdom is not proven in isolated decisions, but in the consistent choosing of truth over impulse.

No one drifts from God suddenly, and no one grows in Him passively; growth comes as we respond to His grace in daily choices. Daily decisions either draw us closer or create quiet distance. Yet direction can be realigned at any moment. Because choices are daily, so is mercy. Because decisions are repeated, so is grace. A single act of awareness, repentance, or surrender can begin to shift trajectory. The direction of a life is hidden in daily choices, but so is the power to realign it.

Truth Is Given, Alignment Is Chosen

God has already given us truth. Through His Word, His Spirit, and the finished work of Jesus on the cross, the way back to life has been clearly revealed. Truth is not hidden. The Lord speaks, guides, corrects, and invites us into His will. Yet knowing the truth is not the same as walking in it. Many understand biblical truth intellectually, yet their lives remain shaped by fear, culture, habits, or past wounds. The issue is not the absence of truth, but the absence of alignment.

God does not force alignment. He invites it. From the beginning, humanity was created with the capacity to choose. Each day, at both small and significant crossroads, we respond, by the help of the Holy Spirit, choosing whether we will follow our own understanding or agree with God's truth, whether we will walk according to the flesh or according to the Spirit. Truth is given by God, and by His grace we are invited and empowered to align our lives with it. The Lord reveals His will, and in response to His grace, we are called to surrender ours. He shows us truth, and we are invited to believe and follow.

Scripture makes this responsibility clear: "Choose for yourselves this day whom you will serve" (Joshua 24:15 NKJV). Transformation, therefore, requires more than knowledge; it requires a yielded agreement that expresses itself through obedient living. Truth must not only be understood but embraced and lived through a surrendered heart. When our thoughts, decisions, and actions align with God's truth, our lives begin to move in the direction He has designed.

Alignment is not a one-time decision, but a daily response of surrender flowing from the finished work of Christ. Every U-Turn begins at this point of choice, where we recognize the gap between our way and God's way and intentionally turn toward Him. As we choose alignment again and again, His truth reshapes our thinking, steadies our steps, and transforms us from the inside out.

The Mercy of God at the Turning Point

"The LORD *is* merciful and gracious, Slow to anger, and abounding in mercy." (Psalm 103:8 NKJV).

At every turning point, mercy is already present. It does not wait for clarity or strength. It meets us in weakness. The crossroads are not where God measures failure, but where He draws near with compassion. Long before our decision forms, His mercy has already moved toward us. Scripture shows that God meets people in places of vulnerability, not strength.

Hagar was seen in the wilderness. Elijah was cared for in exhaustion. The woman caught in adultery was restored before she was instructed. Mercy meets us before direction, preparing our hearts to receive both His truth and His leading. God tends to the heart even as He redirects the path.

Many fear God will meet them with disappointment, yet His mercy creates the space where repentance becomes possible. It does not ignore truth but removes fear so truth can be received. God's mercy does not erase the pain of the journey, but it changes how we carry it. We are not defined by the moment we are in or by the choices that brought us there, but by who we are in Christ. His presence remains steady, patient, and near. The crossroad is not the end of the journey, but the beginning of redirection.

Mercy does not promise ease, but it offers belonging. God does not require full understanding before we turn. He invites trust. When we respond, even imperfectly, He meets us with grace and begins restoring what has been misaligned. Direction is not reclaimed through willpower, but through yielded trust, one surrendered step at a time.

Every crossroad reveals a choice, but it also reveals the nearness of a God who is already reaching toward us. As long as we turn to Him, restoration remains available and the invitation to return is never withdrawn. God is always inviting us back and always making a way forward. This leads into the next step of the journey. In Chapter 7, The U-Turn: God's Pathway to Lasting Transformation, we will explore how turning toward God becomes a sustained process of transformation, where surrendered choices form a new way of living.

Reflection Questions

1. Where in my life do I sense a quiet crossroad forming within my heart, even if nothing outward has changed yet?

2. When I face moments of decision, am I more aware of fear and self-protection, or trust and surrender?
3. What patterns in my recent choices reveal whether I am aligning with truth or relying on my own understanding?
4. How have I experienced God's mercy meeting me before I changed, and how does that shape the way I respond to Him now?
5. What is one small, specific step of obedience God may be inviting me to take today to realign my heart with Him?

Prayer

Heavenly Father,

Thank You for meeting me at every crossroad with mercy and truth. Give me a heart that is willing to turn toward You, even when surrender feels costly. Teach me to recognize Your voice, to choose truth over fear, and to walk in trust one step at a time. I surrender my will to You and invite You to lead me in Your way.

In Jesus' name, Amen.

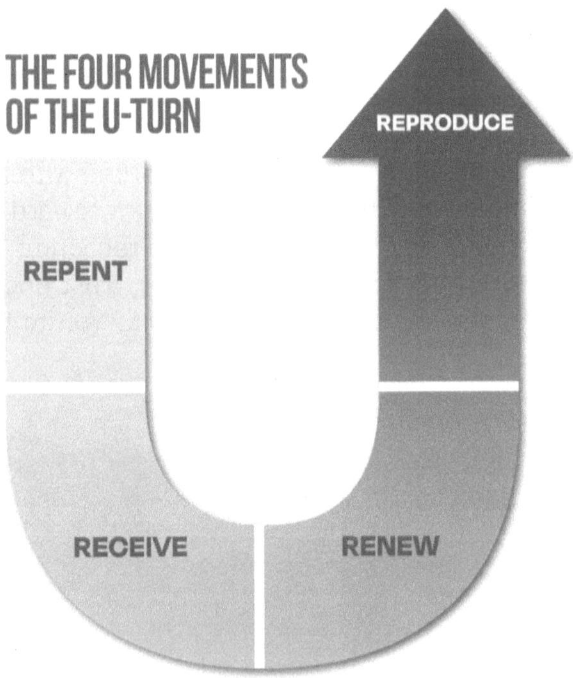
THE FOUR MOVEMENTS
OF THE U-TURN
REPRODUCE
REPENT
RECEIVE
RENEW

Chapter 7 — The U-Turn: God's Pathway to Lasting Transformation

"The U-Turn is the lived expression of repentance, where surrender becomes direction and truth begins to shape how we think, choose, and live."

Awareness brings us to the crossroad, but it is the U-Turn that determines our direction.

In the previous chapter, we saw that every moment carries a choice and every choice forms a trajectory. We became aware of how drift begins through subtle internal agreements that shape our lives over time. Yet awareness is not the destination. It is the invitation.

This chapter reveals the pathway God provides for returning. The U-Turn is both a decisive turning and a Spirit-led ongoing process through which God restores alignment, renews the inner life, and reestablishes a life anchored in truth. The U-Turn is the lived expression of repentance, where surrender becomes direction and truth begins to shape how we think, choose, and live.

Through this pathway, God does more than correct behavior. He restores trust, reshapes belief, and forms a life that reflects His nature. In the pages that follow, we will walk through four movements: Repent, Receive, Renew, and Reproduce. These are not steps to complete, but rhythms to live, revealing how God faithfully leads us back, step by step, into the life we were created to live.

The Biblical Meaning of a Returning

"Return to Me, and I will return to you," Says the LORD (Malachi 3:7 NKJV).

Throughout Scripture, returning to God is not portrayed as a dramatic leap, but as a decisive turning of the heart. It is a reorientation toward truth, love, and life. Biblical repentance emphasizes alignment with God that includes both a transformed heart and a turning away from sin, placing direction above mere external performance. God's invitation is relational before it is behavioral, yet it always leads to a changed life. He calls the heart first because transformed steps flow from renewed devotion.

From Genesis to the Gospels, His pattern remains consistent. He pursues before He instructs, invites before He corrects, and restores relationship as He reshapes behavior. In Luke 15 NKJV, the prodigal son is embraced before he can explain himself, and Israel is led long before they learn to trust. Again and again, God graciously initiates relationship and invites belonging, and as that invitation is received through faith, He forms obedience within the heart. Restoration begins with presence, not pressure.

In this light, a U-Turn is not primarily about changed circumstances, but about a changed orientation. Returning begins when the inner posture shifts, when the soul moves from self-protection to trust and responds to love. Grace, revealed through Christ, becomes the foundation of transformation, and from that foundation a new direction unfolds as the heart realigns with God. God does not drive the returning heart by force; He draws and leads it faithfully, step by step, back into alignment with Him. This understanding moves us from decision into discipleship. The One who calls us to return is already near, inviting us to turn, trust, and come home.

God's Invitation — The U-Turn

Many people hear the word returning and associate it with failure or spiritual defeat. Scripture presents it differently. Returning is not shameful; it is the evidence of a heart responding to God's conviction and grace. God is still speaking, and the soul is still capable of listening. The call to return is not a sign of defeat, but a sign that grace is actively at work.

The invitation is universal: "For all have sinned and fall short of the glory of God" (Romans 3:23 NKJV). Returning is not reserved for the visibly broken; it is the ongoing posture of every believer who desires alignment with God. Repentance is not only a response to sin, but an ongoing rhythm of relationship that keeps the heart aligned with Him. The U-Turn is not a punishment; it is an invitation rooted in covenant love. God meets us at the crossroad not with accusation, but with mercy. His welcome is grounded in grace that invites us into restored relationship through faith, not in our performance.

This invitation often comes quietly through conviction, holy unrest, or a growing awareness that something is misaligned. Though it may feel exposing, it is never without purpose. God does not shame the turning heart; He brings conviction with patience, leading us toward restoration. His aim is not to condemn, but to restore and realign.

I encountered this invitation personally at a crossroads where outwardly little was changing, but inwardly everything was shifting. I knew I could continue as I was or turn and come home. Returning required honesty and surrender without knowing the outcome. Yet what met me was not rejection, but restoration. God revealed Himself as a faithful Father who receives the returning heart and, in that place of grace, begins to reform and instruct it. That moment did not end the journey; it began a steady realignment shaped by love. This is the heart of the U-Turn: it begins with grace that restores relationship with God, and from that restored relationship a transformed life begins to take shape. When the heart turns, God receives, restores, and faithfully leads forward.

What the U-Turn Is / What the U-Turn Is Not

The U-Turn is not a reactionary moment but a relational movement. It is the deliberate reorientation of the heart back toward God, where alignment replaces self-reliant striving and truth reshapes direction through the work of the Spirit. A U-Turn is not failure; it is wisdom responding to the invitation of God's love. It begins when we release our insistence on self-direction and return to His leadership, where clarity forms and peace replaces striving.

What the U-Turn Is

A U-Turn is a loving reorientation toward God. It is not a dramatic overcorrection but a deliberate turning of the heart back toward Him. It begins when we stop insisting on our own direction and allow Him to realign us with the life He designed. Returning is not failure; it is wisdom responding to love. At its core, the U-Turn restores rightful leadership. It is the decision to come back under God's authority rather than continuing under self-direction, fear, or distorted beliefs. When alignment is restored, clarity follows, and peace replaces striving as trust is rebuilt and God's voice is welcomed again.

The U-Turn is not behavior management but renewal at the level of belief, trust, and desire. God reshapes the inner framework that governs how we think, choose, and respond. As truth takes root internally, outward change becomes the fruit rather than the focus.

Returning is often misinterpreted as regression, but it is spiritual strength. Every heart drifts, and every life requires recalibration. A U-Turn is not moving backward but coming home to clarity, truth, and right direction.

What the U-Turn Is Not

The U-Turn does not begin with condemnation. Shame pushes the heart into hiding, but love draws it back into relationship. God's conviction exposes sin truthfully and leads to restoration, not accusation that drives us away from Him. His correction preserves dignity because it is anchored in covenant love. A U-Turn is not a quick fix or a mechanical reset. Restoration unfolds as God patiently rebuilds trust and reshapes the heart over time. Growth develops in layers, and direction becomes clearer as surrender deepens and trust is formed through relationship.

Alignment cannot be sustained by effort alone. Trying harder may modify behavior temporarily, but it cannot restore the inner life. The U-Turn is sustained by grace, where what surrender begins, God faithfully empowers and completes as we continue to walk with Him. This is not passive transformation, but a Spirit-led partnership where dependence replaces self-reliance. Stopping destructive patterns without restoring inner alignment only delays drift. The U-Turn addresses the root, not merely the symptoms. It restores the center of the heart, the place from which decisions, desires, and direction flow.

The U-Turn is not a singular moment but an ongoing rhythm of life with God. Whenever misalignment appears, He invites us to return again. Each return deepens trust, sharpens discernment, and strengthens intimacy. The aim is not instant perfection, but a life of faithful responsiveness that steadily grows in holiness.

Rebuild the Life Operating System

When God calls us to return, He is not calling for superficial change, but for transformation at the level of the inner life. The phrase life operating system is not a biblical term, but an illustration to describe what Scripture reveals about the heart and mind being formed and renewed before God.

> Transformation does not begin with behavior; it begins within, as the heart is guarded and the mind is renewed according to His truth (Proverbs 4:23 NKJV; Romans 12:2 NKJV).

The life operating system refers to this internal framework that governs how we think, interpret, and respond. It shapes how we process pain, relate to authority, define security, and determine worth. Much of it is formed over time through family, culture, and lived experience. What once served as a means of coping or protection can, if left unexamined, begin to distort how we live. A believer may sincerely love God, yet still function from patterns of fear, striving, control, or self-reliance when these operate apart from trust in Him.

In a U-Turn, God does not merely adjust behavior or refine existing patterns. He brings what is misaligned to light, removes its authority, and renews the inner life according to His truth. Scripture describes this as putting off the old self and being renewed in the spirit of the mind (Ephesians 4:22–23 NKJV). This work is not condemning, but redemptive. God does not shame what was formed in weakness; He transforms it through truth. What is brought into the light is not rejected but restored under His Lordship. This restoration unfolds relationally. God restores the heart before He redirects the life, because direction flows from devotion, and devotion is formed through trust. Throughout Scripture, identity is established before assignment. Israel was delivered before they were formed. Peter was restored before he was strengthened. The disciples were called before they fully understood. God consistently works from the inside out.

Rebuilding the inner life requires surrendering the places where patterns were formed and allowing God to redefine them through His Word. The mind is renewed, the will is yielded, and trust replaces self-reliance. Even healthy functions such as planning, guarding, and responsibility are brought under His authority, no longer driven by fear or control, but ordered by wisdom and trust. This restoration is not mechanical but Spirit-led. God leads us through a consistent pattern seen throughout Scripture: repentance restores rightful authority under the Lordship of Christ, receiving establishes identity through grace, renewing transforms the mind through truth, and reproducing expresses His life through obedience and fruit. These are not steps to complete, but movements of transformation lived out in relationship with Him.

Rebuilding the life operating system is not self-improvement. It is the work of the Holy Spirit, realigning the whole of life under the Lordship of Christ. The U-Turn is not sustained by striving, but by surrender. As the inner life is renewed, decisions change, patterns shift, and direction aligns with truth, leading us into the life we were created to live in Him.

The Four Movements of the U-Turn

Transformation unfolds through four interwoven movements that reveal the work God does within us as He leads us from self-reliance into a life shaped by His Spirit. These are not abstract ideas or phases of self-improvement. They reflect the pattern we see throughout Scripture, where God restores hearts, redirects lives, and forms His people over time. Lasting transformation is not instant. It is the ongoing work of God, as we are being changed from one degree of glory to another by the Spirit (2 Corinthians 3:18 NKJV). We are not formed by trying harder, but by turning — turning away from sin and self-rule and turning toward God in repentance and faith (Acts 3:19 NKJV).

The U-Turn is not a single emotional moment, but a Spirit-led progression through which God restores, renews, and redirects a life. Each movement reaches deeper into the heart. God works patiently, establishing what is foundational before entrusting what is visible. He forms identity before assignment and calls us to faithfulness in what is hidden before what is seen (Luke 16:10 NKJV). This work invites surrender, yet it is sustained by His grace, "for it is God who works in you both to will and to do for *His* good pleasure." (Philippians 2:13 NKJV).

This pattern reflects the way of discipleship. We turn from what does not belong, learn to hear His voice, and allow His truth to shape how we think, live, and love. Over time, what God forms within us begins to bear fruit through us. Jesus said that those who abide in Him will bear much fruit, and in this the Father is glorified (John 15:5, 8 NKJV). Growth is not measured by speed, but by abiding, obedience, and the steady formation of Christlike character (Galatians 5:22–23 NKJV).

Scripture shows us that God works from the inside out. The heart is the source from which life flows (Proverbs 4:23 NKJV), and what fills the heart is what is expressed in life (Luke 6:45 NKJV). This is why transformation begins within. God humbles before He exalts (James 4:10 NKJV), calls us to die to self in order to live (Luke 9:23–24 NKJV), and forms us in the hidden place before bringing forth visible fruit (Matthew 6:6 NKJV).

The four movements of the U-Turn are not steps to complete, but a continual rhythm of life with God. Repentance restores us to His authority. Receiving anchors, in us through relationship and identity. Renewal reshapes the mind according to His truth. Reproduction expresses His life through us in fruit and obedience. As we walk with Him, the Holy Spirit continues to reveal deeper areas of the heart, leading us again to return to Him. In this way, the U-Turn becomes a lifelong pattern, as we are continually being conformed to the image of Christ (Romans 8:29 NKJV). The four movements: Repent, Receive, Renew, and Reproduce are not separate ideas, but a unified work of grace. Through them, God faithfully leads us step by step into a life aligned with Him.

1. Repent — Surrendering to His Lordship

Repentance is the return to God's authority. Before anything else can be restored, the heart must come back under His rule. Repentance is more than feeling sorrow. It is a turning away from sin and a turning toward God. Jesus began His ministry with the call, "Repent, for the kingdom of heaven is at hand." (Matthew 4:17 NKJV). Peter likewise declared, "Repent therefore and be converted, that your sins may be blotted out, so that times of refreshing may come from the presence of the Lord" (Acts 3:19 NKJV). In repentance, sin is confessed, the old way is laid down, and the heart yields again to God. Authority shifts, and everything that follows flows from this restored foundation.

2. Receive — Hearing and Following God's Voice

As we return to God, we are restored to relationship with Him. He is not distant. He speaks, leads, and makes Himself known to His people. Jesus said, "My sheep hear My voice, and I know them, and they follow Me." (John 10:27 NKJV). Through Christ, we receive our identity as children of God, not by effort but by grace (John 1:12 NKJV). The Spirit leads those who belong to Him (Romans 8:14 NKJV). Receiving is not passive. It is a posture of listening, trusting, and responding. As we walk with Him, He directs our steps and instructs us in the way we should go (Psalm 32:8 NKJV).

3. Renew — Living from a Transformed Mind

Renewal is the ongoing work of God in the inner life. Scripture calls us not to be conformed to this world, but to be transformed by the renewing of our minds (Romans 12:2 NKJV). This includes putting off the old self and being renewed in the spirit of the mind (Ephesians 4:22–23 NKJV). As God's truth reshapes how we think, we learn to make our thoughts captive and bring them into obedience to Christ (2 Corinthians 10:5 NKJV). Renewal brings alignment between what we believe and how we live. Over time, the truth of God becomes the steady foundation from which we respond to life.

4. Reproduce — From Personal Transformation to Kingdom Impact

What God does within us; He intends to express through us. Jesus said, "He who abides in Me, and I in him, bears much fruit" (John 15:5 NKJV). Fruitfulness flows from abiding, not striving. As we remain in Him, His life produces character, obedience, and impact through us. This includes the fruit of the Spirit (Galatians 5:22–23 NKJV) and participation in His mission to make disciples (Matthew 28:19 NKJV). Reproduction is not about striving to do more, but about living from a life that is rooted in Christ, where His work in us becomes a blessing to others.

Together, these movements reveal how God works in the life of a believer. He restores us to Himself through repentance. He establishes us in relationship and identity. He renews our minds through His truth. And He produces fruit through our lives.

These movements are not a task to complete, but a way to walk with God, as He faithfully forms our lives to reflect Christ.

Movement One: Repent — Surrendering to His Lordship

Repentance is the doorway into the U-Turn. Transformation begins not with effort, but with surrender. To repent is to return governance to God, a decisive turning of authority from self-rule to Spirit-rule. This is not humiliation; it is holy realignment. Repentance restores rightful authority in the heart, allowing God to lead where self once governed.

Repentance reaches beneath visible behavior into the deeper structures of identity, motivation, and governance. It asks not only what we are doing, but what is leading us. When Christ is not fully governing, authority quietly shifts. Repentance restores His leadership across every layer of the inner life, bringing the heart back into alignment with truth.

Movement One unfolds through three decisive reckonings:

Repent — Surrendering to His Lordship

- The Old Self — Reckoning with the flesh
- Fear — Rejecting the spirit of fear
- Control — Relinquishing self-reliance

1. The Old Self — Reckoning with the flesh

Authority first shifts in how we see ourselves. Scripture describes the flesh as the part of us shaped by self-rule rather than surrender, by wounds rather than healing, and by pride or insecurity rather than truth. The Old Self is the version of us formed apart from full trust in God. It learned to survive, protect, strive, and manage, yet what once felt necessary can quietly become misaligned. Reckoning with the flesh is not self-rejection, but discernment. It is recognizing what can no longer remain in authority.

In repentance, we allow the Spirit to expose these patterns, not to condemn us, but to free us from their rule. We acknowledge what has shaped us and release its claim over our identity.

2. Fear — Rejecting the spirit of fear

Authority also shifts in what drives us. Fear becomes a hidden motivator when trust weakens, shaping decisions around safety, approval, preservation, or avoidance. Outward obedience may remain yet inwardly fear sets the pace. Rejecting the spirit of fear is not denying its presence, but refusing its leadership. Repentance confronts fear's influence and brings it under the Lordship of Christ. We choose trust over anxiety, obedience over avoidance, and love over self-protection.

As fear loses authority, the heart steadies in the security of God's character rather than its own defenses.

3. Control — Relinquishing self-reliance

Authority finally shifts in how we manage outcomes. Control seeks certainty apart from surrender. It plans without yielding and moves without waiting. What appears responsible can often mask self-governance. Relinquishing self-reliance is an act of worship. We release the need to manage every detail and entrust both direction and results to God. This does not produce passivity; it produces dependence. We move from striving to trusting, from managing to following.

Repentance is not behavior modification; it is restored governance.

- The Old Self no longer defines us.
- Fear no longer drives us.
- Control no longer directs us.

In their place, the Spirit leads. This is the sacred beginning of transformation. When authority is restored, direction can follow.

Movement Two: Receive — Hearing and Following God's Voice

If Repent restores authority, Receive restores intimacy. After lordship is reestablished, the heart becomes capable of hearing again. What has been yielded to God in repentance creates space for communion. This is not passivity, but attentiveness—the quieting of self-rule so that relationship can deepen. Without this movement, repentance can remain merely corrective. Authority may be acknowledged, yet the heart stays restless, striving to determine its own path.

Receive anchors transformation in relationship, where we do not simply submit to God's rule but learn to recognize His voice.

This movement guards the U-Turn from becoming behavior-driven. We are not adjusting our lives to meet religious expectations; we are responding to a Shepherd who knows us. As His voice becomes familiar, internal pressure begins to quiet. The need to prove, perform, or prematurely resolve begins to fade. Instead of asking, what must I do, the heart begins to ask, what is God saying? Guidance is no longer something we strive to produce, but something we learn to receive.

Movement Two unfolds through four interwoven expressions of divine guidance, each received rather than achieved:

Receive — Hearing and Following God's Voice

- Identity — Who am I in Christ?
- Purpose — What is my calling?
- Gifts — What has God given me?
- Direction — What is my next step?

1. Identity — Who am I in Christ?

Divine guidance begins with identity. Before God clarifies assignment, He establishes belonging. Identity in Christ is not earned through performance or sustained by effort; it is given through covenant love. As authority is restored in repentance, identity is reestablished in relationship. We are no longer defined by the old self, fear, or control, but by sonship. From this place, God's voice is no longer distant instruction, but relational leading. The soul learns to rest, and from that rest it listens.

2. Purpose — What is my calling?

As identity stabilizes, purpose begins to surface. Calling is no longer shaped by comparison, ambition, or the pressure to create significance. It emerges from communion. We begin to discern how God expresses His Kingdom through who we are becoming. Purpose shifts from striving to build something visible to faithfully walking in what God has already prepared. Urgency gives way to obedience and striving yields to discernment.

3. Gifts — What has God given me?

As purpose becomes clearer, the gifts entrusted to us come into view. These gifts are stewardships of grace, not measures of worth. When identity is secure, gifts no longer define value; they express it. They are given for service, for strengthening others, and for revealing God's character through love in action. What we carry is not for comparison or control, but for faithful contribution.

4. Direction — What is my next step?

Guidance then becomes specific. God rarely reveals the entire path; He gives light for the next step. Direction is received through trust rather than complete certainty, and through obedience rather than full visibility. We learn to walk with God instead of moving ahead of Him. Faithfulness is measured not by speed, but by responsiveness. As we obey the light given, further clarity follows. The Shepherd who speaks is also the Shepherd who leads, and at the center of this movement, the heart learns a new posture: not my will, but Yours.

Divine guidance is not merely instruction; it is relationship. God does not simply provide direction. He forms identity, awakens purpose, reveals gifts, and leads us step by step into a life aligned with His Kingdom, His timing, and His love. Here, we discover that guidance is not something we chase, but something we receive.

Movement Three: Renew — Living from a Transformed Mind

Movement One, Repent — Surrendering to His Lordship, reestablished rightful governance. Movement Two, Receive — Hearing and Following God's Voice, restored relational direction. Movement Three builds upon both, bringing what has been surrendered and received into daily life.

Renewal is where surrendered authority and received direction become an established way of life. The inner life is reshaped so that truth governs thought, response, and rhythm. This is not a refined version of the old self, but a life reordered by truth, shaped by grace, and governed by the Spirit.

Transformation moves from conviction into consistency. What we have agreed with and discerned begins to shape how we interpret circumstances, make decisions, and respond under pressure. Obedience flows from identity, belonging, and trust rather than fear or obligation. What once felt like sacrifice becomes alignment as the Spirit forms within us what striving never could.

Renewal is not behavior modification; it is the transformation of the inner life until truth becomes our natural way of living. Movement Three unfolds through renewed belief, transformed thinking, and the daily practice of walking in the Spirit, where truth becomes lived reality.

Renew — Living from a Transformed Mind

- Belief — Agreeing with God's truth
- Mind — Renewing thought patterns
- Practice — Walking in the spirit

1. Belief — Agreeing with God's truth

Renewal begins with agreement. Transformation deepens as we align our beliefs with what God declares true, even when it challenges long-held assumptions or personal wounds. This is not merely intellectual assent but the surrender of interpretive authority to God's Word. As belief aligns with truth, identity stabilizes and the inner life is anchored. Freedom follows because truth becomes the governing reality of the soul.

2. Mind — Renewing thought patterns

As belief stabilizes, the Holy Spirit reshapes thought patterns. Frameworks formed by fear, striving, or self-protection are replaced with wisdom, discernment, and peace. Renewal brings emotion under the authority of truth and redirects internal dialogue. Over time, we pause instead of reacting, discern instead of assuming, and choose faithfulness over urgency. What once felt chaotic becomes governed, and peace emerges through sustained trust.

3. Practice — Walking in the spirit

Renewal becomes visible through practice. Walking in the Spirit becomes a daily posture where decisions flow from alignment and relationships are shaped by grace. Obedience becomes the natural expression of trust rather than forced discipline. Truth becomes habit, and the Spirit-led life shifts from exception to norm. This is not perfection but partnership, where patterns formed in survival are replaced with patterns formed in grace.

Movement Three establishes a steady way of walking. A life once ruled by self and confusion becomes governed by truth and trust, preparing us for both personal wholeness and faithful Kingdom impact.

Movement Four: Reproduce — From Personal Transformation to Kingdom Impact

Movement Four is the natural overflow of a life that has been surrendered, guided, and renewed. Reproduction is not a burden to carry or a quota to meet; it is the quiet evidence of abiding. This movement shifts us from the world's definition of success, measured by visibility and achievement, to Heaven's definition of significance, measured by faithfulness, love, obedience, and fruit that remains.

Reproduction is not about doing more for God but allowing what He has formed within us to continue through us. Fruitfulness is not forced; it is cultivated through connection. By this stage of the U-Turn, the need to prove or perform has lost its authority. What emerges instead is steadiness, a settled heart, and a life that quietly carries God's presence into every space it enters. Movement Four unfolds through overflow, not ambition, as a life rooted in Christ naturally extends His life to others.

Reproduce — From Personal Transformation to Kingdom Impact

- Abiding — Remaining in the vine
- Modeling — Living what we believe
- Discipleship — Walking others toward Christ
- Legacy — Leaving kingdom fruit that remains

1. Abiding — Remaining in the vine

Jesus makes fruitfulness unmistakably clear: connection precedes multiplication. "Abide in Me, and I in you...for without Me you can do nothing." (John 15:4–5 NKJV). Abiding is not productivity but proximity, the deliberate choice to remain in relationship rather than drift into self-sufficiency. When abiding becomes central, pressure dissolves because life flows from union with Him. Our pace softens, striving quiets, and fruit grows in ways we do not orchestrate. Abiding reminds us that God is more committed to fruitfulness than we are and that remaining with Him is the most fruitful work we will ever do.

2. Modeling — Living what we believe

Overflow becomes visible through lived integrity. Paul writes, "Imitate me, just as I also *imitate* Christ" (1 Corinthians 11:1 NKJV), revealing that influence flows from authenticity rather than perfection. Modeling is not performance but congruence, allowing repentance, trust, surrender, and renewal to shape everyday life. When Christ governs the heart, others encounter stability, humility, and peace before they hear instruction. A life aligned with Christ becomes permission-giving, demonstrating that faith is not arrival but ongoing transformation.

3. Discipleship — Walking others toward Christ

Reproduction deepens through relational investment. Jesus did not mass-produce followers; He walked with them. His commission to "make disciples" (Matthew 28:19 NKJV) flowed from shared life, long before it became a mandate. Discipleship is patient and consistent, formed through listening, prayer, teaching, correction, encouragement, and modeled obedience over time. We do not reproduce by pressure or persuasion but by presence, walking with others toward Christ and trusting the Spirit to do the transforming work.

4. Legacy — Leaving kingdom fruit that remains

Legacy reflects the quiet confidence that God completes what we cannot. "One sows and another reaps." (John 4:37 NKJV) reminds us that the Kingdom advances through shared obedience across generations. Legacy is not built through control but entrusted through faithfulness. Much of what God grows through our lives will continue beyond our awareness, as seeds planted in obedience bear fruit over time. Significance is measured not by what we accumulate but by what remains rooted in Christ.

Movement Four reveals that reproduction is not a demand placed upon us but a promise fulfilled through us. A life deeply rooted in Christ will bear fruit because His life is flowing through it. As we remain with Him, grace extends beyond us, truth strengthens others, peace steadies environments, and faith multiplies quietly. This is significance in God's Kingdom, not what we construct for Him, but what He grows through surrendered lives.

Scripture also calls us to vigilance. Alignment can erode subtly through neglect, fear, distraction, self-reliance, or unresolved wounds that quietly reassert authority. Before learning how to sustain a healthy U-Turn, we must understand how drift begins. This framework is not mechanical; the movements overlap and repeat as God revisits deeper layers of the heart. Yet the pattern remains steady: He turns us through repentance, establishes us through grace, renews us through truth, and reproduces His life through us.

The beauty of the U-Turn is not only that God leads us back, but that He faithfully sustains us as we walk with Him. Yet Scripture reminds us that drift is rarely sudden; it is often subtle, quiet, and unrecognized in its early stages. We do not lose our way in a moment, but through small shifts in what we trust, follow, and allow to lead us. What begins as neglect, distraction, or self-reliance can gradually reshape the heart's alignment if left unexamined. This is why understanding the reverse matters. Not to produce fear, but to cultivate discernment. Not to question God's faithfulness, but to guard our responsiveness to Him.

In Chapter 8 — *The Reverse U-Turn: How We Lose Our Way*, we will uncover how misalignment begins, how it progresses, and how awareness becomes a safeguard for the life God is faithfully forming within us.

Pre–U-Turn Assessment

Before beginning the U-Turn journey, take time to consider where you are. Scripture calls us to examine ourselves and walk in the truth. This assessment is designed to help you reflect on your current patterns of thinking, responding, and living. This is not a measure of your worth. Your standing before God is secure in Christ. This is a tool for clarity, helping you recognize where your life is aligned with God's ways and where you may need to return to Him. God reveals not to condemn, but to lead us into truth and restoration.

Why This Assessment Matters

The Believer's Life Operating System shapes how you live from the inside out. It influences your decisions, responses, and daily walk with God. When your life is ordered by God's truth, it produces clarity, steadiness, and obedience. When it is not, life can become reactive, unsettled, or inconsistent.

This assessment helps you:

- Recognize areas of alignment with God's truth
- Identify patterns that need to change
- Respond to God's call to return
- Prepare for lasting transformation

How to Use This Assessment

Read each statement and respond based on your current experience.

- Answer honestly

- Do not overthink your response
- Let truth guide your answer

After completing all questions, add your total score.

Rating Scale

Score	**Description**
1	Rarely true
2	Sometimes true
3	Often true
4	Consistently true
5	Established pattern

Pre–U-Turn Assessment Questions (Appendix B)

Score Summary

Add your responses and record your total: Total Score: ______ / 100. This score provides a general picture of how your life is currently functioning.

#	Category	Sub-category	Statement	Score
1	**Awareness**	Spiritual Awareness	I am aware when my thoughts, attitudes, or actions are not aligned with God's truth	
2		Spiritual Awareness	When I recognize misalignment, I turn to God rather than ignoring or justifying it	
3		Openness	I am willing to acknowledge areas where I need repentance and change	
4		Readiness	I am willing to submit every area of my life to God's authority	
5	**Repent**	Old Self	I recognize patterns of the old way of living that are not consistent with my life in Christ	
6		Old Self	When sin or misalignment is revealed, I confess it and turn from it before God	
7		Fear	I choose to trust God and do not allow fear to direct my decisions	

8		Control	I entrust my plans and outcomes to God rather than relying on my own control	
9	**Receive**	Identity	I understand that my identity is found in Christ and not in my performance or circumstances	
10		Purpose	I seek God's will in my decisions through His Word and prayer	
11		Gifts	I use the abilities and opportunities God has given me to serve others faithfully	
12		Direction	When I understand what God is leading me to do, I choose to obey	
13	**Renew**	Belief	I choose to believe what God's Word says even when it challenges my own thinking	
14		Mind	I allow my thinking to be shaped and renewed by God's truth	
15		Practice	I maintain regular practices such as prayer and Scripture that keep me grounded in God	
16		Practice	In difficult situations, I seek to respond in a way that honors God rather than reacting impulsively	
17	**Reproduce**	Abiding	I maintain a consistent relationship with God	

			through prayer and His Word	
18		Modeling	My daily life reflects my faith in Christ in both words and actions	
19		Discipleship	I intentionally encourage and help others grow in their faith	
20		Legacy	I desire my life to bear lasting fruit that honors God and impacts others	

Understanding Your Total Score

Score Range	**Condition**	**Description**
80–100	Aligned	Your life is generally ordered by God's truth and expressed with consistency. Continue to remain faithful and attentive to Him.
60–79	Strengthening	There is evidence of alignment, though not yet consistent. Continue to return to God and walk in what you know to be true.
40–59	Unsettled	You understand truth but do not live it consistently. This is a call to return and allow God to restore order within.
20–39	Disordered	Your life is not functioning in its intended order. This is an invitation to turn back to God and begin again with Him.

Reflection Questions

1. What is God inviting you to release right now, fear, control, self-reliance, or a pattern formed in survival rather than trust?
2. In your current season, how are you making space to listen to God before acting or deciding?
3. Where have you noticed gradual change in your thoughts, reactions, or beliefs as the Holy Spirit works patiently in you?
4. How might God be using your story, healing, or obedience to quietly bless others—even in ways you may not fully see yet?
5. When transformation feels difficult, what helps you remember that God is a loving Father who is gentle with you in the process?

Prayer

Father God,

Thank You for loving me with patience and kindness. Thank You that repentance is an invitation home, not a place of shame. Teach me to listen for Your voice, to trust Your guidance, and to rest in Your gentle work of renewal. When the journey feels hard, remind me that You are near and that Your love is steady. Let my life overflow with the fruit of abiding in You, so others may encounter Your grace through me. I place my steps in Your hands and choose to walk in Your way.

In Jesus' name, Amen.

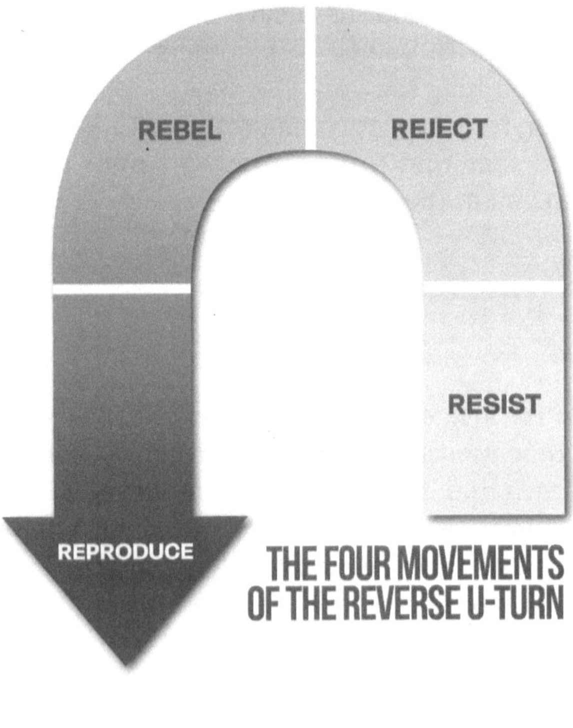

THE FOUR MOVEMENTS OF THE REVERSE U-TURN

Chapter 8 — The Reverse U-Turn: How We Lose Our Way

"Drift is rarely the result of a single decision, but rather a quiet and gradual loss of responsiveness to God."

Chapter 8 examines how believers can gradually drift from God's direction, even after seasons of clarity, healing, and restoration. Building on the U-Turn framework introduced in Chapter 7, this chapter offers a pastoral and scriptural warning. Just as the U-Turn unfolds through four movements toward alignment, drift unfolds through four movements away from it. Renewal is a gift of grace that must be stewarded through ongoing dependence on God. What God restores is not only received with gratitude but also lived out through faithfulness.

The Reverse U-Turn describes a gradual turning of the heart, not through open rebellion, but through subtle resistance, delayed obedience, and a diminishing responsiveness to the Holy Spirit, who continues to convict, guide, and call His people back. As self-reliance begins to replace dependence, and comfort or distraction starts to outweigh faithfulness, the heart can slowly lose its sensitivity to God's leading. Drift is rarely obvious. It often develops quietly beneath sincere faith, familiar language, and ongoing spiritual activity.

Drift often begins not with open defiance, but with inattention to God's voice and a gradual shift in the heart. This chapter calls for reflection, not condemnation. It uncovers how small, often unnoticed shifts, can redirect the heart over time. By recognizing these early patterns, believers are invited to return with humility and renewed surrender. **Drift is rarely**

the result of a single decision, but rather a quiet and gradual loss of responsiveness to God.

God's grace remains present even in seasons of drift, faithfully calling His people back to Himself. His call is not only compassionate, but also holy, inviting realignment with truth. This chapter affirms that awareness itself is an act of mercy and that returning to God is always met with His readiness to restore and lead again.

When Our Hearts Begin to Drift

"Therefore we must give the more earnest heed to the things we have heard, lest we drift away." (Hebrews 2:1 NKJV).

No one begins their journey with God intending to lose their way. In Scripture, drifting is rarely loud or sudden. It unfolds quietly, often while life still appears faithful and productive. Worship continues, service remains steady, and the language of faith remains, yet beneath the surface attentiveness weakens and responsiveness softens. Direction often begins to shift long before behavior visibly changes. What appears steady on the outside can be quietly drifting on the inside.

I have seen this not only in Scripture, but also in my own life. Even with deep gratitude for what God has done, familiarity can begin to replace reverence, and responsibility can slowly crowd out dependence. Drift is not always overt rebellion; more often, it takes the form of quiet neglect, which Scripture treats with great seriousness. Scripture reveals that drift begins in the heart. When the heart is no longer fully yielded, dependence gives way to self-reliance, and intimacy is replaced with familiarity.

This pattern is seen throughout Scripture. Though God was present among Israel, fear entered, trust weakened, and unbelief began shaping their response to Him. Their drift was not first marked by open rejection, but by a failure to fully trust what God had spoken. We see the same pattern in King

Saul. He began in humility, yet under pressure he leaned on his own understanding rather than fully trusting the Lord. His downfall was not sudden, but the gradual result of a heart no longer fully surrendered to God. Jesus later addressed this same condition, describing those who honored God outwardly while their hearts remained distant from Him. This kind of drift is dangerous precisely because it often goes unnoticed, as spiritual activity gradually replaces attentiveness and inward surrender.

Yet, this is the mercy of God: He sees our drift clearly and still calls us back to Himself. In both holiness and compassion, He reveals what is misaligned, not to condemn, but to restore. Every Reverse U-Turn begins in the heart, and the God who warns us is also the One who faithfully leads us home.

The Reverse U-Turn: Four Movements Away from God

Drifting away from God rarely begins with open rebellion or deliberate rejection. More often, it begins with subtle internal shifts that feel reasonable in the moment. What begins as self-protection gradually becomes self-direction, and coping slowly replaces communion. The heart does not turn away all at once; it leans little by little until distance forms. Scripture reveals this pattern clearly. Samson did not lose his strength in a single moment, but through the gradual erosion of consecration until the presence of the Lord departed from him. King Saul did not openly renounce God, yet he increasingly relied on his own judgment and feared people more than he trusted the Lord. In both lives, inward drift preceded visible collapse, and independence took root before disobedience fully emerged. Drift is rarely a sudden departure from God, but a gradual movement toward life without wholehearted dependence on Him.

The Reverse U-Turn often reflects not only defiant choices, but sincere people gradually learning to live apart from abiding in Christ, no longer remaining in active and dependent relationship with Him. It reveals how self-reliance becomes normalized, how fear gains quiet influence, and how independence slowly replaces intimacy with God. Like Martha, devotion may remain while attentiveness is redirected. Like the church in Ephesus, outward faithfulness may continue while first love quietly fades. The heart stays active, yet it no longer stays close.

Where the U-Turn restores alignment through relationship, the Reverse U-Turn creates misalignment when relationship is replaced by self-management. Life may still appear responsible, disciplined, and faithful, yet its rootedness in God quietly weakens. Like the older brother in Jesus' parable, one can remain near the Father's house while living distant from the Father's heart.

"Take heed to yourselves, lest your hearts be weighed down..." (Luke 21:34 NKJV).

Scripture warns us about drift not to condemn us, but to awaken us. This chapter gives language to what many believers sense but struggle to name, revealing how drift unfolds gradually and why awareness is often the first mercy God gives. As Nathan awakened David and Jesus restored Peter, awareness is not the end of the story; it is often the moment God interrupts the drift and calls the heart back to Himself.

The Four Movements of the Reverse U-Turn

Spiritual drift often follows a recognizable progression. What begins quietly in the heart eventually shapes beliefs, decisions, and direction. Scripture consistently shows that when the heart begins moving away from God, life soon follows. What is left unaddressed inwardly will eventually be revealed outwardly in the direction of one's life. These movements are rarely obvious at first and often develop beneath outward expressions of faith and spiritual activity.

The Reverse U-Turn unfolds through four movements, each revealing a growing distance from God. These shifts often feel subtle, reasonable, or even justified in the moment, yet they gradually build upon one another, redirecting the heart away from wholehearted dependence on Him. What begins as resistance can eventually shape the entire course of a person's thinking, living, and influence.

Reverse Movement One: Resist — The Hardened Heart

Drift often begins when the heart resists conviction. The Holy Spirit continues to speak, but responsiveness gradually weakens over time. What once stirred repentance becomes easier to ignore. Justification begins to replace obedience, and the heart slowly loses its tenderness toward God.

Reverse Movement Two: Reject — Human Independence

As resistance becomes familiar, dependence on God gradually gives way to self-reliance. Decisions are made with little regard for seeking Him, and control begins to replace surrender. God is not openly denied, yet His leadership is no longer actively pursued or followed. The relationship grows distant, shaped more by habit than by living dependence.

Reverse Movement Three: Rebel — The Conformed Life

As independence deepens, life increasingly conforms to pressure, fear, or cultural influence rather than God's truth. Obedience becomes selective, and compromise begins to appear reasonable. Faith may still remain outwardly, but the heart is no longer fully yielded to God.

Reverse Movement Four: Reproduce — From Significance to Self-Focus

What is formed inwardly will eventually be expressed outwardly. Independence begins shaping influence, and life gradually turns inward toward personal priorities and self-preservation. What once flowed from devotion begins to reflect self-direction instead. What we consistently live from within will ultimately shape what flows through our lives.

Reverse Movement One: Resist — The Hardened Heart

"Today, if you will hear His voice, Do not harden your hearts." (Hebrews 3:15 NKJV).

The Reverse U-Turn rarely begins with open rejection of God. More often, it begins with resistance. Resistance is subtle, quiet, and often unintentional. It is not always expressed through open unbelief, but through hesitation, delay, and a weakening trust in God. It is not denying God, but postponing obedience. The heart does not harden suddenly; it tightens gradually, often in response to disappointment, pressure, fatigue, pain, or unmet expectations. What we repeatedly postpone in obedience, we eventually begin to drift from in intimacy.

Scripture makes clear that hardness of heart does not develop because God stops speaking, but because His voice is heard and not answered. Repeated resistance to His prompting slowly creates distance in our attentiveness to Him. This is not written as condemnation, but as loving wisdom. God reveals the condition of the heart not to shame us, but to heal and restore us. Even in resistance, His voice continues to call, inviting us back to softness, trust, and surrender.

Resistance often hardens the heart not through obvious rebellion, but through growing independence from God. A hardened heart is rarely formed in a single moment; it develops through many small moments of resisted obedience, delayed surrender, and quiet self-reliance.

Reverse Movement One: Resist — The Hardened Heart Reveals Itself Through Three Patterns

Self-Reliance — Trusting in the Flesh

Resistance often begins with self-reliance. As life becomes heavier or more complex, we begin compensating in our own strength. We manage what we once entrusted to God. We carry what we once surrendered. What begins as responsibility can gradually shift into independence.

This pattern is seen in Israel during the wilderness journey. God delivered them with power, provided manna daily, and dwelled among them, yet under pressure they leaned on their own reasoning, questioned His provision, and doubted His intentions. They did not openly renounce God, but through unbelief they stopped fully relying on Him. **Self-reliance rarely feels sinful at first. It often appears practical, responsible, and necessary.** Yet Scripture reminds us that the arm of flesh will fail, and those who trust primarily in their own strength gradually drift from a life of faith and dependence.

Fear — Yielding to a Spirit of Fear

Where self-reliance grows, fear often follows. Fear whispers that surrender is unsafe and that control is wisdom. It suggests vulnerability is dangerous and that obedience carries too much risk. Fear rarely presents itself openly. More often, it disguises itself as caution, discernment, or realism.

In the life of King Saul, fear of people eventually outweighed trust in God, leading him to act on his own understanding rather than wait on the Lord. Fear reshapes perception. It narrows trust while widening anxiety, training the heart to resist what once felt safe and sacred.

Control — Clinging to Autonomy

Fear often expresses itself through control. **Control becomes the flesh's attempt to create security in uncertainty.** Decisions are rushed, outcomes are tightly managed, and prayer subtly shifts from surrender to consultation. God is still acknowledged, but His leadership is no longer fully trusted or followed.

This pattern appears in Martha. She loved Jesus and served Him faithfully, yet anxiety and pressure drew her into distraction and frustration. Her activity replaced attentiveness, and service slowly crowded out surrender. Control is often quiet and internal, but over time autonomy replaces intimacy. The heart may remain active, productive, and even spiritual, yet no longer fully yielded to God. God's invitation at this stage is gentle and merciful. A hardened heart is not a final condition. When we respond to His voice, surrender begins loosening what resistance has tightened. Grace restores what self-reliance has strained, and trust rebuilds what fear has weakened. The U-Turn back toward life begins as God softens the heart and we choose to respond to His voice today.

Reverse Movement Two: Reject — Human Independence

"There is a way *that* seems right to a man, But its end *is* the way of death." (Proverbs 14:12 NKJV).

When resistance becomes familiar and conformity feels normal, rejection quietly takes root. This rejection is rarely verbal or emotional. It does not deny God's existence or question His goodness. Instead, it no longer yields to His leadership in daily life. Life continues. Decisions are made. Responsibilities are carried, yet submission begins to fade. The will remains strong while dependence weakens. Rejection in this stage is not the absence of God, but a life that is no longer actively yielded to His leadership.

This movement marks a critical shift. God is still acknowledged but is no longer consistently trusted as the source. Prayer becomes secondary. Discernment yields to efficiency. Life is no longer primarily formed through abiding, but through self-management. Scripture consistently warns that independence from God is not strength, but deception. Human wisdom, when detached from dependence on God, can feel right, appear effective, and still lead away from life. The danger of this stage is not obvious disorder, but quiet confidence apart from God.

Reverse Movement Two: Reject — Human Independence Reveals Itself Through Four Patterns

Identity — Forgetting Who I Am in Christ

When identity is no longer anchored in Christ, it begins attaching itself to roles, performance, productivity, or survival. Worth becomes conditional, and belonging starts to feel fragile. The soul strives to secure what has already been freely given through Christ.

This pattern is seen in the older brother in Jesus' parable. Though he remained in the father's house, he related more like a servant than a son. **He worked faithfully and obeyed outwardly, yet his identity had become rooted in performance rather than relationship.** Independence causes the heart to forget what is already true. In Christ, we are already loved, chosen, accepted, and secure. When identity drifts, we begin striving for what grace has already provided.

Purpose — Ignoring God's Calling

As identity shifts, purpose soon follows. Calling is gradually replaced with obligation. The question changes from "What is God leading me into?" to "What must I accomplish?" Service may continue, but it is no longer sustained by joy, intimacy, or obedience. Fatigue increases while delight diminishes. This pattern appears in Moses when he struck the rock instead of speaking to it as God instructed. The work of God still continued, yet obedience was compromised. Pressure replaced attentiveness. **What once flowed from communion became driven by frustration and demand.**

When purpose becomes disconnected from abiding, even holy work becomes heavy. The work of God cannot be spiritually sustained apart from the presence of God.

Gifts — Neglecting What God Has Given

Spiritual gifts were never meant to function apart from intimacy with God. When independence grows, those gifts are often neglected through insecurity or overextended through striving, comparison, and self-effort. What was intended to be overflow slowly becomes performance.

This is seen in Saul, who was anointed and empowered by God, yet gradually shifted toward self-reliance. He acted impulsively, sought the approval of people, and became consumed with protecting his position. The gift remained visible, but the evidence of God's empowering presence diminished. Gifts without dependence often lead to burnout, pride, or exhaustion, while abiding keeps them fruitful, humble, and aligned with God's purpose.

Direction — Choosing My Own Way

At this stage, decisions are often made confidently and quickly, but without discernment. God is no longer sought first; He is consulted later. Direction becomes shaped by urgency, emotion, logic, opportunity, or past success rather than prayerful dependence.

Samson's life illustrates this sobering reality. Though called and empowered by God, he repeatedly chose his own way, and Scripture records that he did not realize the Lord's empowering presence had departed from him. Independence blinded him to what had been lost. Life continued, but spiritual strength was gone. This form of rejection is not hostility toward God, but life increasingly lived apart from Him. Independence may appear effective outwardly, but inwardly it slowly drains intimacy and dulls spiritual awareness.

God's invitation in this movement is not merely to do less, but to return. He calls His people from independence back to dependence, from self-direction back to surrender. Scripture reminds us that apart from Him we can do nothing of lasting spiritual value, yet abiding in Him produces enduring fruit. As we pause, listen, and yield again to His leadership, rejection begins to lose its hold. Identity is restored, purpose is clarified, gifts are renewed, and direction is realigned. The U-Turn forward begins when we choose trust over control and relationship over autonomy, returning to the life that flows from abiding in Him.

Reverse Movement Three: Rebel — The Conformed Life

"Do not be conformed to this world, but be transformed by the renewing of your mind." (Romans 12:2 NKJV).

When independence becomes normalized, conformity soon follows. What began as resistance and slowly matured into self-reliance now begins shaping the way a person thinks, believes, and lives. At this stage, rebellion is rarely loud or outwardly obvious. It is often subtle, respectable, and quietly reinforced by culture, comfort, fear, or self-protection. The issue is no longer merely resisting God's voice but gradually allowing other voices to shape truth and direction.

This form of rebellion does not usually reject God outright. Instead, it reshapes truth to fit personal reasoning, emotional comfort, or cultural pressure. Faith may still remain outwardly active, yet the mind is no longer consistently being renewed by God's truth. Conviction softens, compromise becomes easier to justify, and obedience becomes increasingly selective. Conformity begins when truth is no longer allowed to govern the mind.

Scripture makes clear that transformation is not automatic. Without continual renewal, the mind naturally drifts toward conformity. The heart will always be shaped by whatever it consistently listens to, agrees with, and practices. When God's Word no longer holds its rightful authority, culture, emotion, and personal reasoning quietly take its place. Yet even here, God's mercy remains active. He exposes conformity not to condemn His people, but to awaken them and call them back into transformation.

Reverse Movement Three: Rebel — The Conformed Life Reveals Itself Through Three Patterns

Belief — Agreeing with Lies

Rebellion often begins in the realm of belief, as the heart slowly agrees with thoughts that are misaligned with God's truth. These are rarely loud or obvious deceptions. More often, they appear subtle, reasonable, protective, or necessary, especially during seasons of pressure, disappointment, fear, or exhaustion. Thoughts may begin forming such as: *I have to carry this on my own. God helps, but I must stay in control. Rest is irresponsible. Obedience is too risky right now.* These beliefs rarely feel dangerous at first, yet Scripture shows that deception often begins through persuasion rather than defiance.

In the garden, Eve did not openly rebel against God in a single moment. She listened, reasoned, questioned, and gradually agreed with a distorted version of truth. **Once belief shifted, action soon followed.** Every belief we embrace shapes our direction, and what the heart consistently agrees with, the life will eventually embody.

Mind — Distorting the Truth

As belief shifts, the mind begins supporting and defending those agreements. Truth is no longer received as final authority, but increasingly filtered through emotion, experience, culture, and personal reasoning. Conviction softens while justification grows. The mind becomes practiced at explaining away obedience instead of yielding to it.

This pattern is seen during the time of the judges, when everyone did what was right in his own eyes. God's truth had not disappeared, but it was no longer governing the thinking of His people. Instead of asking, *"What is God saying?"* the heart begins asking, *"What feels reasonable or manageable right now?"*

Spiritual sensitivity dulls not because truth is absent, but because truth is no longer leading.

Practice — Walking in the Flesh

Belief eventually produces behavior. What the heart agrees with, the life will ultimately practice. At this stage, life may still appear disciplined, productive, and spiritually active, yet inwardly it becomes strained and disconnected. Activity begins replacing intimacy, and spiritual life becomes functional rather than relational.

This was evident in the Pharisees. They were diligent in outward practice and religious discipline, yet their hearts remained distant from God. Their lives reflected conformity to a system rather than transformation by the Spirit.

This form of rebellion rarely appears chaotic or openly rebellious. More often, it appears consistent, responsible, and outwardly faithful, while inward surrender quietly fades. A person can remain spiritually active while slowly drifting from true dependence on God.

God's invitation at this stage is renewal. He does not simply call His people to resist conformity, but to be transformed through the renewing of the mind. **Transformation begins as the Holy Spirit uses truth to confront false agreements and realign the heart with God's Word.** As surrender replaces self-protection, rebellion begins losing its hold. Renewal restores what conformity has dulled, and alignment returns as the mind is once again shaped by truth. The U-Turn forward begins here, where the mind is renewed and the heart chooses transformation over comfort and truth over self-preservation.

Reverse Movement Four: Reproduce — From Significance to Selfishness

"You will know them by their fruits." (Matthew 7:16 NKJV).

Every life reproduces something. This is shaped not merely by intention, but by formation. What consistently forms us will eventually flow through us. Jesus taught that fruit always reveals the root. A healthy root produces living fruit, while a disconnected root may still produce activity, but not true life. By this stage of the Reverse U-Turn, inward drift no longer remains internal; it begins reproducing itself outwardly through influence, priorities, relationships, and legacy.

This movement is not about measuring visible success or judging outward outcomes, but about spiritual discernment. Fruit reveals what we are truly abiding in. When the flesh becomes the guiding force, the fruit of life begins reflecting disconnection rather than vitality. What once flowed from intimacy with God gradually begins flowing from effort, self-preservation, and striving. What once carried eternal weight slowly turns inward toward personal significance and self-focus. What is formed in the heart will eventually be reproduced through the life.

Yet even here, God's purpose is not exposure for shame, but revelation for restoration. He reveals the fruit so He can heal the root. What is formed through independence will eventually reproduce itself through influence, whether intentionally or unintentionally.

Reverse Movement Four: Reproduce — From Significance to Selfishness Reveals Itself Through Four Patterns

Isolation — Disconnecting from the Vine

When independence matures, abiding quietly fades. Striving replaces dependence, and activity replaces intimacy. Life may remain full, productive, and outwardly connected, yet inwardly the soul becomes increasingly detached from God.

Jesus' teaching in John 15 NKJV is clear: branches do not wither because they stop working, but because they disconnect from the vine. "Apart from Me you can do nothing" does not mean activity ceases; it means spiritual life does. Prayer becomes occasional rather than relational. Scripture remains familiar, yet no longer formative. **Communion with God becomes functional rather than life-giving. Isolation at this stage is rarely physical; it is spiritual disconnection hidden beneath responsibility, busyness, and productivity.**

Modeling — Living Contrary to God's Word

What we live always teaches more deeply than what we say. As drift deepens, the gap between confession and conduct widens. Language may remain spiritual and faithful, yet life begins communicating something different. Jesus warned about the Pharisees not because they lacked knowledge, but because their lives contradicted the truth they taught. Their words honored God, but their hearts remained distant from Him.

This is not usually open defiance, but quiet misalignment formed through neglect. Truth may still be known intellectually, yet it is no longer consistently embodied. Over time, inconsistency weakens credibility, first within the heart and eventually before others.

Influence — Leading Others Away from Christ

Influence never disappears; it reproduces whatever forms us. When intimacy with God diminishes, influence gradually begins shaping others through fear, pressure, control, performance, or self-reliance rather than trust, surrender, and dependence on Christ.

What once remained personal drift now becomes multiplied impact.

This pattern is seen in Jeroboam, whose fear and insecurity led him to establish false worship, causing others to turn away from God. His independence did not remain private; it reproduced itself through influence. **Without realizing it, we can begin modeling autonomy instead of abiding, teaching others through our example to depend on striving more than surrender.** What appears effective outwardly may no longer be leading people toward Christ inwardly.

Legacy — Leaving Temporary, Empty Fruit

The final outcome of this movement is a legacy marked by activity without eternity. Effort increases, systems function, responsibilities continue, and visible achievements accumulate, yet the fruit does not remain.

Paul describes works that are tested by fire, where some endure and others are consumed. The issue is not visibility, but source. What is built apart from abiding may appear impressive, productive, or significant, yet it lacks eternal substance. This is not necessarily failure in the world's eyes, but loss in the eternal sense. Life continues, but it no longer multiplies spiritual life in others.

Yet even here, grace remains. God's invitation is not simply to produce more, but to return deeper. He calls His people back to abiding, where fruitfulness flows from relationship and legacy carries eternal weight. Jesus reminds us that the Father is the Vinedresser, pruning not to punish, but to restore life and increase lasting fruit.

As we return to the Vine, significance is redeemed, selfishness loosens its hold, and fruit that remains begins growing again. **The U-Turn is always possible because God's invitation to return is always present.**

Early Warning Signs

Drift rarely begins with dramatic decisions; it begins with small shifts in attention, affection, and response. Because what we are calling the "Reverse U-Turn" develops gradually, its early signs are often subtle. Recognizing them is not cause for alarm, but an invitation to remain tender and attentive before distance deepens.

Early warning signs may include:

- A diminishing hunger for Scripture or prayer
- Irritation or defensiveness when lovingly corrected
- Justifying attitudes or behaviors that once stirred conviction
- Prayer becoming reactive in crisis rather than relational in daily life
- Busyness replacing abiding
- Comparison replacing communion

- Increased self-reliance in decisions once surrendered to God
- Delayed obedience when the Spirit prompts clearly
- Serving outwardly while neglecting inward formation

These signs do not define spiritual failure or our standing before God in Christ; they reveal where the heart may be quietly shifting. None of these signs alone define failure. Rather, they serve as invitations to respond early, before distance deepens. The Spirit's conviction is not condemnation but a gracious work that leads us back to truth and restores alignment with Him. Awareness is mercy, and what is brought into the light can be realigned before drift becomes distance.

The Mercy of Awareness

The purpose of revealing the Reverse U-Turn is not shame but awakening. Awareness itself is mercy. When God brings drift into the light, He is not condemning His people but calling them back. Conviction does not crush; it guides the heart toward truth and restores alignment with Him. Scripture shows that drift begins in the heart, settles in the mind, strengthens in the will, and multiplies in influence.

"Return to Me, and I will return to you," says the LORD of hosts (Malachi 3:7 NKJV).

Restoration does not begin with perfection, but with recognition. The moment we see where we have grown distant is evidence that grace is already at work. God, in His mercy, reveals what is misaligned, not to shame us, but to draw us back, reminding us that the way home remains open through His grace. He meets us with invitation, not accusation, and with correction anchored in love.

Chapter 8 reminds us that losing our way is rarely sudden; it unfolds quietly as resistance grows, independence replaces surrender, and attentiveness fades. Yet this awareness is not given to produce fear, but to awaken the heart. God's mercy meets us even in seasons of drift, because He remains faithful to His covenant, and His voice continues to call His children home. This recognition prepares us for the way back, where restoration begins not with striving, but with repentance and a willing return to God. As we move into Part III, The U-Turn Movements, we begin where all true renewal begins, with surrender. Chapter 9, Repent: Surrendering to His Lordship, invites us to turn again with confidence toward the Father and that the Father is already moving toward us.

Reflection Questions

1. Which movement of the Reverse U-Turn most clearly reflects my present spiritual posture? What evidence do I see in my thoughts, choices, or fruit?
2. What beliefs or inner narratives have I accepted that quietly contradict God's truth, even if they seem reasonable or practical?
3. In what ways have my identity, purpose, or decisions been shaped more by responsibility, necessity, or survival than by Christ and His calling?
4. What kind of fruit is my current way of living producing in my relationships, spiritual life, and influence on others?
5. Where have I sensed the Spirit's gentle conviction but delayed my response?

Prayer

Father God,

Thank You for Your patience and mercy when my heart drifts. Thank You that even when I lose my way, You never lose sight of me. Search my heart and reveal where resistance, independence, or fear has taken root. I choose to turn back to You, not with shame but with trust. Restore my sensitivity to Your voice, renew my dependence on Your Spirit, and lead me again in the way of life. I surrender my will to Yours and return to You with an open heart.

In Jesus' name, Amen.

Part III — TRANSFORMATION

The U-Turn Movements from Surrender to Life

> "Therefore, if anyone *is* in Christ, he *is* a new creation; old things have passed away; behold, all things have become new." — (2 Corinthians 5:17 NKJV).

Awakening opens our eyes, and alignment restores direction. Transformation is where truth, by the work of the Holy Spirit, becomes lived reality in us. This is where God reshapes how we think, live, and walk with Him, forming not only new patterns of behavior but a renewed heart that responds to Him in faith.

The U-Turn begins with a decisive turning to God and continues as a daily rhythm of walking with Him. Through repentance, receiving God's truth, renewal of the mind, and a life that bears fruit in others, God, in His grace, restores the heart and realigns the inner life. What begins in surrender grows into obedience and lasting change, not through striving, but through abiding in Him. Together, these movements form a way of life. The U-Turn becomes a rhythm we return to again and again, as God faithfully forms in us a life marked by freedom, trust, and joyful obedience in relationship with Him. This is not merely change in behavior, but transformation that reflects the life of Christ being formed within us.

Chapter 9 — Repent: Surrendering to His Lordship

"Repentance is not the work of repairing ourselves; it is the surrender of the heart that returns us to God, where true restoration begins."

Movement One: Repent — Surrendering to His Lordship

<u>The Descent Where Surrender Begins</u>

Transformation begins when we recognize that self-direction cannot produce a life formed by the Spirit. Repentance is not merely sorrow for sin; it is a decisive turning back to God. It is the moment we step away from self-reliance and realign under His Lordship. What may feel like a descent is, in truth, the beginning of freedom. As we become aware of old patterns, release control, and resist fear as a guiding influence, repentance restores a life of dependence on God.

Scripture makes the promise clear:

> "Repent therefore and be converted, that your sins may be blotted out, so that times of refreshing may come from the presence of the Lord." (Acts 3:19 NKJV).

Refreshing follows returning. As we turn to God, our hearts are positioned to receive His guidance. Without repentance, transformation is hindered; with it, we move forward with clarity and alignment. Every true U-Turn begins here, when we choose to return to God and trust His direction. Repentance is the sacred moment we stop asking God to follow our plans and instead choose to follow His. This work is often internal before it is visible. We may notice how quickly we interpret life through self-protection rather than trust. Fear can influence decisions related to safety, approval, and control, and what appears to be wisdom may at times be rooted in anxiety. Repentance brings these patterns into the light, allowing us to realign with God's truth and place our confidence in His care.

As we remain in this posture, what is confronted within begins to shift:

- Old Self — Reckoning the flesh and turning from former patterns
- Fear — Rejecting fear as a guiding influence
- Control — Relinquishing self-reliance and yielding to God's authority

Repentance does not produce shame; it restores relationship. It leads us back into freedom, where clarity increases, the soul steadies, and trust in God's leading is renewed. As we come under His Lordship, we are repositioned to walk forward in peace, alignment, and obedience.

The Two Ways We Live: Flesh and Spirit

Scripture reveals that the believer lives with an ongoing tension between the flesh and the Spirit. These are not equal sources of life, but opposing influences that shape how we think, respond, and walk each day. The flesh represents patterns formed apart from surrendered trust in God, while the Spirit leads us into truth, dependence, and life under His authority.

The question is not whether both influences are present, but which one is leading. Even as believers, if we are not attentive to the Spirit and do not intentionally yield the flesh to Him, we will continue to experience unnecessary struggle and inner conflict. What Christ has made possible positionally may not be fully expressed practically. In those moments, we become more vulnerable to the enemy's influence in our thoughts, perceptions, and responses, not because he has authority over us, but because we are not actively walking in the authority God has given.

The flesh draws us toward self-reliance, control, and fear. It reacts quickly, seeks to protect, and depends on what feels manageable. The Spirit leads us into trust, surrender, and obedience. He anchors us in truth, steadies the heart, and guides us in alignment with God's will. These two ways of living produce very different fruit, not only in outward behavior but in the condition of the inner life. Scripture makes this distinction clear.

"Walk in the Spirit, and you shall not fulfill the lust of the flesh." (Galatians 5:16 NKJV).

The call is not to improve the flesh, but to walk in the Spirit. The flesh cannot produce the life of God. It may imitate strength or wisdom, but it cannot bear spiritual fruit. Only a life yielded to the Spirit produces love, peace, and lasting transformation. If we do not yield the flesh to the Spirit, we cannot bear the fruit that comes from the Spirit.

Repentance is where this shift begins. It is the moment we recognize where the flesh has been leading and intentionally return authority to the Spirit of God. This is not a one-time correction, but a daily surrender. As we yield, the Spirit works within us to form what we cannot produce on our own, shaping our thoughts, desires, and responses according to God's truth. Over time, what we yield to shapes what we produce. A life led by the flesh becomes marked by striving, instability, and limitation. A life led by the Spirit becomes marked by peace, clarity, and fruit that reflects the character of Christ. The life we experience is shaped by who we allow to lead.

Restoring Authority Over Your Life

Every U-Turn begins with recognition. We may sincerely love God, yet still find ourselves reacting from fear, striving, or self-reliance. Repentance is the moment we recognize the need to return to God and once again live in surrender under His Lordship. It is not only a turning away from what is misaligned, but a turning back to the One who leads with truth and love. Repentance is the turning of the heart that brings us back under God's leadership in our daily lives.

As we surrender to His Lordship, the inner life begins to change. Peace begins to replace pressure, not because circumstances immediately shift, but because trust is being restored. As we return to honoring God in His rightful place, we begin to experience clarity, stability, and confidence in His guidance.

Repentance Is a Return, Not a Repair

"Return to Me, and I will return to you," says the LORD of hosts. (Malachi 3:7 NKJV).

Scripture expresses this relational reality clearly. Throughout Scripture, repentance is presented as a return to God, not an effort to fix ourselves. He invites us to come as we are and to turn our hearts back to Him. Restoration flows from relationship, not self-effort. When we respond to His invitation, we encounter His grace and are brought back into alignment under His Lordship.

For a time, I approached repentance as something I needed to manage carefully. I would examine myself, identify what was wrong, and try to correct it before returning to God, rather than responding to His grace with surrender. Without realizing it, I was relying on my own effort. Over time, I came to understand that true repentance is not about repairing ourselves, but about returning to Him in humility and trust.

Scripture consistently reveals this pattern. When Adam and Eve hid, God sought them. In the parable of the prodigal son, the father welcomed his son with compassion when he returned. King David, when confronted, turned to God and asked for mercy. In each case, repentance was a return to God, and restoration followed.

Repentance is not the work of repairing ourselves; it is the surrender of the heart that returns us to God, where true restoration begins. As we return to Him, we discover that He is ready to receive us, guide us, and lead us forward step by step.

The Real Gap We Must Face: Reality and God's Original Design

At the heart of repentance is the recognition of a gap, not only between right and wrong, but between the life we are living, and the life God has called us to walk in with Him. Repentance brings us face to face with this gap, not to bring shame, but to lead us back to Him. As we bring our lives honestly before God, we open ourselves to His restoring work.

From the beginning, Scripture shows that we were created for relationship with Him, to live in trust and dependence under His care. In the garden, life flowed from fellowship with God. When sin entered, that fellowship was disrupted. Trust gave way to fear, and Adam and Eve hid from God. The gap was not only about wrongdoing, but about broken fellowship and loss of alignment with Him. Repentance is the invitation to step out of hiding and return to restored relationship with God. This pattern continues throughout Scripture. Though God's people knew His promises, they often turned to what felt familiar instead of trusting Him fully. God continually called them back to Himself, reminding them of His faithfulness and inviting them to return. Repentance was always about coming back to God.

Jesus addressed this same gap in His ministry. He met people where they were and called them into a new life. He did not shame them but invited them to follow Him. Grace did not ignore what was broken; it made restoration possible. Repentance requires the humility to acknowledge where we are and the trust to return to God.

In the U-Turn journey, repentance is where we release what is misaligned and return to God, trusting Him to restore and lead us forward. This is not about striving for perfection, but about returning to Him, where He restores, guides, and leads us step by step.

Repentance and the Life Operating System

Repentance is not about condemnation; it is God's invitation to return to living under His Lordship. Each of us lives from an inner framework that shapes how we think, respond, and make decisions. When God is at the center of our hearts and decisions, life flows from trust and obedience, and peace steadies the heart. However, over time fear, self-reliance, or past disappointments can begin to shape our responses, gradually drawing us away from active dependence on Him.

Repentance is the moment we recognize this drift and return our hearts to God's leadership. It is not driven by pressure or self-effort, but by surrender. We turn back to Him, releasing what we have relied on and entrusting ourselves again to His care. Scripture consistently reflects this pattern. When God's people returned to Him, He restored their direction. When Jonah turned back, he walked again in obedience. When Peter turned to the Lord after his failure, he was restored and strengthened.

Repentance carries hope because it brings us back into a trusting relationship under God's care and guidance, where our lives can be realigned with His will. As we return to Him, striving gives way to rest, confusion to clarity, and anxiety to peace. Repentance does not diminish us; it restores us to walk with God, where growth and fruit flow from a life surrendered to Him.

The Function of Repentance in the U-Turn

Repentance anchors the U-Turn because God leads through surrender, not resistance. Movement without surrender may appear productive, but it often remains misaligned. Direction pursued apart from a yielded heart results in striving, confusion, or delayed obedience. God is not withholding guidance. In His wisdom, He leads us to alignment before we clearly discern direction.

The U-Turn unfolds through four movements: repent, receive, renew, and reproduce. Repentance comes first because it repositions the heart under God's authority. It is not merely behavioral correction. It is the yielding of our hearts back under His leadership. Until that shift occurs, the remaining movements cannot function as they were intended. We cannot fully receive while still resisting. We cannot be renewed while clinging to self-rule. We cannot reproduce spiritual fruit if the root system remains misaligned.

Repentance restores the fullness of relational communion and realigns the heart so that God's voice, not self-direction, determines the course of our lives. Scripture consistently reflects this order. Israel's hearts were shaped in the wilderness before they entered the promise land. Isaiah was cleansed before he was sent. Peter was restored before he was commissioned. Throughout Scripture, God addresses alignment before assignment. He brings us back under His authority before entrusting us with greater responsibility.

In the U-Turn, repentance is the decisive turning point where resistance gives way to surrender and control yields to trust. It is where we stop negotiating with partial obedience and entrust the leadership of our lives fully to Him. This shift may feel quiet, but it changes everything that follows. This movement is not burdensome; it is freeing. Repentance does not demand perfected obedience or complete clarity about the future. It asks for willingness. It positions us to receive what we cannot produce and to be renewed beyond what effort can accomplish. It anchors every subsequent step in relationship rather than performance. At its core, repentance turns us back toward God's authority so that everything that follows flows from His leadership instead of our own. It is not loss. It is grace in motion. It is the return that makes the U-Turn possible and sustains our forward movement under His rule.

Movement One: Repent — Surrendering to His Lordship

Movement One is the foundation of the U-Turn and the beginning of the journey back to God. Repentance is His invitation to return, releasing whatever has taken His place and returning to live in surrender under His Lordship. It is not loss, but the restoration of our lives in relationship with Him. Repentance is the moment we turn back to God and surrender our lives to His leadership. Throughout Scripture, God brings His people back to Himself before leading them forward. The pattern is clear: He prepares the heart before He directs the path.

Repentance is the turning point where striving gives way to trust, and self-direction yields to God's leading. When we return to God, peace begins to replace pressure and obedience flows from relationship rather than fear. What we lay down was never meant to sustain us. As we return to Him, we find renewed dependence, clearer direction, and a restored walk with Him. This is where the U-Turn truly begins, when we turn from self-direction and return to walk under His leadership.

Core Areas of Repentance in This Movement

1. The Old Self: Reckoning with the Flesh

"And those who are Christ's have crucified the flesh with its passions and desires." (Galatians 5:24 NKJV).

Awareness is a gift, but it does not determine what leads our lives. We may recognize patterns and understand our reactions, yet transformation begins as we realign our hearts under Christ's authority. Repentance moves us beyond insight into surrender, bringing our lives back under His leadership. The old self is not merely behavior; it is a pattern of self-reliance where fear, pride, or control subtly lead, reacting before seeking God and attempting to manage what was never meant to be self-governed. Repentance is not deeper self-understanding; it is the surrender of the heart to Christ's authority.

For a season, I mistook self-awareness for transformation. I could explain my tendencies, yet explanation did not produce freedom. Scripture consistently reveals that God is not calling us to perfect self-analysis, but to surrendered trust. Throughout Scripture, personality is not erased, but authority is realigned. What once influenced our decisions is no longer meant to direct them as we yield to God.

Reckoning the flesh is not self-condemnation; it is clarity about lordship. The old self may still present its impulses, but it no longer defines who we are or directs our lives. This is the quiet work of repentance, where we no longer allow fear, pride, or control to shape our decisions. The issue is not activity, but authority: who is leading the heart in that moment. As we yield again to Christ, what is brought into the light can be surrendered, and what is surrendered begins to lose its influence over us as we continue to yield to God. Repentance becomes a continual return, placing the heart again under His faithful leadership.

1.1 Recognizing the Old Self

The old self is more than sinful behavior; it is a pattern of living shaped by self-reliance rather than surrendered trust in God's authority. For many believers, it remains hidden because it can appear responsible, disciplined, and productive. Yet what appears mature outwardly may still function from self-governance within. The old self reveals itself in subtle ways, when we rely on experience instead of seeking God, react defensively rather than listening, or move quickly to solve rather than pausing in trust. The issue is not activity, but authority, who is leading the heart in that moment.

In one season of leadership, I recognized that competence had quietly replaced dependence. Outwardly, responsibilities were fulfilled and goals were met, yet inwardly I was drawing from personal strength rather than surrendered trust. Scripture describes this as the flesh, meaning patterns of life formed apart from dependence on the Spirit. It develops through self-protection and becomes a default way of responding, often operating before we consciously recognize it.

In my own journey, the flesh did not appear rebellious; it appeared capable. I had equated maturity with independence and strength with control, yet beneath it was fear. Scripture reflects this pattern consistently. Adam hid, Abraham struggled to trust fully, Israel longed for what felt familiar, and Peter reacted under pressure. In each case, fear influenced decisions where trust was required, and God responded by restoring relationship and drawing them back to dependence on Him.

The old self resists surrender because it was shaped to protect. It clings to what feels manageable, even when it limits obedience. Recognizing it is not condemnation; it is clarity. The Holy Spirit reveals these patterns not to shame us, but to bring them into the light. What is brought into the light can be surrendered, and what is surrendered begins to lose its influence as we continue to yield to God. Repentance begins with an honest return, yielding ourselves again to God's leadership and realigning the heart under His authority, where life was always meant to flow.

1.2 How the Old Self Operates

If the old self were obvious, it would be easier to confront. Instead, it often hides in what feels familiar, sounding like instinct and blending into personality. It justifies itself with quiet assumptions such as, "This is just how I am." Since it does not always appear outwardly sinful, it can remain unchallenged. At its core, the old self is self-governance shaped by self-preservation, seeking control, avoiding vulnerability, and relying only on what feels manageable. It reacts before we pause or pray because it operates as though authority belongs to us. These patterns are not random; they reveal a life being shaped apart from active, surrendered trust in God. Scripture reminds us, "There is a way *that* seems right to a man, But its end *is* the way of death." (Proverbs 14:12 NKJV), highlighting how easily self-direction can feel right while leading us away from God's design.

For a season, I misidentified what was operating within me. I called drivenness responsibility, perfectionism excellence, defensiveness strength, and anxiety discernment. While these appeared admirable on the surface, they revealed a deeper issue of who was functionally leading my life. My sense of security was rooted more in personal effort than in trusting God's rule. Scripture reflects this pattern consistently. Sarah moved ahead of God's timing, Saul acted under pressure rather than waiting, and Jonah resisted when God's direction conflicted with his preference. The issue was not lack of knowledge, but self-direction. The old self assumes it must secure outcomes and protect identity because trust in God has been weakened.

Certain responses reveal what is shaping our decisions. Striving often reflects reliance on self-effort. Defensiveness can indicate that identity feels unsettled. People-pleasing may reveal a search for affirmation apart from God. These are not behaviors to condemn, but indicators that we are not yielding to God's leadership in that moment. They expose what we are depending on for security and significance. The question beneath every pattern is not simply what we are doing, but who is leading in that moment.

The old self also expresses itself through deeply rooted internal beliefs, such as feeling alone, needing to prove oneself, or struggling to trust. These beliefs quietly shape decisions and relationships when left unexamined. Recognizing these patterns is not about behavior modification, but about discerning what is governing our responses. Repentance begins as we acknowledge where self-preservation has been leading and return to yielding ourselves to Christ's authority. Though old patterns may still present themselves, they no longer define who we are or need to direct our lives. As we return to living under His leadership, the heart realigns, and life begins to flow again under His direction.

1.3 When the Flesh Takes the Lead

The flesh, meaning patterns within us shaped apart from dependence on God, is not passive. Scripture shows that these patterns seek to influence our decisions, reactions, and priorities, often drawing us toward control, predictability, and self-effort. When we begin to follow the impulses of the flesh, even sincere spiritual activity can become burdensome because we are attempting to sustain in our own strength what only God can govern. The issue is not activity, but alignment.

This shift is often subtle and emerges under pressure. King Saul illustrates how easily this happens. When Samuel delayed, Saul acted out of urgency and offered the sacrifice himself. What appeared practical was rooted in fear. Anxiety began to drive his decision, and urgency replaced obedience.

Similarly, Peter, in his desire to protect Jesus, spoke from human instinct rather than submission to God's plan. His intention was sincere, but his perspective was misaligned.

The flesh rarely presents itself as open rebellion; it often appears reasonable while quietly replacing trust with self-direction. When fear dictates timing, when pressure drives decisions, or when outcomes feel dependent on our effort, it reveals that we are not yielding to God's leadership in that moment. Scripture reminds us, "It is God who works in you both to will and to do for *His* good pleasure." (Philippians 2:13 NKJV). What God initiates, He also sustains.

Repentance brings us back into alignment, where we yield ourselves again to God's leadership and allow Him to direct our lives. This exposure is not condemnation but mercy. The flesh was never designed to carry the weight of ruling a redeemed life. Self-effort leads to weariness, but God's leadership produces peace and clarity. Repentance is the turning point where we step aside and yield ourselves again to His leading.

1.4 Living from the Finished Work

Living from the finished work is not an emotional moment or an immediate change in behavior. It is a settled agreement with what Christ has accomplished and what His authority has secured, expressed through a life that continues to respond in trust and obedience. Repentance, in this light, is not striving to overcome the old self, but returning to live under the authority of the One who has already overcome. We are not fighting to earn victory; we are learning to stand in a victory already won.

> "Knowing this, that our old man was crucified with *Him*, that the body of sin might be done away with, that we should no longer be slaves of sin." (Romans 6:6 NKJV).

Scripture does not instruct us to crucify the old self; it reveals that it has been crucified with Christ. This truth reshapes repentance. We are not contending with an equal power but aligning with what God has already declared. The power of sin has been broken through Christ, and its rule no longer defines us. What remains is the daily choice to walk in that reality. The old self may still present familiar patterns or thoughts, but it no longer defines our needs or identity to direct our lives. Its voice can be recognized without being followed.

After the resurrection, the disciples still faced fear and uncertainty, yet Christ did not return to the cross. He revealed Himself as the risen Lord and invited them to live from what had already been accomplished. Their transformation unfolded as they anchored their identity in His finished work rather than in their changing emotions. Repentance becomes the ongoing return to His authority, where identity shapes behavior rather than the other way around.

Living from the finished work is often quiet and consistent. Each time we choose truth over reflex, surrender over control, and trust over fear, we are aligning ourselves with Christ's lordship. The influence of old patterns weakens as we depend on the Spirit and continue to yield to God. When repentance flows from this place, change is no longer driven by performance but sustained by identity. We yield not to earn acceptance, but because we already stand accepted in Him. As we continue returning to His authority, His life is more fully expressed in us, and obedience becomes the natural fruit of alignment.

2. Fear: Rejecting the Spirit of Fear

"For God has not given us a spirit of fear, but of power and of love and of a sound mind." (2 Timothy 1:7 NKJV).

In the U-Turn journey, repentance reaches beyond outward behavior into the inner structures that shape our decisions and direction. As self-reliance is confronted, fear is often revealed as a hidden influence. Fear does not simply visit the heart; it can begin to shape how we respond. It may present itself as wisdom, caution, or responsibility, yet its deeper effect is to draw us away from trust in God. Repentance in this area is the deliberate choice to yield again to the Spirit of God rather than allowing fear to shape our direction.

Fear often forms quietly through disappointment, pain, or uncertainty, and over time it becomes a lens through which we interpret life. It can lead us toward control, withdrawal, or striving, persuading us that safety depends on our effort. When fear shapes our responses, obedience narrows and trust weakens. Scripture shows how fear distorts perception when it leads. Elijah, after a great victory, fled in despair under threat, believing he was alone, yet God met him with gentleness and restored his perspective. Jehoshaphat, facing overwhelming opposition, sought the Lord, and God brought victory as worship led the way. In both accounts, the circumstances were real, but the outcome was shaped by whether they responded in fear or in trust.

Fear often surfaces at the threshold of obedience. Moses hesitated when called, and Joshua was repeatedly encouraged to be strong and courageous. In each case, the presence of fear was not the issue; the question was what would shape their response. Rejecting fear does not mean denying its presence but refusing to let it define reality or direct our decisions. Fear may speak, but it is not given authority in a life surrendered to God.

God deals with fear patiently, not condemning the heart but calling it back to trust. Repentance becomes the quiet yet decisive act of yielding again to His leadership, acknowledging that He alone directs our steps and secures our lives. Courage then is not the absence of trembling, but the fruit of restored trust. As we return to living under His authority, fear loses its influence and obedience flows from confidence in who God is.

2.1 Fear as a Governing Influence

Fear often becomes more noticeable as self-reliance is confronted. As we begin to release control, fear can surface, attempting to shape our responses. It rarely sounds defiant; it sounds careful, responsible, and strategic. Yet its fruit is restriction. Where God invites trust, fear demands certainty. Where God speaks promise, fear calculates risk. Instead of asking what God has said, fear focuses on what might happen. In doing so, it shifts attention from God's Word to imagined outcomes. When fear shapes our decisions, faith is reduced to managing risk rather than trusting God.

Fear does not always stop movement; often it redirects it. We may remain active and responsible, yet our decisions become shaped by what feels safest rather than by what God has spoken. What appears wise on the surface can be rooted in self-protection rather than surrender. Scripture reminds us, "For we walk by faith, not by sight." (2 Corinthians 5:7 NKJV). Obedience flows from trust in God's authority, not from the need for certainty. Israel's response at the edge of the Promised Land reveals this clearly. God had already declared the land theirs and demonstrated His faithfulness, yet fear shifted their focus from His promise to the size of the opposition. Perception overruled revelation, and what was meant to be advancement became delay. The issue was not God's ability, but which voice they responded to. Fear magnifies threats and minimizes awareness of God's presence.

Recognizing fear as a shaping influence is essential. Repentance begins when we discern that fear has been influencing our direction and we return to yielding ourselves to God's leadership. He responds not with condemnation, but with invitation, calling us back to His Word and His character. As we return to living under His authority, fear loses its influence and the heart is steadied in trust. Freedom grows as we learn to follow His voice rather than our uncertainties.

2.2 The Nature of Fear

> "Fear not, for I *am* with you; Be not dismayed, for I *am* your God. I will strengthen you, Yes, I will help you, I will uphold you with My righteous right hand." (Isaiah 41:10 NKJV).

Fear is more than an emotion; it is an influence that shapes how we interpret circumstances, make decisions, and understand ourselves. It often presents itself as caution or responsibility, yet at its root is the belief that we must secure our own safety and outcomes. In this way, fear subtly shifts reliance away from God's authority and toward self-protection. Fear becomes destructive not by its presence, but when it is allowed to shape and direct our response.

Fear became deeply embedded in the human experience when trust in God was broken. After sin, Adam said, "I was afraid," and he hid. From that moment, fear became closely tied to self-preservation. Throughout Scripture, fear is shown not merely as a feeling to manage, but as an influence that can shape how we see ourselves and respond. It whispers that we are alone, that we must strive to be accepted, or that we are not enough. Left unchallenged, these thoughts can quietly limit obedience and hinder intimacy with God.

In my own journey, fear rarely appeared as panic. It surfaced in overthinking, striving, and subtle insecurity. What I once labeled as discernment or sensitivity was often rooted in fear of rejection. When brought honestly before the Lord, its hold began to weaken. What seemed strong in secrecy lost its influence in His presence. Fear often forms around places where security once felt uncertain, becoming an internal pattern that influences responses and relationships. Scripture reflects this repeatedly, as individuals responded to pressure with fear rather than trust, until God met them and restored their perspective. God consistently meets fear not with condemnation, but with the assurance of His presence. His command to "fear not" is not a demand for emotional strength, but an invitation to return to trust. Repentance in this area is not suppressing fear but returning to live under God's authority so that fear no longer defines our response. As fear is brought into the light and surrendered, it begins to lose its influence. Peace steadies the heart, and obedience flows again from trust rather than self-protection.

Understanding the nature of fear becomes the beginning of freedom. Each place where fear once shaped our thinking becomes an opportunity to trust God more deeply. As we return to living under His authority, confidence grows from His character, and the heart becomes anchored in His presence rather than in uncertainty.

2.3 The Subtle Strategies of Fear

Fear rarely announces itself with alarm. It slips in quietly through thoughts that appear responsible, strategic, or mature. It sounds like careful planning or wise caution, yet beneath the surface it seeks to shape decisions and redirect trust by anticipating loss. Its goal is not merely to caution, but to influence.

Fear operates through anticipation and interpretation. It imagines worst outcomes and conditions the heart to expect disappointment. Like Israel at the edge of the Promised Land, it magnified giants while minimizing God's proven faithfulness. The land had not changed, and neither had God's promise, yet perception was distorted. Fear enlarges threats and diminishes the memory of God's works. It persuades us that retreat is safer than obedience and that control feels wiser than surrender. Over time, it forms internal agreements such as, I am not enough, or if I trust, I will lose. These thoughts repeat until they feel true, even though they are not anchored in God's Word. Fear seeks our agreement, but it does not carry God's authority. Fear may speak, but it has no rightful place in directing a surrendered heart.

In my own life, fear often appeared subtly. A delayed response could stir questions about value or belonging, and situations beyond my control exposed deeper insecurities. What I once labeled as responsibility was, at times, fear of not measuring up. Yet when brought honestly before the Lord, its influence weakened. What feels powerful in secrecy loses strength in His presence. The disciples experienced this in the storm; though Jesus was with them, fear distorted their perception and made them feel abandoned.

"For the LORD *is* on my side; I will not fear. What can man do to me?" (Psalm 118:6 NKJV).

God consistently meets fear not with condemnation, but with the reassurance of His presence. He does not demand the absence of fear but calls us to trust Him in the midst of it. Repentance in this area is the decision to refuse agreement with fear's conclusions and return to living under God's leadership. As we do, what once shaped our thinking begins to lose its influence, and the heart is steadied under His care rather than driven by anxious calculation.

2.4 Rejecting the Spirit of Fear

"There is no fear in love; but perfect love casts out fear." (1 John 4:18 NKJV).

Rejecting what Scripture describes as a "spirit of fear," referring to a pattern or influence that opposes trust in God, is not becoming someone who never feels afraid. It is discerning fear's voice and refusing to let it direct our response. Fear may attempt to speak, but it no longer defines identity, establishes boundaries, or determines direction. Repentance in this area is the conscious return to living under the leadership of God's love.

Fear often grows through quiet internal agreements such as, I must protect myself, or if I stay small, I will remain safe. Though these thoughts can appear wise, they are rooted in distrust of God's care and shift reliance from His presence to self-preservation. Rejecting fear is not the removal of emotion, but the restoration of trust in God's leadership over the heart. Scripture shows that fear does not always disappear before obedience begins. Moses felt inadequate, Joshua carried the weight of leadership, David faced Goliath while others trembled, and Peter stepped onto the water while the storm still raged. In each moment, the circumstances were real, but the decisive question was whose voice would shape their response. God did not promise the absence of difficulty, but He consistently promised His presence within it.

In my own journey, fear often surfaced in subtle ways through insecurity, hesitation, and the weight of responsibility, especially as my mother's dementia progressed while I was far away. Fear whispered that I was failing her. Yet in prayer, the Lord reminded me that He holds her life more securely than I ever could. Peace did not come all at once but grew steadily as I released the illusion of control and returned to living under His authority. Fear says, you are alone. Love answers, I am with you. Fear says, you will fail. Grace answers, my strength is sufficient. As truth replaces distortion, fear shifts from something that once strongly influenced us to something we can now discern and respond to, and obedience becomes possible again.

Perfect love does not remove every challenge, but it removes fear's control over our decisions. As trust deepens, the soul is steadied under God's leadership, and life is shaped by His faithful care rather than anxious calculation.

2.5 When Faith Takes the Lead

"The LORD *is* my light and my salvation; Whom shall I fear?" (Psalm 27:1 NKJV).

When faith leads, fear no longer directs our response. This is not the denial of emotion, but a decision about what shapes our lives. Feelings may still arise, but they no longer determine direction. Leadership shifts from anxiety to trust, from self-preservation to surrendered alignment under God's rule. Faith does not eliminate fear's presence, but it removes its role in guiding our decisions.

Faith does not wait for circumstances to settle before it moves. It anchors itself in the unchanging character of God. As trust grows, peace returns, and obedience becomes possible again, not because outcomes are guaranteed, but because God's nature is secure. The internal dialogue begins to change. Instead of asking what could go wrong, the heart asks what God has spoken. Instead of shrinking back, it steps forward with quiet confidence that the Lord goes before it.

This shift is sacred. Fear may still whisper, but it no longer sits at the center of our decisions. Faith shapes the response, trust steadies the soul, and courage grows as the fruit of alignment rather than effort. Repentance in this movement is the return to yielding to God's voice. As faith leads, the heart rests under His care, and fear becomes a passing influence rather than a shaping force. Yet as fear loosens its grip, a deeper layer often emerges, the tendency toward control, the attempt to secure outcomes through self-reliance. Repentance continues as we surrender even this, allowing God alone to lead our lives.

3. Control: Relinquishing Self-Reliance

Control often appears as responsibility, diligence, or wisdom, yet beneath the surface it is frequently rooted in fear and the belief that outcomes ultimately depend on us. When life feels uncertain, control promises safety, but it produces exhaustion. It tightens the inner life, strains relationships, and places upon us a weight we were never designed to carry.

> "Trust in the LORD with all your heart, And lean not on your own understanding; In all your ways acknowledge Him, And He shall direct your paths." (Proverbs 3:5–6 NKJV).

Relinquishing control is not passivity or disengagement; it is a return to living under God's authority. It is the movement from grasping to trusting, from clenched fists to open hands. It acknowledges that calling, growth, and fruitfulness are sustained by God, not by human striving. Releasing control is not weakness; it is repentance from self-reliance and a return to His leadership. When we stop attempting to be the source and yield to His guidance, peace replaces pressure and freedom begins to grow. What we release is not responsibility, but the illusion that everything depends on us.

3.1 Control as False Security

Control is often the final layer surrendered because it appears virtuous. It convinces us that careful management, constant anticipation, and diligent effort will produce stability. Yet beneath this effort lies a subtle assumption that security depends on us. Control promises stability but produces vigilance, keeping the soul striving rather than resting. What feels like strength is often fear expressed through competence.

Moses wrestled with this early in his calling. Attempting deliverance in his own strength, he acted ahead of God's timing and fled into obscurity. In the wilderness, dependence was formed, and from that surrendered place he was entrusted with authority. Control feels like security, but surrender is where true authority is received and expressed.

3.2 The Roots of Control

Control is not merely behavior; it is a posture shaped by wounds, unmet needs, and the fear that safety must be created rather than received. It can resemble strength and leadership, yet underneath it is vulnerability. When trust has been broken or life has felt unstable, control becomes a strategy for protection.

In my early years of leadership, I called it diligence. I anticipated problems, carried responsibility quietly, and rarely allowed space for weakness. Self-reliance appeared noble, yet it produced constant pressure and an inability to rest. What I labeled strength was, in reality, guardedness. Control did not produce peace; it confined it. Scripture contrasts these responses. Saul grasped for control when insecurity surfaced, acting ahead of God's instruction. David, though imperfect, chose to wait on God's timing rather than seize what had not been given. Jesus, in Gethsemane, prayed, "Not My will, but Yours be done," revealing that surrender is alignment with the Father's will.

"Commit your way to the Lord, Trust also in Him, and He shall bring *it* to pass." (Psalm 37:5 NKJV).

Control promises security, but only trust produces peace. Repentance at this level is the recognition that self-reliance has quietly replaced trust. Freedom begins when we release the illusion that everything depends on us and entrust our lives again to God's faithful care.

3.3 The Inner Mechanics of Control

"Be still, and know that I *am* God." (Psalm 46:10 NKJV).

Control begins internally long before it becomes visible. It is rooted in the belief that outcomes depend on personal effort. It seeks to reduce uncertainty and shield the heart from disappointment, yet it is sustained by fear of what might happen if we loosen our grip. It often appears as responsible planning, but it carries an underlying urgency that demands certainty before obedience.

Scripture illustrates this pattern. Sarah believed God's promise yet struggled to trust His timing and introduced her own solution. Martha served Jesus faithfully, yet her service became anxious because she was managing the moment rather than receiving from Him. In both cases, devotion was present, but trust was strained. We attempt to cooperate with God while quietly retaining final authority over outcomes.

Freedom begins when we recognize that control is not strength but self-protection. As we release the burden of outcomes, striving gives way to stillness and trust replaces tension.

3.4 When We Carry What God Never Asked Us To

Many believers are weary not because God has overburdened them, but because they are carrying responsibilities He never assigned. What appears as maturity can quietly become striving, shifting us from obedience into managing outcomes.

Jesus declared that His yoke is easy and His burden is light. If the inner life is marked by constant pressure, it is wise to ask whether we have stepped outside His yoke. Self-reliance insists everything depends on us, but Scripture teaches that obedience is ours while outcomes belong to God. Peace returns when we lay down what He never asked us to carry. Repentance is realignment, releasing self-appointed responsibility and returning to the One who sustains all things. Obedience is ours, but outcomes belong to God.

3.5 Letting God Be God

Letting God be God is the sacred culmination of surrender. It is the moment we stop assuming responsibility for what only He can govern. This is not resignation, but active trust. The impulse to control often grows from the belief that if we do not intervene, something essential will be lost. Yet every attempt to manage what belongs to God adds weight the soul was never meant to carry.

"Cast your burden on the LORD, And He shall sustain you." (Psalm 55:22 NKJV).

Casting is intentional. We release what we were holding and entrust it fully to Him. In that exchange, pressure lifts and peace steadies. We do not lose what was ours to steward; we release what was never ours to carry and return to alignment under God's authority. As we trust Him with outcomes, we discover that the future is safer in His hands than it ever was in our own. Surrender is not the loss of control, but the restoration of trust in the One who has always been faithful.

Three Areas Where Authority Shifts

Repentance becomes clearer when we recognize where our hearts most often drift. The old self, fear, and control are not separate struggles but interconnected expressions of misplaced leadership within us. When we are not fully yielded to Christ's lordship, our lives begin to reflect misalignment in three primary areas: how we see ourselves, what motivates us, and how we respond to responsibility and outcomes.

Self-Perception — The Old Self

Misalignment often begins in how we see ourselves. When our self-understanding is shaped by wounds, performance, or survival instead of surrender to Christ, the old self begins to influence how we live. We operate from learned patterns rather than yielded trust, drawing identity from what we have experienced rather than from who God is.

Repentance restores our self-perception by bringing it back under Christ's lordship. Our identity becomes rooted in who we are in Him and expressed through surrender to Him. We are no longer defined by fear, strength, or independence, but by our relationship with Him and our position in Him.

Motivation — Fear

Misalignment also reveals itself in what drives us. Fear becomes a hidden motivator when trust weakens, quietly shaping decisions around safety, approval, preservation, or control. Outward obedience may remain yet inwardly fear begins to shape our pace and decisions. Over time, this creates a disconnect between action and trust, producing activity without rest.

Repentance exposes false motivation and restores the heart to trust as its foundation. True obedience flows not from fear of outcomes, but from confidence in God's character. As trust is renewed, the heart finds rest even while remaining faithful in action.

Response and Direction — Control

Misalignment is also seen in how we respond to responsibility and outcomes. Control attempts to secure what only God can sustain. It plans without surrender and moves without waiting, often appearing responsible while functioning independently of dependence on God. Control is self-reliance expressed through the need to manage outcomes. Repentance releases the illusion of control and restores us to living under God's rightful place as Lord over both direction and results. It is not merely behavior correction; it is the realignment of the heart to trust Him fully in every area.

These three areas reveal the same root issue: who we are yielding to in daily life. Self-perception shapes how we respond, motivation shapes why we move, and our response to responsibility shapes how we live. When any of these fall out of alignment, repentance brings us back to living under Christ's authority.

When we drift, direction often becomes unclear. We may continue moving and serving, yet internally something feels strained because the deeper issue of surrender has not been settled. As long as the old self shape's identity, fear drives motivation, or control governs our responses, we experience competing influences that make it harder to discern God's voice. Repentance quiets that internal noise by restoring the heart to a place of surrendered trust. When Christ is truly Lord in the heart, clarity increases and obedience becomes steady and life giving. This is why surrender must precede guidance. We more clearly recognize His leading where He is trusted. In this movement, repentance restores our alignment with Him. In the next chapter, we learn to recognize and follow His voice.

Once the heart is realigned, direction can be received with clarity, and obedience becomes relational rather than reactive.

As we return to living under His authority, the heart becomes steady enough to listen. Repentance is not the end of the journey; it is the restoration of alignment that makes guidance possible. When self, fear, and control no longer shape our lives, space is created for God's voice to be recognized and followed. Surrender restores our sensitivity to His leading, and what once felt unclear begins to come into alignment as the heart rests in Him. Repentance does not end the journey; it makes a life of listening and following possible.

Chapter 10 — Receive: Hearing and Following God's Voice flows naturally from this place, where a surrendered life begins to discern and respond to the voice of the Lord.

Reflection Questions

1. Where is God inviting you to return to Him in surrender rather than continue in self-direction?
2. In which area do you sense misalignment, self-perception, motivation, or control, and how is that affecting your trust in God?
3. What patterns of the old self, fear, or self-reliance has the Holy Spirit been gently revealing to you?
4. When God brings conviction, how do you typically respond, with surrender, delay, or self-effort?
5. What would it look like for you to live each day with a posture of repentance, allowing God to continually realign your heart to Him?

Prayer

Father,

Thank You that repentance is an invitation to return to You. Today, I surrender again and bring every area of my life before You. Search my heart, realign what is out of place, and teach me to trust You. Where fear or control has shaped my responses, restore my heart to live under Your authority. Lead me step by step in Your truth.

In Jesus' name, Amen.

Chapter 10 — Receive: Hearing and Following God's Voice

"A surrendered heart does not strive to create direction; it learns to recognize and respond to the voice of the Lord."

Movement Two: Receive — Hearing and Following God's Voice

The Bottom of the U Where Surrender Becomes Listening

After authority is restored, alignment must follow. Movement Two unfolds at the bottom of the U-Turn, the quiet center where striving ceases and listening begins. Repentance relinquishes control and receiving welcomes God's guidance. A surrendered heart becomes a listening heart. To receive is not to construct meaning for us, but to welcome what God reveals through His Word, by His Spirit, and in alignment with His truth. What was once driven by effort begins to be reordered through relationship, and the heart becomes attentive to His leading.

A surrendered heart does not strive to create direction; it learns to recognize and respond to the voice of the Lord. At this stage, the inner life is not instantly perfected but begins to be renewed and realigned. Identity is received in Christ through His finished work rather than built through performance. Purpose flows from belonging. Gifts are stewarded with humility. Direction unfolds one faithful step at a time as we walk in obedience.

Scripture assures us that God leads those who trust Him. The bottom of the U is not a place of stagnation but of recalibration. Alignment begins internally before it becomes visible externally. As striving gives way to trust and resistance is laid down, the soul becomes attentive. Guidance is no longer forced or chased; it is received as we learn to wait on Him.

In this movement, what is reordered within begins to express itself outwardly.

- **Identity** is anchored in Christ before assignment is pursued.
- **Calling** flows from restored relationship rather than pressure.
- **Gifts** are stewarded faithfully for the building up of the body, not for self-promotion.
- **Direction** is revealed step by step as discernment grows through a life that listens and obeys.

As Jesus said, His sheep hear His voice, and they follow Him. This hearing is not merely emotional or subjective but is grounded in His Word and guided by His Spirit. Receiving is not passive. It is active trust expressed through attentiveness and obedience. Faithfulness is formed before function is clarified. At the bottom of the U-Turn, we discover that when the heart is yielded, God is faithful to lead.

Resetting Your Life Operating System

At the bottom of the U-Turn, surrender becomes listening. Once authority is restored to God, the inner life begins to be renewed. Receiving is the posture that allows this transformation to unfold. To receive means welcoming God's truth, His leading, and His shaping work with a yielded heart rather than striving to produce them through self-effort. Here,

God, by His Spirit, renews and reorders the inner life as we learn to listen and respond to Him.

Identity is received as sons and daughters through Christ. Purpose is clarified through relationship with Him. Gifts are recognized as entrusted stewardship. Direction unfolds step by step as we walk in obedience. This renewal does not happen through effort alone but through ongoing trust and surrender, as self-direction gives way to Spirit-led attentiveness.

God does not merely give direction; He forms a heart that can recognize and follow His voice. The inner framework that shapes belief, emotion, and decision begins to align with truth as we learn to discern His leading above competing influences. The life that was once self-managed becomes increasingly Spirit-led, not perfectly, but progressively, as we grow in responsiveness to His presence. In this way, we are no longer driven by pressure but guided by relationship, learning to walk with God in a way that is steady, faithful, and rooted in trust.

The Lord Is My Ultimate Source

To receive and follow God's voice as revealed in Scripture and illuminated by the Holy Spirit, one confession must settle deeply in the heart: the Lord is my ultimate source of life, wisdom, and direction. Until this becomes established within us, we may pray and seek Him sincerely, yet still filter His leading through logic, experience, or self-protection apart from surrendered trust. We ask for guidance yet quietly retain final authority. Receiving requires more than hearing. It requires surrendering our need to remain in control so that we can truly follow where He leads.

In my own journey, I discovered how easily faith and self-reliance can coexist. I trusted God, yet I depended on planning, strategy, and outcomes for security. When clarity was delayed, I responded by trying harder. The result was not peace, but exhaustion. God gently revealed the tension within me. I was asking Him to bless my direction rather than waiting for His. I wanted certainty before obedience, yet Scripture consistently calls us to trust before we fully understand.

> "Thus says the Lord: 'Stand in the ways and see, And ask for the old paths, where the good way *is*, And walk in it; Then you will find rest for your souls.'" (Jeremiah 6:16 NKJV.)

Receiving begins when we surrender not only our decisions, but our need to be the source of our own direction. Direction flows from dependence on God, and it becomes clearer as we continue to seek Him and walk in obedience to what He has already revealed in His Word. God does not always unveil the entire path at once. More often, He leads step by step, forming trust as we follow Him faithfully in what we know. When I released control and acknowledged Him as my source, my posture began to change. I stopped demanding immediate answers and began to wait with expectation. Silence no longer felt like absence, because His Word remained steady even when specific direction was not yet clear. In that place, trust deepened. Waiting became part of the formation, not a barrier to it.

When the Lord is our source, guidance becomes relational rather than transactional, and obedience flows from trust rather than pressure. We no longer strive to extract direction, but learn to walk with Him, responding to what He reveals through Scripture and by His Spirit. Decisions become less driven by urgency and more shaped by peace as we remain submitted to Him. We learn to wait without fear, to move without striving, and to obey even when we do not yet see the full picture.

Receiving His voice begins with surrender, not only of outcomes, but of ownership. As we yield our need to control direction, we discover that He is faithful to lead. What once felt uncertain becomes steady, not because every detail is known, but because the One who leads is trustworthy.

Movement Two: Receive — Hearing and Following God's Voice

Movement Two is the turning point of the U-Turn. After repentance restores rightful authority, the surrendered heart becomes attentive. Receiving is not about pursuing direction with urgency, but about positioning ourselves to hear and follow God according to His Word, as the Holy Spirit faithfully guides and applies it in our lives. God's voice is relational, flowing from our relationship with Him, and it never contradicts His revealed truth in Scripture. As fear, control, and self-direction are laid down, we become more able to discern His guidance with clarity and steadiness.

Scripture consistently reveals this pattern. As hearts yield, God's direction becomes clearer. He does not typically reveal the entire future at once but provides light for the next faithful step. In this way, dependence is formed as we walk with Him. Receiving shifts, us from striving to listening, from self-definition to being shaped by God's truth, and from independence to dependence on Him. Direction becomes less about securing outcomes and more about responding in obedience to what God has already made clear.

Jesus describes this pattern plainly: "My sheep hear My voice, and I know them, and they follow Me." (John 10:27 NKJV). Hearing and following belong together. We listen because we belong to Him, and we follow as we trust His Word and yield to His leading. Receiving is not the pursuit of guidance, but the posture of a life that is yielded, attentive, and ready to obey.

In this movement, identity is established before assignment, and calling is clarified before action. Direction unfolds step by step as trust deepens and obedience is practiced. God does not merely give direction; He forms a people who can recognize His voice and walk in it faithfully. Receiving is where surrender becomes lived out through ongoing responsiveness to the Spirit, and the believer learns not only to discern God's guidance, but to follow it with humility, trust, and consistency.

Core Areas of Receiving in This Movement

Receiving God's voice as revealed in Scripture and applied by the Holy Spirit becomes tangible in four foundational areas of formation. These are not tasks to achieve, but places where we learn to hear, trust, and follow. As we receive, our lives begin to align with how God defines us in His Word rather than how we have defined ourselves through experience, culture, or past patterns.

1. Identity: Who Am I in Christ?

> "Therefore, if anyone *is* in Christ, *he is* a new creation; old things have passed away; behold, all things have become new." (2 Corinthians 5:17 NKJV).

Before God clarifies direction, He establishes identity. Many believers follow Christ sincerely, yet continue to live from performance, comparison, insecurity, or past labels. Identity is often shaped by experience long before it is grounded in truth. When identity is unstable, obedience becomes inconsistent because it is influenced by shifting perceptions rather than anchored in what God has declared.

Receiving God's voice begins with receiving who He says we are in Christ through His Word. Identity is not earned or proven; it is given through our union with Christ and His finished work. We are no longer ultimately defined by fear, weakness, or history, though we continue to be transformed as we grow in Him. From this foundation, transformation becomes steady and lasting. We no longer strive to become accepted; we begin to live as those who already belong.

The deeper question is not simply who I am, but whose Word defines me. When our identity is shaped by Scripture, we are positioned to discern God's guidance more clearly and follow Him with greater steadiness.

1.1 Receiving Identity Before Receiving Direction

> "But now, thus says the LORD, who created you, O Jacob, and He who formed you, O Israel: 'Fear not, for I have redeemed you; I have called *you* by your name; you *are* Mine.'" (Isaiah 43:1 NKJV).

In receiving and following God's guidance, identity comes before direction. Before God reveals what we are to do, He establishes who we are in Him. When identity is uncertain, direction can feel pressured or driven by performance. When identity is secure in Christ, guidance is received with trust rather than anxiety.

Many believers seek God's will while still living from identities shaped by fear, achievement, or comparison. These internal beliefs influence how we hear and interpret what God reveals. If worth feels dependent on performance, direction can be misunderstood as something to prove rather than a path to walk in obedience.

When identity is secure in Christ, we follow from belonging rather than striving. Scripture consistently reveals that God anchors His people in relationship before entrusting them with responsibility. Receiving identity means aligning our hearts with what God has already declared in His Word. As this alignment deepens, clarity increases. We no longer seek direction to gain significance but respond as those who already belong.

1.2 How Identity Is Formed

Scripture reflects that what we internalize in the heart shapes how we live. Identity begins forming long before we are fully aware of it. In early life, when the heart is impressionable, identity is influenced by words spoken over us, experiences we internalize, and beliefs we come to accept about ourselves. Words carry weight, and repeated messages can form patterns of thinking that influence how we see ourselves and respond to life.

Experiences often reinforce these patterns. When love feels conditional, we may begin to measure our worth by performance. When acceptance feels uncertain, we may strive for approval or withdraw to protect ourselves. Culture also contributes to identity formation, often defining value through achievement, appearance, or independence. Without recognizing it, we can begin to measure ourselves by standards that are not rooted in God's truth.

Identity may be influenced by life experiences, but it must be grounded in what God has revealed in His Word. Over time, patterns that once felt protective can become limiting, and that tension becomes an invitation to realignment. As we receive God's truth, false beliefs are replaced and our thinking is renewed. In place of striving, we learn to rest in belonging. In place of fear, we grow in trust. As our hearts align with God's truth, our identity becomes increasingly established in who He says we are.

1.3 Hearing Who God Says You Are

"But as many as received Him, to them He gave the right to become children of God." (John 1:12 NKJV).

In this movement of receiving, identity is strengthened as we align our hearts with what God has already declared in His Word. Before we follow God's direction, we must be anchored in who we are in Christ. Scripture consistently shows that identity is established before assignment, forming a foundation for faithful obedience.

Many voices shape how we see ourselves, including past experiences, relationships, and cultural expectations. Over time, these influences can form beliefs that do not fully align with God's truth. Without realizing it, we may begin to live from these beliefs rather than from what God has revealed in Scripture.

When we receive what God has declared, we stop striving to become and begin living from who we already are in Christ. This requires humility and a willingness to allow Scripture to shape our thinking more than past experiences or personal assumptions. It is not positive thinking, but alignment with truth.

As identity is grounded in Christ, obedience becomes a response of trust rather than an effort to prove worth. Direction becomes clearer because it flows from a secure foundation. In the U-Turn, receiving God's voice is not only about knowing what to do next, but about walking in truth as we follow Him. When identity is established in Christ, the path forward becomes steady, anchored in His Word, and sustained by His grace.

2. Calling: What Is My Calling?

2.1 Calling from the Father Who Knows You

"Where there *is* no revelation, the people cast off restraint; But happy is he who keeps the law." (Proverbs 29:18 NKJV).

In the movement of receiving, calling is not determined by pressure but discerned through a growing relationship with God and alignment with His revealed Word. Calling flows from the Father who knows you and is made clear as we walk in obedience to Him. Where God's revelation is neglected, direction is lost, but where His Word is honored, life is anchored. When calling is not rooted in Him, life becomes reactive, and we begin to measure ourselves by productivity, comparison, or fear of missing His will. Instead of listening, we attempt to define direction on our own.

Biblical calling begins with alignment to God and is expressed through faithful obedience to what He has already made known. Throughout Scripture, calling unfolds in the context of relationship with Him. David was anointed before he ruled, and Moses was called before he led. Their calling was not absent in hidden seasons; it was being formed according to God's timing. The One who calls is also faithful to shape, guide, and sustain. Anxiety around calling often comes from believing we must secure it ourselves, yet God is not uncertain about our lives. He directs those who seek Him and walk in obedience to His Word, often through Scripture, wisdom, and the steady leading of His Spirit, one step at a time.

Calling received from God produces steadiness and peace because it is rooted in His Word and formed through relationship, not pressure or striving. It may not answer every detail, but it establishes the direction of the heart. The focus shifts from achievement to faithfulness, from recognition to obedience. In the U-Turn journey, hearing your calling means remaining attentive to God and walking with Him according to what He has revealed.

2.2 Calling Revealed Through Relationship

> "For we are His workmanship, created in Christ Jesus for good works, which God prepared beforehand that we should walk in them." (Ephesians 2:10 NKJV).

Calling is not first uncovered through strategy but revealed through relationship with God. Before God entrusts assignment, He draws us into closeness with Him. Scripture teaches that we are His workmanship, and the works we are called to walk in are prepared by Him. Our role is not to create our calling, but to remain aligned with the One who has already established it.

Calling is revealed as we remain rooted in relationship with God and walk in obedience to what He has made known. When relationship is primary, calling becomes steady rather than stressful. Roles may change and seasons may shift, but a life anchored in God remains aligned. David learned who he was in God's presence long before he stepped into public leadership, and those hidden years were part of God's preparation, not a delay of calling.

Calling is not defined by position alone but is expressed through faithfulness wherever God places us. As we remain attentive to God through His Word, prayer, and a surrendered heart, direction becomes clearer. Calling is not something we manufacture through effort, but something we faithfully walk out as we respond to God in obedience. As we stay close to Him, our sensitivity to His leading grows. The focus shifts from achieving to obeying, and from striving to trusting. In that posture, calling unfolds with clarity and peace.

2.3 When Calling Is Misaligned

Sincerity and activity do not always mean alignment with God. It is possible to love God, remain active, and even see results, yet drift from obedience to His Word. Not every opportunity is from God, and not every desire reflects His will. At times, what appears to be calling may be shaped by fear, pressure, or the need to prove ourselves rather than by faithful obedience.

When calling is misaligned — when our direction moves outside of obedience to God's Word — striving replaces peace. We may begin to act from self-reliance, seeking approval, control, or security. Over time, this leads to weariness. Scripture shows how subtle this drift can be. Saul's calling remained, but his disobedience led him away from God's direction. Martha served yet became distracted and anxious. Jonah received clear instruction but resisted. In each case, the issue was not activity, but alignment with God.

Misalignment often brings a sense of heaviness, urgency, or pressure. These are not meant to condemn, but to prompt reflection and return. God, in His faithfulness, calls us back to

Himself so that we may walk in obedience to His will. The U-Turn is not a place of shame, but a return to truth.

True calling is not something we achieve, but something we walk in through ongoing surrender and faithful obedience to God's Word. As we come back to hearing and following God through Scripture and the Spirit's leading, calling is realigned, identity is strengthened, and obedience becomes steady. What once felt driven becomes directed, and what once felt heavy becomes sustained by grace.

3. Gifts: What Has God Given Me?

3.1 What the Father Has Entrusted to You

> "As each one has received a gift, minister it to one another, as good stewards of the manifold grace of God." (1 Peter 4:10 NKJV).

Every gift in your life begins as something received, entrusted by the Father, and distributed through the Holy Spirit according to His will. Before it is recognized, developed, or affirmed, it is given according to His purpose. In this movement of hearing and following God's voice, this foundation matters deeply. We cannot steward rightly what we have not first received with humility. Spiritual gifts are not proofs of our worth, but expressions of God's grace, revealing both our identity in Him and His generosity through us.

The gift is not the ultimate goal; faithful obedience to God is, and gifts serve that purpose. When we lose sight of the Giver, gifts can become burdens. We may strive to prove ourselves or withdraw in uncertainty, questioning whether what we carry is enough. Both responses distract from listening to God's leading. Striving seeks recognition, and fear questions sufficiency, but stewardship listens. It asks, Lord, how would You have me use what You have given? As we remain attentive to Him through His Word and prayer, He brings clarity in timing, direction, and use. What once felt pressured becomes peaceful, and what once felt uncertain becomes steady.

What the Father has entrusted to you is meant to serve others and reflect His work, not define your identity. As you follow His leading, your gifts function with clarity and humility. Your gifts no longer carry the weight of self-definition but become instruments for His purposes. When stewarded in dependence on Him, they bear fruit in ways that honor God and build up others.

3.2 The Gift Refined by Relationship

Spiritual gifts are not developed in isolation. They are shaped over time as we walk with God. In a life committed to hearing and following His voice, the growth of a gift is closely connected to the formation of character. Gifts are expressed through the heart and empowered by the Spirit, and when the heart is influenced by fear, comparison, or self-protection, even good gifts can become difficult to carry. But when the heart is yielded to God, those same gifts can serve with clarity and peace.

Scripture shows that God often develops both calling and character together. Joseph demonstrated leadership and discernment early in life, yet his journey included seasons of testing that shaped his humility and trust in God. The Lord did not remove the gift but matured the person. This pattern reflects God's wisdom and care. He forms us so that what He has entrusted can be expressed rightly.

As we continue to walk with Him, He gently corrects motives, strengthens trust, and teaches us to depend on Him. Growth may be gradual, but it is purposeful. When we remain grounded in His Word and responsive to His leading, our gifts are expressed with greater wisdom and balance. They are no longer driven by pressure or comparison but guided by obedience. In this way, what God has entrusted becomes a means of serving others faithfully, and the fruit reflects His work rather than our effort.

3.3 Stewarding the Gifts God Has Given

Once gifts are recognized, the question shifts from what has God given me to how am I caring for what He has entrusted to me. Scripture presents gifts as trusts given for service and the building up of others, not as personal possessions. Stewardship is measured by faithfulness to God and dependence on His strength, not by visibility or recognition. Some may hide their gifts out of fear or insecurity, while others may misuse or overextend them. In each case, the issue is not the gift, but the posture of the heart.

When gifts are not grounded in humility and trust, they can become burdensome or misdirected. The fruit of a gift is shaped by the condition of the heart and our willingness to follow God's leading. Faithful stewardship involves both dependence and participation. Gifts are developed over time through practice, correction, and patience as we remain attentive to God. He refines what He entrusts, forming both character and wisdom.

Scripture also calls us to remain watchful, as strengths can be misapplied when they are not yielded to Him. As we stay rooted in His Word and dependent on His guidance, our gifts are expressed with balance and clarity. God is not concerned with how impressive our gifts appear, but whether they are surrendered and shaped by love. In the U-Turn journey, stewardship is not about doing more, but about walking faithfully with what has been given. As we hear and follow His voice, our gifts become expressions of His grace, serving others and reflecting His work.

4. Direction: What Is My Next Step?

4.1 Understanding the Importance of Divine Guidance

"In all your ways acknowledge Him, And He shall direct your paths." (Proverbs 3:6 NKJV).

Divine guidance is not simply about making correct decisions. It is about learning to live in dependence on God rather than self-direction. His guidance anchors our lives in His wisdom instead of our own understanding, emotions, or urgency. Without His direction, even sincere intentions can lead to confusion and unnecessary strain. Scripture presents guidance as essential for alignment, protection, and faithful obedience, through which fruit is borne in His timing.

From the beginning, God has revealed Himself as One who leads His people. He delivered Israel and guided them through the wilderness, not leaving them to rely on their own judgment. His direction was an expression of His care, protecting and sustaining them. Scripture also shows the consequences of acting without seeking the Lord. Joshua's agreement with the Gibeonites and Saul's impatience both reveal how acting apart from God's counsel leads to misalignment. In contrast, David inquired of the Lord and was guided step by step. His strength was not perfection, but dependence on God.

In my own journey, I have learned that when direction feels unclear, the issue is often not only God's silence, but also the temptation to move ahead of trust. I wanted clarity before obedience, yet Scripture teaches that God directs those who walk with Him in faith. God gives light for the next step as we trust Him rather than revealing the entire path at once. Leaning on our own understanding can be subtle, especially when we are capable and experienced, but it often produces pressure rather than peace. Divine guidance invites us to slow down and remain attentive to God rather than driven by urgency. Direction matters because it keeps our lives rooted in relationship with God, not merely outcomes. He does not guide us only to accomplish something, but to walk with Him. In the U-Turn journey, following His direction marks the shift from self-reliance to trust and from striving to faithful obedience.

4.2 God Reveals Himself Through Process and Steps

"The steps of a good man are ordered by the LORD, and he delighteth in his way." (Psalm 37:23 NKJV.)

God often leads through process rather than full visibility. He guides step by step, forming trust as we walk with Him. This pattern is consistent throughout Scripture. Abraham was called to go without knowing the destination. Peter stepped out in faith at Jesus' command. Paul made plans, yet remained responsive as the Lord directed his steps. In each case, direction became clear as they moved in obedience.

Over time, I have learned to pray more simply: Lord, show me the next step. As I release the need for certainty and seek Him through His Word and prayer, clarity comes in its proper time. God meets a humble and willing heart with guidance through His Word, His Spirit, and the counsel of His people, not always immediately, but faithfully.

God's direction is grounded in His Word and discerned through a life of prayerful dependence. As we remain rooted in Scripture, seek Him consistently, and walk in humility, we grow in discernment. Wise counsel within the body of Christ provides protection and confirmation, helping us remain aligned with God's truth. These means work together to guide us in a way that is steady and trustworthy. God is not withholding direction; He is leading us as we walk with Him. As we remain attentive to His Word, respond in obedience, and take one step at a time, the path becomes clearer. Direction is not something we control or determine on our own, but something we receive as we follow Him.

4.3 When You Are Not Walking in Divine Direction

"There is a way *that* seems right to a man, But its end *is* the way of death." (Proverbs 14:12 NKJV).

When we are not walking in alignment with God's direction, it rarely appears as open rebellion. More often, it reveals itself through quiet exhaustion, lingering confusion, or an internal strain that persists even when life appears productive. Many sincere believers experience this tension, continuing to pray and serve while sensing something unsettled within. This is not failure, but often an invitation to return to dependence on God rather than relying on personal understanding.

One common sign is decision paralysis. Fear of making the wrong choice becomes so weighty that movement feels difficult. We overanalyze, hesitate, and wait for complete certainty before obeying. Yet Scripture consistently shows that faith involves movement, even when clarity is partial. Another indicator is a life marked by constant noise and urgency. When we become reactive instead of responsive, discernment weakens. We shift from listening to managing, from trusting to controlling. Even good desires can lead us when they are no longer submitted to God.

Direction without surrender produces pressure, even when outcomes appear successful. This is not the way God leads His people. He corrects with gentleness, not condemnation, inviting us back into alignment with His heart. Jesus said,

> "Come to Me, all *you* who labor and are heavy laden, and I will give you rest... For My yoke *is* easy and My burden is light." (Matthew 11:28–30 NKJV).

This does not mean the path is without challenge, but that true alignment replaces striving with grace. When we return to listening with humility and trust, clarity begins to emerge again.

4.4 Divine Direction and the Personal Operating System

"A man's heart plans his way, But the LORD directs his steps." (Proverbs 16:9 NKJV).

Divine direction is processed through the life operating system we live from, the internal framework of the heart and mind that shapes how we interpret uncertainty, respond to pressure, and make decisions. A self-directed life tends to rely on control, urgency, and visible outcomes, while a Spirit-led life is shaped by listening, trusting, and a willingness to follow God one step at a time.

For much of my life, my default posture was driven and disciplined. While these qualities are not wrong, they can quietly compete with discernment when they are not surrendered. I planned carefully and moved quickly yet did not always make space for God's pace. Over time, I realized that what felt like a lack of clarity was often the result of internal noise rather than God's silence. As the heart becomes quieter before Him, direction becomes clearer.

Scripture affirms this pattern:

> "Then He said, 'Go out, and stand on the mountain before the LORD.' And behold, the LORD passed by, and a great and strong wind tore into the mountains and broke the rocks in pieces before the LORD, *but* the LORD was not in the wind; and after the wind an earthquake, *but* the LORD was not in the earthquake; and after the earthquake a fire, *but* the LORD was not in the fire; and after the fire a still small voice." (1 Kings 19:11–12 NKJV).

The issue was not God's absence, but the posture required to hear Him. In the same way, discernment grows where the heart is attentive and surrendered. Planning and responsibility remain important, but they are no longer driven by pressure and are instead submitted to God's leading.

Divine direction becomes clearer when our posture shifts from control to trust and from urgency to attentiveness. In this alignment, obedience takes priority over speed, and peace becomes a steady confirming witness alongside God's Word and wisdom (Colossians 3:15 NKJV). God's guidance is not merely directional; it is relational. He leads not only to guide our steps, but to keep us near to Him. In the U-Turn journey, this realignment is essential. Direction flows most freely when our life operating system is yielded to the Spirit and shaped by ongoing dependence on Him.

The Pivot: Trusting God Enough to Move

Surrender prepares the heart, and trust calls it into action according to what God has revealed in His Word. The Pivot is the decisive moment in the U-Turn where agreement with God becomes movement with God. Faith shifts from internal conviction to outward obedience, and belief begins to shape daily life rather than remain an idea. Trust is not ultimately grounded in what we fully understand, but in our willingness to obey what God has revealed. As we respond, grace meets us in our obedience, strengthening us to walk in what God has made known.

Throughout Scripture, God's people move forward without full visibility. "Abraham obeyed when he was called to go out...not knowing where he was going." (Hebrews 11:8 NKJV). Peter stepped out onto the water in the midst of the storm (Matthew 14:29 NKJV). Israel followed the Lord through the wilderness one step at a time (Exodus 13:21–22 NKJV). In each account, direction often unfolded through obedience as they moved forward, rather than being fully revealed beforehand. Faith was expressed in movement, not merely agreement.

The Pivot bridges hearing God's voice through His Word and Spirit and walking in His direction. As we respond to His leading, truth begins to shape our habits, decisions, and direction. The U-Turn moves from yielding to living, from listening to walking. Obedience becomes the pathway through which alignment is sustained and deepened, not as a striving effort, but as a response to God's grace and leadership.

From here, the journey rises into the next movement: Renewal. In Chapter 11, we will explore how the heart, mind, and life are transformed from the inside out as obedience to God's guidance reshapes patterns of thinking and daily living.

Reflection Questions

1. Where am I relying on my own understanding instead of acknowledging the Lord and trusting Him to direct my path (Proverbs 3:5–6 NKJV)?
2. What beliefs or past experiences may be shaping how I hear and respond to God's Word in this season?
3. Is there an area where I am seeking clarity before obedience instead of responding to what God has already made clear in Scripture?
4. When has God been faithful as I obeyed Him step by step, even without full understanding?
5. What is one next step of obedience the Lord may be calling me to take as I listen and follow Him?

Prayer

Lord,

I come before You with a willing heart. I surrender my need to control outcomes and my desire for full understanding. Teach me to trust You and to walk according to Your Word. Quiet every voice that competes with Your truth and help me to discern Your leading clearly. Give me grace to obey what You have already revealed, even when I cannot see the whole path. Lead me step by step in humility, faith, and dependence on You.

In Jesus' name, Amen.

Chapter 11 — Renew: Living from a Transformed Mind

"Renewal is not self-improvement but living from the new identity already established in Christ through Spirit-empowered obedience."

Movement Three: Renew — Living from a Transformed Mind

The Ascent Where Truth Reshapes Life

What is received in surrender must now reshape thinking. Movement Three unfolds in the ascent of the U-Turn, where the believer begins to live from a transformed inner framework rather than old patterns. Receiving establishes alignment, renewal sustains it. A surrendered and listening heart becomes a transformed mind. To renew means allowing the Holy Spirit, through God's Word, to bring our beliefs, thoughts, and responses into agreement with His truth rather than allowing them to be shaped by fear, culture, or past experiences. At this stage, the inner operating system is renewed and reshaped by the Spirit through God's truth. What was once driven by reaction is now governed by truth. Identity stabilizes. Discernment sharpens. Obedience strengthens. Life begins to reflect what has been received.

Transformation is sustained through renewal, not by human effort, but by the ongoing work of the Holy Spirit through the Word of God. The ascent of the U is not striving; it is formation. Alignment that begins within now becomes visible in how we think, respond, and live. When truth replaces false beliefs and consistency replaces instability, the mind becomes steady. We no longer interpret life through circumstances alone, but through what God has spoken. Renewal trains the soul to respond with wisdom instead of fear, and trust instead of self-protection.

In this movement, what is transformed within begins to express itself outwardly in three ways:

- **Belief** — We agree with God's truth over every area of life. What He says becomes our foundation, shaping how we see ourselves, others, and our circumstances.
- **Mind** — Thought patterns are renewed and brought into alignment with Christ. Old ways of thinking are gradually replaced as the Spirit uses Scripture to reshape our understanding.
- **Practice** — Daily living reflects spiritual alignment. Walking in the Spirit becomes consistent rather than occasional, as obedience flows from a renewed mind.

Renewal is not self-improvement; it is Spirit led transformation. What the Spirit forms within becomes evident in how we live, bearing fruit that reflects His work. As the mind aligns with truth, life aligns with God's design.

Stabilizing Your Life Operating System Through Truth

A reset must be stabilized. Without renewal, the Life Operating System can return to familiar patterns under pressure, even after sincere surrender. Renewal strengthens what God has already restored, allowing transformation to become steady rather than temporary. Scripture teaches that transformation comes through the renewing of the mind, not through outward effort alone (Romans 12:2 NKJV). As we remain in God's Word, in prayer, and in dependence on the Holy Spirit, what was once reactive becomes anchored in truth. Old thought patterns are gradually replaced as Scripture reshapes how we think and respond.

Emotional responses are gradually brought under the guidance of the Spirit and shaped by truth rather than ruled by impulse, and identity becomes rooted in Christ rather than in circumstances. As perspective is formed by Scripture, the inner life grows more stable and consistent. Renewal does not remove struggle, but it changes how we respond, anchoring us in truth rather than allowing us to be led by shifting emotions or external pressure.

God leads step by step, and renewal supports each step by aligning our thinking with His truth. What once produced anxiety begins to give way to peace, not because circumstances have changed, but because the mind is being renewed (Romans 8:6 NKJV). Decisions begin to flow from conviction shaped by God's Word rather than from fear or uncertainty. The Life Operating System becomes increasingly governed by the Spirit rather than by fluctuating emotions or past patterns. In this way, renewal establishes stability, forming a life that is grounded in truth and responsive to God's leading.

What Renewal Really Means

Renewal is far more hopeful than we often imagine. It is not God asking us to fix ourselves or become disciplined enough to live a godly life. Scripture presents renewal first as a gift before it becomes a process. It begins with the truth that something real has already changed within us. In Christ, we are new creations learning to live from what God has already made true (2 Corinthians 5:17 NKJV). The old self, shaped by sin and separation, was decisively dealt with at the cross, and its authority has been broken, even as we continue to grow in freedom through the Spirit. Renewal is not improving that old identity but learning to walk in the new life given through the Spirit.

Renewal is not self-improvement but living from the new identity already established in Christ through Spirit-empowered obedience.

Scripture consistently shows that God establishes identity before transformation is fully expressed. When Gideon was hiding in fear, God called him a "mighty man of valor." His behavior had not yet aligned, but God spoke truth first and then led him into it. Peter's restoration reflects the same pattern. After denying Jesus, he was restored through relationship before responsibility. "Do you love Me?" came before "Feed My sheep." Renewal begins with connection, not performance.

This is why renewal does not rely on willpower alone, but on the work of the Holy Spirit through God's Word as we abide in Christ. As we remain in Him, the Spirit renews our thinking, shapes our responses, and strengthens our obedience. Old patterns gradually lose their influence as truth takes root. Transformation is sustained through abiding in Christ, not striving in the flesh. Renewal is a steady, ongoing work. God is faithful to complete what He has begun (Philippians 1:6 NKJV). Each step is supported by grace, not condemnation. As the mind is renewed, faith moves from belief into daily living, and life increasingly reflects the truth of who we are in Christ.

Why Renewal Is Essential in the U-Turn Journey

Renewal is essential because what has been restored in surrender must be sustained in daily living. It is not God asking us to fix ourselves or strive harder to become godly. It begins with the truth that something real has already changed within us. In Christ, we are new creations learning to live from what God has already made true. Renewal is not the improvement of the old self but the daily practice of living from the new life given through Christ. Instead of focusing on what is still broken, renewal redirects our attention to what God has already accomplished. The old life shaped by sin, fear, and striving has been dealt with, and a new life, empowered by the Holy Spirit, has begun. Renewal becomes the steady alignment of our thinking with this truth.

Scripture shows that God establishes identity before transformation is fully expressed. Gideon was called a mighty man of valor while still hiding in fear. Peter was restored in relationship before being entrusted with responsibility. In the same way, renewal begins with what God declares to be true and continues as our thinking and responses come into alignment with it.

Renewal is the ongoing work of aligning our minds with God's truth so that what He has already established in Christ becomes increasingly expressed in how we live.

This is why renewal is not sustained by willpower. It flows from abiding in Christ and walking in obedience to His Word. As we remain in Him, the Holy Spirit reshapes our thinking and responses. Old patterns lose influence, not simply because we resist them, but because new life is growing stronger within us. God is patient and faithful, completing the work He begins. Ultimately, renewal is the steady alignment of the mind with God's truth, so that what we believe is increasingly reflected in how we live. It is the ongoing journey where faith becomes lived experience. God is not calling us to strive for a transformed life, but to receive it, walk in it through obedience, and trust Him to bring it to completion.

Movement Three: Renew — Living from a Transformed Mind

Movement Three is the sustaining movement of the U-Turn. If repentance restores authority and receiving clarifies direction, renewal establishes stability. This is where transformation moves from decision to formation. The heart has turned and

God's voice has been received, but now the mind is being renewed so that alignment becomes consistent rather than occasional. Renewal establishes stability as the Holy Spirit aligns our thinking with God's truth through His Word, so that transformation is sustained rather than temporary.

Renewal is not striving to improve behavior; it is the ongoing work of the Holy Spirit reshaping the inner life through God's Word so that what He has spoken becomes how we live.

What He has spoken begins to influence how we interpret circumstances, process emotions, and make decisions. Old patterns formed through fear, control, or self-reliance are gradually replaced as we yield to the Holy Spirit and learn to agree with His truth. This work is often gradual, and while growth may not always feel immediate, God is faithful to form what He has begun. As the mind is renewed, life becomes steadier, and obedience flows more consistently from within.

This movement engages belief, thought, and practice. What we believe shapes what we agree with, what we think influences how we interpret life, and what we practice reflects what governs us. The Holy Spirit teaches us to live intentionally from truth rather than unconsciously from habit. He forms a life that responds with wisdom rather than reacting from emotion, where faith is expressed in daily decisions and inward transformation becomes outwardly visible. Renewal is not a single moment but a continual process of aligning the mind with God's truth, forming a life that remains steady and responsive to Him. Through this ongoing work, the U-Turn becomes a way of life, and the transformed mind becomes the foundation for lasting spiritual growth.

Core Areas of Renewal in This Movement

Renewal is expressed in daily life through three connected areas: belief, mind, and practice. These work together under the guidance of the Holy Spirit to sustain transformation from the inside out.

Renew — Living from a Transformed Mind

- Belief — Agreeing with God's Truth
- Mind — Renewing Thought Patterns
- Practice — Walking in the Spirit

1. Belief: Agreeing with God's Truth

1.1 Belief: Where Alignment Begins

"For as he thinks in his heart, so *is* he." (Proverbs 23:7 NKJV).

Belief is never neutral. What a person truly believes will eventually surface in choices, emotional responses, and repeated patterns, especially under pressure. In moments of stress or uncertainty, beliefs reveal themselves without effort. We often default to what we truly believe in those moments, unless our hearts have been strengthened and renewed by God's truth. Belief is more than mental agreement. It is the inner alignment that shapes how reality is interpreted long before visible decisions are made.

Scripture shows that walking with God requires agreement: "Can two walk together, unless they are agreed?" (Amos 3:3 NKJV). Alignment with God begins at the level of belief, and is sustained through the transforming work of His Spirit. We may desire to follow Him, yet true spiritual movement requires agreement with His truth. When belief quietly disagrees with God, distance may begin to form in our awareness and responsiveness to Him, even if outward activity continues. Yet He remains near and continually invites us back into alignment. The issue is not effort but alignment. Belief functions like the operating system of the heart. It determines how we process truth, emotion, and experience.

When belief aligns with God's Word, transformation is no longer sustained by effort alone but by conviction shaped and strengthened by the Spirit. As belief shifts, obedience becomes less forced and more natural. Trust begins to replace control, and the Spirit leads rather than the flesh reacting. Agreement leads to alignment, and alignment makes it possible to walk with God.

1.2 Distorted Belief: When the Flesh Governs the Mind

"There is a way *that seems* right to a man, But its end *is* the way of death." (Proverbs 14:12 NKJV).

Distorted belief rarely appears as open rebellion. It often feels reasonable or protective. When thinking is shaped by fear, past pain, or self-reliance rather than the Spirit, belief gradually forms around those influences instead of God's truth. Over time, these beliefs become internal assumptions about God, ourselves, and others. When this happens, self-protection replaces surrender, and performance replaces trust.

A person may still confess truth outwardly yet live from a different internal agreement. This creates inconsistency, not because desire for God is absent, but because belief is divided. Scripture consistently shows that outward failure begins with inward misalignment. Renewal brings these hidden beliefs into the light so they can be realigned with truth. It does not condemn but restores. As truth reshapes belief, fear loses its authority, control loosens, and identity becomes anchored in God. The shift toward Spirit-led thinking may take time, but it establishes lasting transformation. When belief is restored, the U-Turn moves from surface change to deep and stable alignment.

1.3 Projection and the False Self

"Be sober, be vigilant; because your adversary the devil walks about like a roaring lion, seeking whom he may devour." (1 Peter 5:8 NKJV.)

Renewal requires vigilance because what is not brought before God can begin to shape how we see and respond to life. This includes being aware not only of external spiritual opposition but also of internal patterns that influence perception. When pain, disappointment, or unmet expectations remain unaddressed in God's presence, they can affect how we interpret others and situations. What feels like discernment may be influenced by past hurt, and what appears to be strength may reflect self-protection rather than trust.

Projection occurs when we interpret others through our own unresolved experiences rather than through truth and grace. Scripture shows that the inner life matters deeply. Saul allowed fear and insecurity to shape how he viewed David, while David consistently brought his emotions before the Lord and remained aligned with Him. The difference was not the absence of struggle, but the posture of the heart.

When the heart is not anchored in truth, responses are shaped more by self-protection than by trust in God. Renewal begins not with striving to correct behavior, but with bringing thoughts and emotions honestly before Him. As truth reshapes belief, perspective becomes clearer, humility grows, and relationships are strengthened. The result is not outward performance, but a steadier inner life marked by peace and alignment with God.

1.4 Spirit-Led Belief

"For as many as are led by the Spirit of God, these are sons of God." (Romans 8:14 NKJV).

A Spirit-led belief system brings the mind and heart under the guidance of God. Rather than being shaped primarily by circumstances or emotions, belief becomes anchored in God's character and His Word. Emotions are not ignored, but they are brought before the Lord and understood in light of truth. Fear may arise, but it does not determine direction.

Disappointment may be felt, but it does not redefine God's goodness.

As belief aligns with truth, transformation becomes evident in the inner life. Scripture describes the fruit that grows from a life led by the Spirit: love, joy, peace, longsuffering, kindness, goodness, faithfulness, gentleness, self-control (Galatians 5:22–23 NKJV). This fruit is not produced by pressure, but by abiding in God and walking in step with His Spirit.

As we submit to God and align with His truth, we are strengthened to resist the enemy, and he will flee. Spiritual strength grows as we continue to agree with God's truth and walk in dependence on Him. In daily life, this means returning to Scripture and allowing it to shape how we think and respond. As belief is continually realigned, the mind becomes more stable, the heart more at rest, and life more consistent with the work God is doing within us. This is renewal lived out, a life shaped by truth and guided by the Spirit.

2. Mind: Renewing Thought Patterns

2.1 God's Design for the Mind

> "And do not be conformed to this world, but be transformed by the renewing of your mind, that you may prove what *is* that good and acceptable and perfect will of God." (Romans 12:2 NKJV).

From the beginning, God designed the mind as a gift to serve His purposes. It is created for understanding, remembering, and discerning, yet it is not meant to function independently from Him, but in dependence on His truth and guidance. In Scripture, a renewed life reflects proper alignment, where the Spirit leads, the mind is shaped by truth, and life follows in obedience. When this order is present, there is increasing clarity, stability, and peace. When the mind is shaped primarily by surrounding influences rather than God's truth, confusion and inner tension can arise.

Scripture consistently emphasizes the importance of the inner life. What fills the heart and mind will ultimately shape direction and conduct. Renewal is therefore central to transformation. God works not only in outward behavior but also in the renewing of our thinking so that our lives reflect His will. Jesus demonstrated this perfectly. He lived in continual dependence on the Father, responding in perfect alignment with His will rather than being governed by pressure or circumstance.

The renewing of the mind is the ongoing work by which our thinking is brought into alignment with God's truth. Thoughts themselves are not the problem, but they must be guided by what is true according to God's Word. Scripture calls believers to bring their thinking into obedience to Christ (2 Corinthians 10:5 NKJV). As this happens, perspective begins to change. Instead of being led by uncertainty, we learn to seek God's wisdom. Trust grows, and discernment becomes clearer over time.

As the mind is renewed through God's truth, it becomes a steady instrument through which His will is discerned and lived out. Within the U-Turn journey, renewing the mind restores this alignment. As believers continue in God's Word and yield to His Spirit, the mind becomes steady and responsive to truth, supporting a life that reflects God's will rather than being shaped by shifting circumstances.

2.2 When the Mind Drifts from Truth

"For to be carnally minded *is* death, but to be spiritually minded *is* life and peace." (Romans 8:6 NKJV).

When the mind drifts from truth, it does not mean a person has lost faith. Rather, it reflects a shift in focus. Instead of being shaped by the Spirit, thinking becomes influenced by fear, fatigue, or circumstances. When this happens, clarity can give way to confusion, and peace may feel distant. In such moments, the mind may begin to react rather than discern, focusing on immediate concerns instead of being anchored in God's promises.

Scripture describes this as a mindset shaped by the flesh, meaning thinking that is not presently aligned with the Spirit. This is a condition of perspective, not a change in identity. The Scriptures illustrate this with compassion. After a significant victory, Elijah became discouraged and overwhelmed. God, in His compassion, restored him through rest and care before speaking truth to him again. His experience shows that even faithful believers may need renewal in their thinking during seasons of weariness.

When the mind drifts, God's invitation is not condemnation, but a return to His truth and presence. As we come back to Him and allow His Word to reshape our thinking, clarity is restored, the heart becomes steady, and peace returns. Renewal places the mind back into its proper role, shaped by truth and responsive to the Spirit. Where this alignment is restored, life and peace follow, just as Scripture promises.

2.3 Taking Every Thought Captive

> "Casting down arguments and every high thing that exalts itself against the knowledge of God, bringing every thought into captivity to the obedience of Christ." (2 Corinthians 10:5 NKJV).

Renewing the mind requires intentional alignment with truth. Scripture teaches that our thoughts are not meant to lead us independently but are to come under the authority of Christ. Throughout the day, many thoughts pass through the mind, yet some subtly challenge God's truth by stirring fear, accusation, or old patterns of thinking. When left unexamined, these thoughts begin to shape emotions and influence decisions.

Taking every thought captive begins with recognizing that not every thought should be accepted as truth. Instead, each thought is to be examined and measured against God's Word. A guiding question becomes, does this thought align with God's character, His promises, and His revealed truth. If a thought contradicts these, it is to be brought into submission to Christ.

This is not about achieving a perfect thought life, but about cultivating a surrendered one. As we consistently bring our thoughts under Christ's authority, the mind becomes steadier, and peace begins to guard the heart. Within the U-Turn journey, this becomes a daily practice of renewal. As truth replaces false agreement, the mind is trained to support a life led by the Spirit rather than shaped by fear or reaction.

2.4 One Spirit with the Lord

"But he who is joined to the Lord is one spirit *with Him*." (1 Corinthians 6:17 NKJV).

Renewing the mind requires remembering our identity in Christ. Scripture reveals that through Him, we are joined to the Lord in spiritual union, while remaining distinct as His redeemed people. This union is not something we strive to achieve; it is a reality established through His finished work. Our identity is not defined by changing thoughts or emotions, but by our relationship with Him.

When Jesus declared, "It is finished," He completed the work of redemption. Forgiveness, righteousness, and access to God were fully secured. Yet the mind can drift into striving, as though we must earn what Christ has already accomplished. Renewal calls us back to what is already true. As Scripture teaches, Christ lives in us, and from that place we learn to think and live.

Renewal is not striving to become someone new but learning to live from who you already are in Christ. From this place, the mind becomes a faithful servant, aligned with truth, grounded in grace, and responsive to God's leading.

2.5 Living from a Transformed Mind

> "Be transformed by the renewing of your mind, that you may prove what *is* that good and acceptable and perfect will of God." (Romans 12:2, NKJV)

Renewal is not a one-time moment but a continuing work of God in the believer's life. While salvation is complete in Christ, the renewing of the mind unfolds over time as we consistently return to truth and bring our thoughts into alignment with Him. Transformation is not sustained by a single decision, but by a continual agreement with God's truth.

Many believers sincerely love God yet still experience inner tension because old patterns of thinking remain. These patterns may be shaped by past wounds, fear, or habits of self-reliance. When left unexamined, they influence how we interpret people, respond under pressure, and make decisions. At times, what appears to be an external struggle is connected to a mind that has not yet been fully renewed. Scripture reminds us that both spiritual opposition and inner renewal must be addressed in dependence on God.

Renewal requires both honesty and patience. God is not merely correcting behavior; He is restoring how we see, think, and respond. As we learn to pause before reacting, measure our thoughts by Scripture, and trust God's truth above our emotions, the mind begins to change. Each time truth replaces a lie, stability increases. Each time we choose trust over fear, transformation deepens. Over time, this produces visible fruit. Clarity grows, peace becomes steadier, and relationships are strengthened. The mind no longer reacts from old patterns but responds from truth. This ongoing renewal reflects God's faithfulness, as He patiently completes the work He has begun.

3. Practice: Walking in the Spirit

3.1 Practicing Agreement with Truth

"But be doers of the word, and not hearers only, deceiving yourselves." (James 1:22 NKJV).

Spiritual transformation is not complete when truth is understood; it is established as truth is practiced. Agreement with God's Word is essential, but obedience allows that truth to shape daily life. Many believers hold sincere convictions yet feel stuck because truth has not consistently moved into action. Growth begins when what we believe becomes how we live. Scripture consistently reveals that obedience to what God has already made clear in His Word often precedes fuller clarity in direction. When Jesus called His disciples, they followed before fully understanding. Their faith grew as they walked with Him. In the same way, God invites us to respond in trust, even when the full picture is not yet visible. Truth becomes active when it is lived, not simply when it is known.

Walking in the Spirit is formed through daily, Spirit-dependent choices rather than occasional moments. It is choosing to pause instead of reacting, to forgive instead of holding offense, and to trust God's Word over shifting emotions. These small, consistent decisions train the heart to live in alignment with truth. As Scripture teaches, the life of the Spirit is cultivated through ongoing obedience and dependence on God.

Obedience does not earn God's favor; it expresses trust in what Christ has already accomplished. As we practice truth, even imperfectly, we grow in discernment, stability, and freedom. God meets us in that obedience, guiding and strengthening us step by step.

3.2 Responding Rather Than Reacting

"Keep your heart with all diligence, For out of it *spring* the issues of life." (Proverbs 4:23 NKJV).

One expression of a renewed mind is the shift from reacting to responding. Reactions are often immediate and shaped by emotion, while responses are guided by truth and formed under the influence of the Spirit. When the inner life is not guarded, pressure, fatigue, or misunderstanding can quickly shape our words and decisions. But as the heart remains anchored in God, we begin to respond with greater clarity, patience, and discernment. A renewed mind learns to pause, allowing truth to shape the response rather than emotion.

Scripture teaches that what flows outward reveals what is taking place within. When the heart is neglected, reactions become quicker and less measured. But when the heart is guarded, the Spirit brings steadiness. Jesus perfectly modeled this, and as we follow Him, we grow in the same pattern. Though often surrounded by urgency and opposition, He did not respond impulsively. He remained in communion with the Father and spoke with clarity, grace, and purpose.

Learning to respond rather than react requires intentional surrender in the moment. It means allowing space to seek God's perspective before speaking or acting. This does not ignore emotion, but places it under the authority of truth. Over time, this practice reshapes the inner life. Peace becomes more consistent, discernment grows stronger, and relationships are strengthened. This is part of living from a transformed mind, where life's pressures no longer control our responses, but instead become opportunities to reflect the character of Christ.

3.3 Walking Daily in the Spirit

"I say then: Walk in the Spirit, and you shall not fulfill the lust of the flesh." (Galatians 5:16 NKJV).

Walking in the Spirit is not a single moment but a daily posture. It is the steady practice of allowing the Holy Spirit to guide our thoughts, decisions, and responses rather than being led by fear, habit, or self-reliance. Walking in the Spirit is formed through consistent, daily choices to align with God's truth. Many believers sincerely desire to follow God, yet still notice moments where old patterns surface, especially under pressure. This does not mean faith is absent, but that renewal is still taking place.

Scripture calls us not only to believe, but to walk in step with the Spirit. Walking reflects rhythm and consistency, learning to pause when emotions rise, to listen before responding, and to seek God's wisdom in everyday decisions. Jesus demonstrated this life with perfect clarity, and as we follow Him, we grow into that same pattern. He was not driven by urgency but by communion with the Father. Even in demanding situations, He remained attentive and responded with truth and compassion. The same Spirit who led Him now dwells in us, guiding us into a life that reflects God's character. This kind of growth requires patience. Patterns formed over time are renewed through steady alignment with truth. As we remain in Scripture, return to prayer, receive correction with humility, and allow space for rest, our awareness of the Spirit deepens. His guidance becomes clearer as our hearts become more attentive.

Walking in the Spirit does not remove difficulty, but it brings alignment, where peace steadies the heart, discernment replaces assumption, and love shapes our responses. Step by step, the renewed mind becomes evident in daily life.

As renewal takes root, it begins to move beyond the inner life. What God restores within us is meant to be expressed through us. A transformed mind leads to a transformed life, and that life naturally begins to influence others through everyday obedience and relationship. What God forms within you; He intends to express through you. Transformation is not meant to remain personal; it is intended to overflow into the lives of others through faithful witness and discipleship. This leads into the next movement of the U-Turn. If renewal establishes stability, the next movement releases impact. Chapter 12 explores how a transformed life becomes a vessel for Kingdom influence, where discipleship deepens and spiritual multiplication begins.

Reflection Questions

1. Where in my life am I relying more on effort than on agreement with God's truth, and what belief may need to be realigned?
2. What thought patterns or reactions tend to surface under pressure, and how can I begin to bring them into alignment with Scripture?
3. In what areas do I believe God's Word, but struggle to consistently practice it in daily responses or decisions?
4. How do I respond when growth feels slow, and how is God inviting me to trust His ongoing work in me?
5. What simple, daily steps can I take to walk more consistently in the Spirit and allow truth to shape how I think and live?

Prayer

Lord,

Thank You that in Christ I am made new, and that You are faithfully renewing my mind day by day. Help me to agree with Your truth above every fear, thought, and old pattern. Teach me to bring my thinking into alignment with Your Word and to walk in step with Your Spirit. Form in me a steady and surrendered mind, so that my life reflects Your truth in every response and decision. I trust You to complete the work You have begun in me.

In Jesus' name, Amen.

Chapter 12 — Reproduce: From Personal Transformation to Kingdom Impact

"What God forms within you, He intends to express through you."

Movement Four: Reproduce — From Personal Transformation to Kingdom Impact

The Fulfillment of the U-Turn Journey: A Life That Multiplies

The U-Turn journey does not end when a life is restored. It continues as that restored life begins to faithfully multiply. What God begins through repentance, deepens through receiving, and establishes through renewal is never meant to remain contained. It is designed to overflow from the heart of a loving Father who restores not only for healing, but for His redemptive purpose. A life that has been brought back to God becomes a life through which His love is carried to others, reflecting Christ and participating in His Kingdom.

In U-Turn, every movement reveals the kindness of God drawing us back to Himself. He does not rush the process. He leads with patience, restores with compassion, and renews with truth. By the time we arrive at this movement, something has been deeply re-formed within us. Our striving begins to quiet. Our trust begins to grow. From that place, what He has done within us begins to flow outward, not by pressure, but through the steady overflow of His life.

Jesus reveals this pattern with clarity and tenderness:

> "I am the vine; you *are* the branches. He who abides in Me, and I in him, bears much fruit; for without Me you can do nothing." (John 15:5 NKJV).

Fruit is not produced by striving, but it does grow through abiding that is expressed in faithful obedience. As we remain in Christ, His life becomes the source of everything that flows from us. His love shapes our words. His truth directs our decisions. His grace fills our relationships. What we have received from Him begins to be expressed through us in quiet and faithful ways. What once was broken becomes a place where His goodness is revealed.

This is the beauty of God's design. He restores us so that His life may be revealed through us. A healed heart becomes a place of compassion. A renewed mind becomes a place of wisdom. A surrendered life becomes a vessel of peace. What God does in us becomes a testimony of who He is. Jesus also reminds us of the purpose behind this fruit:

"By this My Father is glorified, that you bear much fruit; so you will be My disciples." (John 15:8 NKJV).

A life that multiplies brings glory to God, not through striving or visibility, but through faithful abiding. Much of this fruit may grow quietly, often unseen by others, yet it is never unnoticed by Him. Every act of obedience, every moment of trust, every expression of love carries eternal significance. God, in His faithfulness, uses even the smallest surrender to accomplish far more than we can see.

The fulfillment of the U-Turn is not found in what we accomplish, but in what God faithfully reproduces through a life that remains yielded to Him. As we continue to abide, trust, and walk with Him, our lives become part of something greater than ourselves. His Kingdom advances not through force, but through lives that carry His presence. This is the quiet and powerful continuation of the journey.

In this movement, what has been formed within begins to multiply outwardly in four ways:

- **Abiding** — Remaining rooted in Christ as the source of all fruitfulness
- **Modeling** — Living out truth with consistency and authenticity
- **Discipleship** — Walking with others toward growth and transformation
- **Legacy** — Bearing fruit that endures beyond our lifetime

Reproduction is not an endpoint but a release. A life surrendered, aligned, and renewed becomes a life that multiplies. What began as a personal turning now carries Kingdom impact, as ordinary obedience produces lasting fruit for His glory.

When Transformation Does Not Multiply

Within the journey of the U-Turn, God leads us with patience and kindness, step by step, back to Himself. He restores what was broken, speaks truth where there was confusion, and renews the mind through His Word. Yet in His design, transformation is not meant to remain within us. It is meant to be expressed. There are seasons when a believer is genuinely growing, being healed, and learning to walk in truth, yet that transformation has not yet extended outward. This is not condemnation, but it is an invitation. The same God who restores us in love also calls us forward in obedience.

Scripture reminds us with clarity and grace:

"But be doers of the word, and not hearers only, deceiving yourselves." (James 1:22 NKJV).

God's Word is not only given to guide us, but to be lived through us. When truth is received but not expressed, it remains like a seed that has been planted but has not yet borne fruit. When we begin to respond in simple obedience, even in small and unseen ways, that seed begins to grow. Love is no longer only understood but practiced. Grace is no longer only received but extended. What God has done within us begins to take visible form. Fruitfulness flows from abiding. It is not something we manufacture, but something that grows as we remain in Christ and walk in obedience to Him. When transformation has not yet multiplied, the invitation is not to strive harder, but to remain more deeply and respond more faithfully. As we abide in Him, His life within us naturally extends beyond us in ways that are steady, gentle, and faithful.

Spiritual maturity is seen not only in what God has restored within us, but in how His life begins to flow through us to others. This is where transformation finds its fuller expression. What once brought healing to our own hearts becomes a source of life for someone else. What God has formed in us becomes something He can entrust through us. This is the heart of Movement Four. In the U-Turn, God does not simply bring us back. He brings us forward. What He restores, He releases. What He renews, He multiplies. What began as a personal turning becomes a life that quietly carries His presence, His love, and His Kingdom into the lives of others, for His glory and for their good.

Movement Four: Reproduce — From Personal Transformation to Kingdom Impact

Movement Four carries transformation beyond the individual into the world God loves. What began with repentance and surrender continues through receiving God's truth and renewed patterns of living. As inward transformation is established, reproduction begins to flow as the faithful outworking of a life realigned, restored, and guided by Christ. This movement is not driven by pressure but expressed through abiding and obedience as we participate with God in His purposes.

Four Areas of Reproduction

- Abiding: Remaining in the Vine
- Modeling: Living What We Believe
- Discipleship: Walking Others Toward Christ
- Legacy: Leaving Kingdom Fruit That Endures

1. Abiding: Remaining in the Vine

In the journey of the U-Turn, God lovingly leads us back to Himself, restoring what was lost, renewing what was broken, and realigning our lives with His truth. Yet His work does not end with restoration. In His kindness, He invites us into a deeper life of communion with Him. This is where reproduction begins, not with activity, but with abiding. Reproduction in God's Kingdom does not begin with doing more, but with remaining in Christ. Before life can multiply outward, it must first be sustained inward.

A branch cannot produce fruit by effort or intention alone. It must remain connected to its source. In the same way, our lives bear fruit not because we strive, but because we stay close to Christ and walk in responsive obedience to Him. Abiding is not a spiritual method to master, but a relational posture to live from. It is the daily choice to remain in union with Jesus, drawing from Him as our source of life, direction, and strength. In this place, we experience not only His truth, but His presence and His faithful love.

Fruitfulness in the Kingdom flows from connection to Christ, expressed through a life that remains in Him and responds to Him in obedience. When the branch remains in the vine, life flows, and fruit appears in its proper season. There is no striving for identity or worth, but there is a continual yielding to His life and leading. As we stay rooted in Christ, His life flows through us, shaping our thoughts, guiding our steps, and expressing itself through love, faithfulness, and obedience.

Reproduction apart from abiding may appear fruitful for a time, but it cannot be sustained. Activity may increase while spiritual depth quietly weakens. The heart grows weary, and what is produced may lack the character of Christ. Abiding protects us from this drift. It anchors us in Him, ensuring that what flows from our lives comes from His life within us.

Scripture reminds us with both clarity and comfort:

"For it is God who works in you both to will and to do for *His* good pleasure." (Philippians 2:13 NKJV).

This is the beauty of abiding. We are not the source; He is. Even the desire to follow Him and the strength to obey Him are the result of His work within us. As we remain in Him, we begin to recognize that fruitfulness is not something we achieve, but something we receive and faithfully walk out. Abiding is the foundation of Kingdom multiplication. From this place of closeness, transformation moves outward with grace, producing fruit that endures for His glory and for the good of others.

1.1 From Striving to Shared Life

Many believers, with sincere hearts, pursue fruitfulness through effort. They serve more, give more, and try harder, hoping that increased activity will produce greater impact. Yet Jesus did not call us into striving, but into relationship. Abiding shifts our focus from producing results to living from His presence. It moves us from striving to shared life with Christ.

Union with Christ is not something we earn through discipline or prove through performance. It is established by grace through faith and lived out through ongoing relationship with Him. As we remain in Him, our lives begin to reflect Him, not because we are trying to imitate Him, but because we are living from Him.

Scripture affirms this invitation:

> "As you therefore have received Christ Jesus the Lord, so walk in Him, rooted and built up in Him and established in the faith, as you have been taught, abounding in it with thanksgiving." (Colossians 2:6–7 NKJV).

The same way we received Christ, through grace and faith, is the way we continue to walk with Him. Our growth is sustained not by pressure, but by relationship. Rooted in Him and built up in Him, fruit becomes the natural expression of a life deeply connected to its source.

1.2 Dependence as the Mark of Spiritual Maturity

Abiding is not passive. It is a living dependence on God that expresses itself through trust and obedience. True spiritual maturity does not lead to independence from Him, but to a deeper reliance on Christ and the work of the Holy Spirit within us. As the U-Turn journey unfolds, we begin to recognize that transformation is not sustained by our strength, but by His presence.

Abiding means drawing wisdom, direction, and strength from Christ rather than from ourselves. It is the daily posture of listening before acting, yielding before deciding, and trusting rather than controlling. In this place, there is a quiet steadiness that comes from knowing we are not carrying what only God was meant to carry.

Spiritual maturity is not marked by independence, but by a deep and steady dependence on Christ. This dependence protects the heart from striving and pressure. It allows God to set the pace of our lives and the rhythm of our fruitfulness.

When we remain rooted in Him, obedience becomes a natural response of love, and reproduction flows from alignment rather than effort.

"The steps of a good man are ordered by the Lord, and He delights in his way." (Psalm 37:2, NKJV).

God does not direct from a distance. He leads personally and faithfully. As we depend on Him, we discover that He is both our guide and our sustainer.

1.3 Fruit That Outlives the Season

Not all fruit is measured in the same way. Some outcomes are visible and immediate, shaped by timing, opportunity, or recognition. Yet the fruit that flows from abiding carries a deeper and lasting quality. It is not dependent on visibility or circumstance but rooted in the life of Christ Himself.

As we walk through the U-Turn, God gently shifts our focus from immediate results to enduring fruit. What He forms within us through surrender, renewal, and alignment is not temporary. It is designed to remain. This kind of fruit often grows quietly, beneath the surface, in places unseen by others but fully known by Him. Abiding guards the heart from burnout and from the subtle temptation to measure impact by speed or visibility. Instead, it invites us into a life of faithful obedience, consistent love, and surrendered trust. We learn to release outcomes to God and rest in His faithfulness.

Fruit that remains is not produced by striving, but by a life that stays rooted in Christ and walks faithfully with Him. Kingdom impact endures when it flows from abiding, not from personality, position, or platform. What is formed in Him carries eternal weight because its source is eternal. Abiding is where every outward movement begins. Before lives are influenced, disciples are formed, or legacy takes shape, the branch must remain connected to the Vine. From this place of union, transformation moves outward in a way that is both gentle and powerful, bearing fruit that remains for God's glory and for the good of many.

2. Modeling: Living What We Believe

Within the U-Turn journey, what God restores inwardly is never meant to remain hidden. As repentance softens the heart, receiving aligns us with truth, and renewal reshapes the mind, a new way of living begins to emerge. Modeling is where this inward transformation becomes visible. It is the gentle yet powerful expression of a life that has been formed by Christ. In the Kingdom of God, truth is not merely taught; it is lived. It is not only spoken; it is carried. Modeling becomes the bridge between personal transformation and Kingdom multiplication. Before beliefs are transferred through words, they are revealed through the quiet consistency of a surrendered life. Reproduction flows not through instruction alone, but through lives that remain yielded to Christ, where truth is both taught and lived.

Jesus formed His disciples not only through teaching, but through shared life. They walked with Him, watched Him, and experienced how He responded in every circumstance. They saw how He prayed, how He trusted the Father, how He moved in compassion, and how He remained steady under pressure. His authority, rooted in who He is as the Son of God, was expressed through the perfect alignment between His words and His life. In the same way, Kingdom reproduction flows from alignment between belief and behavior.

What we live consistently will shape others more deeply than what we say occasionally. Modeling ensures that what is multiplied reflects Christ rather than culture. It answers the quiet question in every heart: What does this look like when it is truly lived out?

2.1 A Life Observed Before It Is Explained

Spiritual formation often begins long before words are spoken. It begins through observation. People learn how to follow God by watching how others walk with Him in real life. They notice how we respond in difficulty, how we humble ourselves in repentance, and how we trust God when the outcome is uncertain. These moments, often unseen and unplanned, quietly reveal the reality of our faith.

Within the U-Turn process, as God gently leads us back to alignment with Him, our lives begin to tell a story. What He heals, restores, and renews becomes visible not through perfection, but through a growing consistency of trust and obedience. Others begin to see not just what we believe, but how we live because of what we believe.

Paul expresses this pattern with clarity and invitation:

> "The things which you learned and received and heard and saw in me, these do, and the God of peace will be with you." (Philippians 4:9 NKJV).

Paul did not separate his teaching from his living. He invited others to observe, receive, and follow the same pattern of life shaped by Christ. This is the heart of modeling. It gives quiet permission. It shows that surrender is possible, that obedience is livable, and that God is faithful in the realities of everyday life. Modeling does not require visibility or a platform. It simply requires faithfulness. As we walk closely with God, our lives become a living invitation for others to do the same.

2.2 Congruence Over Perfection

The Kingdom of God does not advance through flawless people, but through surrendered and aligned lives. Modeling is not about presenting an image of spiritual success. It is about living with integrity, where what we believe and how we live begin to come into harmony under Christ. Congruence creates credibility, and credibility builds trust, allowing others to more clearly see the work of God in a life. When there is alignment between belief and behavior, people encounter something real. They sense the authenticity of a life that is being formed by God. This kind of life does not draw attention to itself but quietly points to Him.

God is not calling us to flawless perfection, but to a life that is surrendered and continually being formed and aligned with Him. Perfection often creates distance, but congruence creates safety. When people see lives that are honest about weakness yet anchored in God's grace, they find courage to step into their own journey of transformation. This reflects the true heart of the Gospel. Faith is not about hiding struggle, but about bringing it into the light and allowing God to transform it.

Jesus, fully God and fully man, modeled this perfectly. He did not deny hardship or rush through suffering. He lived in full dependence on the Father, expressing obedience, compassion, sorrow, and joy with complete integrity. His life revealed that true maturity is not self-sufficiency, but faithful alignment with the will of God.

Congruence also guards the heart from hypocrisy, which Scripture consistently warns against. When belief and behavior become disconnected, reproduction is weakened. What is passed on may sound right, but it will lack the life and power of Christ. But when a life is aligned, what is multiplied carries both truth and love, conviction and grace. As the U-Turn journey continues, modeling protects the work God has done within us. It keeps transformation from becoming theoretical and allows it to remain relational, lived, and Spirit-led.

2.3 Renewal Passed On

Within the U-Turn journey, renewal is never meant to remain hidden within the heart. What God restores and reshapes inwardly begins, over time, to gently flow outward into every relationship, every conversation, and every environment we step into. Renewal is not something we contain; it is something we carry. What shapes our inner world will inevitably shape the world around us. As a heart comes under the loving governance of Christ, His character begins to form within us. His peace steadies us, His truth anchors us, and His ways begin to guide our responses. This inner transformation does not remain private. It becomes visible through the way we live, love, and respond to others.

If fear governs the heart, fear will be reproduced. If striving leads, striving will be passed on. But when Christ governs the heart, something different begins to flow. Faith replaces fear, rest replaces pressure, and obedience flows from love rather than obligation. The atmosphere around us begins to change, not because we are trying to influence others, but because His life is being expressed through us.

What is formed within us will, over time, be revealed through us as we continue to yield to God's transforming work, and what flows through us will shape the lives around us. This is why reproduction must follow renewal. Without ongoing inner transformation, influence may unintentionally reflect areas still being healed rather than the fullness of Christ's work. God, in His mercy, does not rush us into influence before He forms Christ within us.

Jesus teaches this with clarity and simplicity:

"A good man out of the good treasure of his heart brings forth good." (Luke 6:45 NKJV).

Fruit is not produced by intention alone, but by the condition of the heart. Renewal changes the root system, and healthy roots produce healthy fruit. This fruit often grows quietly and gradually, but it carries a depth and endurance that only God can produce. Modeling ensures that reproduction remains spiritual, not merely relational or organizational. It passes on not just information, but formation. It shapes how others come to know God, how they trust Him, and how they walk with Him through both joy and suffering.

Within the U-Turn, modeling protects the movement from becoming mechanical or performance-driven. It keeps transformation rooted in relationship, expressed through real life, and sustained by the Holy Spirit. As renewed lives are lived with sincerity and faithfulness, others are not only taught truth, but they are also invited into it. They begin to see that following Christ is not a concept to understand, but a life to live.

3. Discipleship: Walking Others Toward Christ

As renewal overflows and modeling become visible, reproduction moves into something deeply personal. Discipleship is where transformation is no longer observed from a distance but shared in relationship. It is the sacred space where God uses one life to walk alongside another, as Christ is being formed in each life through the work of the Holy Spirit. In the U-Turn journey, God does not only restore us for our own sake. He restores us so that we may walk with others, not as distant experts, but as humble and responsible followers of Christ who walk alongside others. Discipleship is not about producing followers or managing outcomes. It is about faithfully walking with others as God continues His work in them.

Discipleship reflects the heart of God. He does not lead from a distance but draws near. He walks with us patiently, faithfully, and personally. In the same way, He invites us to walk with others. In the Kingdom of God, discipleship is rarely efficient and never rushed. It unfolds through shared moments of life. It grows through conversations, honest questions, prayerful dependence, gentle correction, and timely encouragement. It is built in presence, not pressure. Jesus modeled this beautifully. He did not form His disciples through pressure or performance, but through relationship grounded in truth and authority. He stayed with them in their misunderstandings, their failures, and their doubts. He did not withdraw when they struggled; He remained. His presence became the place where transformation could take root.

Discipleship is not built on pressure, but on presence shaped by truth, love, and obedience. This kind of walking with others is not always easy. It requires patience, humility, and love. It requires us to stay when it would be easier to step back. Yet it is one of the primary ways God multiplies His life through us. What He has formed in us begins to take shape in others, not through control, but through relationship.

3.1 Discipleship Is Relational, Not Transactional

In God's Kingdom, transformation multiplies through relationship shaped by truth, not through control or manipulation. Discipleship is not the transfer of information from one person to another. It is the shared journey of obedience between two people who are both being led by a faithful God. Many have experienced forms of discipleship that felt transactional, where expectations were high but space for growth was limited, and where performance was emphasized more than formation. But this is not the way of Jesus. He invites before He instructs. He walks before He sends.

Within the U-Turn, this is consistent with how God leads us. He does not rush transformation. He does not demand instant maturity. He patiently forms us, step by step, with kindness and truth. Discipleship requires this same posture. It calls for patience because growth is not uniform. Some areas of life align quickly, while others require time, healing, and repeated surrender. Walking with someone in this process means resisting the urge to fix, to rush, or to control outcomes, while still faithfully pointing them to truth. It means trusting that the Holy Spirit is faithfully working in ways we cannot see.

Paul describes this kind of discipleship with deep affection and clarity:

"We were well pleased to impart to you not only the gospel of God, but also our own lives." (1 Thessalonians 2:8 NKJV).

This is the heart of Kingdom discipleship. It is not limited to teaching truth but extended through sharing life. It requires time, emotional investment, and humility. Yet what it produces is not surface-level change, but deep and lasting transformation. This kind of discipleship builds trust. And where trust is present, hearts open. And where hearts are open, God moves. Transformation takes root not through pressure, but through truth expressed in love and faithful presence.

3.2 Pointing to Christ, Not to Ourselves

Within the U-Turn journey, as God gently leads us from repentance to renewal, He continually re-centers our hearts on one truth: everything begins and ends with Him. Discipleship, in its purest form, is not about drawing people toward us, but about lovingly and consistently pointing them to Christ. True discipleship always redirects attention toward Jesus. The moment people begin to depend on us rather than on God, something begins to weaken. God, in His wisdom and love, never intended for us to be the source. We are vessels, not the Vine. Healthy discipleship helps others recognize God's voice, respond to His leading, and trust His faithfulness, even when the path feels unclear.

The goal of discipleship is not to draw people to ourselves, but to lead them into a deep and personal dependence on Christ. This requires humility. It invites us to live honestly before others, acknowledging that we do not have every answer, and that we, too, are being led day by day. It means modeling repentance, dependence, and a listening heart. Often, the most powerful moments in discipleship are not when we speak with certainty, but when we say with sincerity, "Let us seek the Lord together."

Jesus Himself modeled this beautifully. Though He is the Son of God, He lived in continual dependence on the Father. He revealed the Father and called people to Himself as the way to the Father. He prayed openly, withdrew to be with God, and moved in perfect alignment with His will. He prepared His disciples not to rely on His physical presence, but on the Holy Spirit who would guide them.

"However, when He, the Spirit of truth, has come, He will guide you into all truth." (John 16:13 NKJV).

Healthy discipleship is ultimately measured not by how closely people depend on us, but by how faithfully they grow in walking with Christ. When Christ remains at the center, discipleship becomes freeing, not binding. It becomes life-giving, not dependent. It produces maturity that is rooted in Him, sustained by Him, and led by His Spirit.

3.3 Faithfulness Over Visibility

In the Kingdom of God, much of what is most valuable is often unseen. Within the U-Turn, as God reshapes our hearts and aligns our lives, He also gently transforms how we measure fruit according to His Word. What once felt important begins to fade, and what is eternal begins to take root. Some of the most meaningful moments of discipleship will never be recognized or celebrated. They unfold in quiet conversations, in prayers whispered in faith, and in unseen decisions to obey God when it would be easier not to. These are often the places where deep and lasting transformation is formed.

The Kingdom does not ultimately measure success by visibility, speed, or scale, but by faithfulness. Much of what God grows takes time. Roots are formed long before fruit becomes visible, and what is built in hidden places often carries the greatest strength. There are seasons when discipleship feels slow, even invisible. Progress may seem small, and change may feel subtle. In these moments, it is easy to wonder if anything is truly happening. Yet God is always at work, even when we cannot see it.

"Let us not grow weary while doing good, for in due season we shall reap if we do not lose heart." (Galatians 6:9 NKJV).

Faithfulness in hidden places is never wasted in God's hands; it is where He forms the kind of fruit that lasts.

Discipleship calls us to remain present, to continue loving, praying, and walking with others even when outcomes are unclear. What God forms slowly is often what endures most deeply. A life built in quiet obedience will one day stand firm, not because of outward recognition, but because it has been rooted in Him.

4. Legacy: Leaving Kingdom Fruit That Remains

As the U-Turn journey brings us into reproduction, God begins to lift our vision beyond the present moment. Legacy is not something we strive to build in our own strength; it is something God forms as we walk faithfully and intentionally with Him over time. It is the quiet unfolding of a life surrendered to God, bearing fruit that reaches far beyond what we can see. Legacy is reproduction viewed through the lens of eternity. It is the assurance that every act of obedience, every surrendered moment, and every step of faith is being woven into God's greater story. In His love, He allows our lives to become part of something far bigger than ourselves.

Kingdom legacy is not built through recognition or influence as the world defines it. It is built through faithfulness. It is measured not by what is seen in the moment, but by what remains over time. It continues long after roles change, seasons end, and voices grow quiet. Jesus did not pursue human approval or self-exalting visibility. He invested deeply in a few, walked closely with them, and entrusted the future to the Father. What He formed in them did not end with His earthly ministry. It multiplied. His life, poured out in love and obedience, continues to bear fruit across generations.

Legacy is not about how much we are seen, but about how deeply Christ is formed in others through our obedience.

4.1 Legacy Through an Eternal Lens

When we begin to see life through God's perspective, our priorities shift. The questions we ask begin to change. We no longer ask how much was accomplished or how many noticed. Instead, we begin to ask what God is forming and who is being drawn closer to Him. Legacy asks deeper questions. Who is growing in faith because I obeyed? Who is learning to trust God because I remained faithful? These are the questions that carry eternal weight.

Scripture reminds us that our lives are part of something far greater than we can fully see:

"For we are God's fellow workers; you are God's field, *you* are God's building." (1 Corinthians 3:9, NKJV)

This truth frees us from the pressure to control or define results, while remaining faithful in stewardship. It invites us to trust that God is working beyond what we can see or understand. When we live with an eternal lens, obedience becomes our focus, and trust becomes our strength.

4.2 Quiet Faithfulness Multiplied

Much of what God does is quiet, gentle, and often unseen. Yet it is never insignificant. The seeds planted in faith, even in the smallest moments, carry the potential for lasting impact. There are times when obedience feels ordinary, even costly. Conversations that seem small, prayers offered in private, and acts of faith that go unnoticed. Yet in God's Kingdom, nothing surrendered to Him is ever wasted. Over time, He brings fruit from these hidden places. What was planted in faith begins to grow, often in ways we could never have planned or predicted.

This is the kindness of God. He multiplies what we entrust to Him.

What is done in faith and love before God will always bear fruit in His way and in His time. Quiet faithfulness builds deep roots, and deep roots sustain lasting fruit. What grows slowly in God's hands often endures the longest.

4.3 Trusting God with the Increase

At the heart of legacy is surrender. We are called to obedience, but the outcome belongs to God. This truth brings both humility and rest. Paul expresses this with clarity:

"I planted, Apollos watered, but God gave the increase." (1 Corinthians 3:6 NKJV).

We are invited to plant faithfully and to water diligently, but the increase is always God's. When we release control, something shifts within us. Pressure lifts, striving fades, and joy returns to obedience.

We are responsible for obedience, but God alone is responsible for the increase. This trust guards our hearts from comparison and from the need to prove results. It allows us to serve with purity, to love freely, and to remain focused on Christ rather than outcomes. Legacy is not something we manufacture. It is something God grows through lives that remain surrendered to Him. When we live with open hands and deep trust, what He forms through us will endure beyond us, carrying His life into generations to come.

Carrying Transformation Forward

Chapter 12 brings the U-Turn journey into its outward expression as Spirit-empowered overflow, where the work God has faithfully done within begins to flow beyond us and touch the world He so deeply loves. What began with repentance and faith, as we surrendered to His Lordship, was tenderly shaped through receiving His truth and steadily formed through the renewing work of His Word and Spirit. Now, in His grace, that transformation is released through lives yielded to His purposes, becoming a channel through which His love, truth, and life reach others.

Transformation was never meant to end with us; it is God's invitation for His life to flow through us and bring life to others. As we remain aligned with Christ, our lives quietly become vessels through which His presence is made known, carrying hope into homes, strength into relationships, and light into places that long for Him. What He restores within us is not only for our healing, but for His glory and the good of many. Yet in His wisdom, God does not call us to simply move forward with momentum. He invites us to walk with Him in a way that is steady, rooted, and sustained. Lasting fruit is not produced through striving in our own strength, but through abiding in Christ as our true source. As transformation expands, it must be carefully stewarded, guarded by a heart that remains dependent on Him, and shaped by the gentle leading of the Holy Spirit. In this place, fruit is not only produced but sustained by God.

This is why the journey continues. Chapter 13, When the U-Turn Becomes a Way of Life, gathers the foundational truths from each movement and anchors them into daily living. These are not formulas to follow, but wisdom to live by, helping us remain close to God and faithful to what He has begun. They protect the heart from drifting and keep our lives aligned with His Spirit as His work continues to grow.

The U-Turn does not end with transformation; it becomes a way of life marked by surrender, dependence, and faithful obedience to God. Even spiritual multiplication is not the final destination, but part of a greater unfolding. As we continue to walk with Him, what He has begun is carried forward through faithful stewardship, bearing fruit that remains for His glory and extending into generations we may never fully see, yet can trust Him completely to reach.

Reflection Questions

1. Where is God inviting me to allow what He has done within me to gently overflow into the lives of others?
2. In what areas of my life am I striving to produce fruit, rather than abiding in Christ as my true source?
3. What does the pattern of my daily life reveal about my trust in, surrender to, and dependence on God?
4. Who has God intentionally placed in my life that I am called to walk with, encourage, and lead toward Him?
5. Where do I need to release control and entrust the fruit, the timing, and the outcome fully to God?

Prayer

Father,

Thank You for the work You have done in me through repentance, guidance, and renewal. I surrender the fruit of my life to You. Teach me to abide deeply, to live what I believe, and to walk others toward You with humility and love. Guard my heart from striving and keep me faithful in obedience. I release control of outcomes and trust You with the increase. Let my life bear fruit that remains for Your glory and the good of others.

In Jesus' name, Amen.

Chapter 13 — When the U-Turn Becomes a Way of Life

> ***"The U-Turn does not end with transformation; it becomes a way of life marked by surrender, dependence, and faithful obedience to God."***

Chapters 9 through 12 traced the sacred movements of transformation: repent, receive His truth, renew, reproduce. Each movement reflects the tender way God, in His love, draws us back to Himself, restoring alignment and returning the heart to the authority of Christ. What begins as awakening becomes surrender. What is surrendered is gently renewed. And what is renewed begins, by His grace, to overflow into fruitful influence that carries His life to others.

Yet the U-Turn was never meant to remain a single moment of clarity or a brief season of spiritual intensity. In God's kindness, it is designed to become a way of living, a steady, daily returning to Him. A single act of repentance can redirect a life, but lasting freedom in Christ is formed when that return becomes continual. When surrender is no longer occasional but wholehearted. When listening is not reactive but relational. When renewal quietly reshapes our thinking again and again. When obedience flows not from pressure, but from love.

When the U-Turn becomes a way of life, alignment is no longer easily unsettled but formed in the safety of His presence and sustained by His grace. Authority is no longer debated; it is settled in the heart that trusts Him. The believer no longer lives characterized by drifting between clarity and confusion, but begins to walk with increasing steadiness, discernment, and peace under one faithful and loving Lord.

One Governing Authority

When the U-Turn becomes a way of life, it is because one foundational truth has been lovingly established within: God is welcomed to govern the inner life. Transformation is not merely a change in behavior; it is the restoration of rightful authority, the gentle yielding of the heart back to the One who formed it and knows it fully.

Before repentance, the heart often allows other influences to take the lead. Fear may speak loudly. Control may feel necessary. Disappointment, ambition, the desire for approval, or self-reliance can quietly assume places they were never meant to hold. A life may appear disciplined or even spiritually active outwardly, yet inwardly the leadership may remain divided. But in His mercy, God does not leave us there. He invites us into wholeness. Sustained transformation requires more than sincerity; it requires one clear and consistent authority.

"No one can serve two masters." (Matthew 6:24 NKJV).

Jesus speaks with clarity, not to condemn, but to bring freedom. The heart cannot flourish under competing voices. When authority within is divided, clarity begins to fade, and decisions become heavy with internal conflict. Emotions rise, not because they are wrong, but because they begin carrying weight they were never designed to bear. Division often appears quietly, through internal negotiation, delayed obedience, or reasoning that leans toward comfort rather than trust. Yet through every movement of the U-Turn, God faithfully restores what has been misplaced.

Every movement of the U-Turn restores this governance:

- **Repent** surrenders the heart to His Lordship and exposes misplaced trust.
- **Receive** reopens the heart to His truth and His voice, relinquishing self-direction.

- **Renew** reshapes thought patterns and emotional responses through His Word.
- **Reproduce** expresses outwardly what has been reordered inwardly, reinforcing alignment through obedience.

When authority is unsettled, these movements weaken. But when authority is surrendered to Him, they deepen, strengthen, and begin to flow together with quiet strength. Where His rule is welcomed, peace begins to steady the heart, and life comes back into alignment with His love.

Transformation endures not because life becomes without challenge, but because the heart has found its resting place under His authority. As the U-Turn matures into a way of life, something beautiful begins to settle within. Leadership is no longer constantly contested. Emotions are no longer ignored, but they are gently interpreted through truth. Desires are no longer followed blindly but are brought into the light of His wisdom. Decisions begin to flow from trust rather than pressure. In that place, His peace guards, His Spirit leads, and His love sustains every step.

The Threefold Alignment: Spirit, Soul, and Body Under God's Authority

In this final stage of the journey, the U-Turn is no longer a moment; it becomes a way of life. What began as repentance, receiving, and renewal now matures into a steady, daily alignment with God. This is how He faithfully leads us step by step back to the life we were created for, not through striving, but through surrender, truth, and obedient love. God's intention has always been wholeness. He does not transform only one part of us but lovingly restores the entire person. As we continue to walk with Him, His Spirit is faithfully bringing our spirit, soul, and body into increasing harmony under His authority. What was once divided is being unified. What was once led by fear or self-reliance becomes anchored in His truth and presence.

> "Now may the God of peace Himself sanctify you completely; and may your whole spirit, soul, and body be preserved blameless at the coming of our Lord Jesus Christ." (1 Thessalonians 5:23 NKJV).

When the U-Turn becomes a way of life, alignment is no longer occasional but becomes a growing, steady posture of a heart yielded to God. This alignment is not achieved through human effort, but through God's grace at work as we respond in faith. It is the fruit of abiding in Christ, listening to His voice through His Word and Spirit, and responding in trust. As His love leads us, transformation becomes sustained, gentle, and deeply rooted.

1. The Aligned Spirit: Surrendered to His Lordship

The spirit is where our response to God's authority is settled. It is here that we respond to God's invitation to trust Him fully and yield to His Lordship. In the U-Turn journey, repentance is not merely turning from sin but turning toward God's rightful place as Lord over every part of life.

"The humble He guides in justice, And the humble He teaches His way." (Psalm 25:9 NKJV).

An aligned spirit rests in this truth and responds in trust. It does not strive to control outcomes but yields to God's wisdom and timing. Even when understanding is incomplete, the heart chooses obedience because it trusts who God is. This posture keeps the spirit soft, teachable, and responsive. A surrendered spirit establishes the foundation where God's authority is no longer resisted but welcomed.

2. The Aligned Soul: Renewed and Governed by Truth

As the spirit settles under God's authority, the soul must continually be renewed. The mind, will, and emotions often carry patterns shaped by past experiences and assumptions. In the U-Turn, renewal is the ongoing work of bringing those patterns into alignment with God's Word.

> "And do not be conformed to this world, but be transformed by the renewing of your mind, that you may prove what *is* that good and acceptable and perfect will of God." (Romans 12:2 NKJV).

An aligned soul learns to interpret life through truth rather than through fear or feeling. Thoughts are examined, emotions are acknowledged, and the will is gently redirected toward obedience. Over time, the inner life becomes more stable because it is no longer governed by shifting circumstances but by unchanging truth.

3. The Aligned Body: Expressed Through Obedient Living

The body becomes the visible expression of what God has established within. In the U-Turn, obedience is not a burden but a response of love. What God reveals in the spirit and renews in the soul is carried out through faithful action.

> "I beseech you therefore, brethren, by the mercies of God, that you present your bodies a living sacrifice, holy, acceptable to God, *which is* your reasonable service." (Romans 12:1 NKJV).

Obedience in the body expresses and strengthens the transformation God is working within, allowing what He has restored to be lived out faithfully each day. An aligned body walks in consistency. It chooses faithfulness over convenience and truth over impulse. Daily habits, decisions, and responses become acts of worship, reflecting a life that is yielded to God.

The One True Voice and the Inner Life That Responds Under God's Word

As the U-Turn becomes a way of life, discernment is no longer something occasional; it becomes a daily grace. God, in His kindness, does not leave us to navigate the inner life on our own. He speaks through His Word and leads by His Spirit, teaching us how to recognize His truth and walk in it with growing clarity and confidence. His leadership is not harsh or distant, but faithful, patient, and full of steadfast love.

Within our inner life, there are many thoughts, desires, and responses that influence how we think, feel, and act. Yet Scripture makes clear that God alone speaks with final authority, and He has revealed His truth in His Word. The Holy Spirit does not speak independently of Scripture but faithfully illumines and applies it to the heart. Every inner impression, thought, or inclination must therefore be tested and brought into alignment with His Word.

"My sheep hear My voice, and I know them, and they follow Me." (John 10:27 NKJV).

Only God's voice carries true authority, and it will always agree with His Word. As we remain rooted in Scripture and attentive to the Spirit, we grow in discernment and walk in faithful obedience.

1. The Voice of the Holy Spirit: The Authoritative Voice of Truth

The Holy Spirit leads God's people into truth. He does not introduce new revelation that contradicts Scripture, but illuminates what God has already revealed, bringing clarity, conviction, and understanding. His work is to glorify Christ, not to draw attention to Himself, and to guide believers in alignment with God's Word.

"However, when He, the Spirit of truth, has come, He will guide you into all truth." (John 16:13 NKJV).

His leading may come through Scripture brought to mind, through conviction of sin, or through a clear prompting that aligns with God's Word. His voice produces humility, clarity, and a willingness to obey. He convicts but does not condemn. He corrects but does not reject. In every way, His leading draws us closer to Christ and deeper into truth.

2. The Witness of the Spirit: The Assurance That Confirms

The Spirit of God also bears witness within the believer, confirming what is true according to God's Word. This is not a separate source of truth, but an inner assurance that aligns with what God has already revealed.

"The Spirit Himself bears witness with our spirit that we are children of God." (Romans 8:16 NKJV).

This witness brings a settled confidence in our relationship with God. It strengthens assurance, anchors identity, and steadies the heart. It does not override Scripture or replace discernment but confirms truth in a way that produces peace and strengthens faith.

3. The Mind: Renewed and Brought into Obedience to Christ

The mind is constantly forming thoughts, interpretations, and conclusions. Because it can be shaped by past experiences, fears, and worldly patterns, it must be continually renewed through God's Word.

"And do not be conformed to this world, but be transformed by the renewing of your mind." (Romans 12:2 NKJV).

Scripture also calls us to actively examine and submit our thoughts to Christ.

"Bringing every thought into captivity to the obedience of Christ." (2 Corinthians 10:5 NKJV).

As we walk with God, we learn not to trust every thought automatically, but to test and align our thinking with Scripture. Over time, the mind becomes clearer, more discerning, and increasingly shaped by truth rather than by fear or assumption.

4. The Will: Strengthened Through God's Work and Our Obedience

The will is where decisions are made. It is the place where we choose whether to obey God or follow our own desires. Scripture teaches that both our desire and our ability to obey are shaped by God's work within us.

"For it is God who works in you both to will and to do for *His* good pleasure." (Philippians 2:13 NKJV).

At the same time, we are called to respond actively in obedience.

"Work out your own salvation with fear and trembling." (Philippians 2:12 NKJV).

As we continue in the U-Turn, the will is gradually aligned with God's purposes. What once resisted begins to yield. What once clung to control begins to trust. Obedience becomes not merely an obligation, but a response shaped by love and reverence for God.

5. Emotions: Realigned and Anchored in Truth

Emotions are part of how God created us. They reflect what is happening within and can reveal important aspects of the heart. However, Scripture consistently teaches that they must be brought under the guidance of truth and not allowed to govern our lives.

"You will keep *him* in perfect peace, *Whose* mind *is* stayed on *You*, Because he trusts in You." (Isaiah 26:3 NKJV).

The Psalms demonstrate that emotions are to be brought honestly before God, not suppressed, but also not followed without discernment. As we walk with Him, we learn to bring our feelings into His presence and allow His truth to shape our response.

When emotions are brought under God's truth, they no longer lead the heart but are steadied by His peace and directed by His Word. Fear is answered with His promises. Anxiety is met with His faithfulness. Confusion is clarified through His truth. Over time, emotional life becomes more stable, not because feelings disappear, but because they are anchored in what is unchanging.

The Four Listening Postures That Sustain the U-Turn

As the U-Turn becomes a way of life, discernment is no longer something occasional; it becomes a daily grace. God, in His kindness, does not leave us to sort through the noise of life on our own. He draws near, teaching us through His Word and by His Spirit how to recognize His voice and follow Him with confidence. His leadership is not harsh or distant, but faithful, patient, and full of love. Within our inner life, there are different influences that shape how we think, feel, and respond, yet only God's Word carries final authority over them all. As we walk with Him, He lovingly brings clarity, helping us discern what is from Him and what must be brought into alignment with His truth.

"My sheep hear My voice, and I know them, and they follow Me." (John 10:27 NKJV).

The more we remain grounded in His Word and rest in His love, the more clearly, we recognize His voice and walk in faithful obedience.

1. Resistant Listening

Resistant listening occurs when truth is heard, yet the heart quietly pushes back. God may be speaking through His Word or through conviction, but something within holds onto control, comfort, or self-protection. In these moments, conviction can feel uncomfortable, and correction may seem difficult to receive. Yet even here, God's love remains steady. He does not withdraw when we resist; He patiently calls us to return. His correction is not to shame, but to restore.

"He who...hardens *his* neck, Will suddenly be destroyed, and that without remedy." (Proverbs 29:1 NKJV).

This warning reminds us of the seriousness of resisting truth, yet it is given so that we may turn and live. When the heart resists, repentance is hindered because repentance requires humility. But as resistance softens, the heart becomes teachable again. Truth begins to penetrate more deeply, gently exposing what needs to change. When the heart yields, even in small ways, the grace of God leads it back into alignment. This posture also shapes relationships. A heart that resists God often becomes guarded with others, but as humility grows, listening becomes more open and love begins to flow more freely.

2. Selective Listening

Selective listening allows truth to enter, but only partially. The heart receives what feels comfortable yet filters out what challenges control or requires deeper surrender. In this posture, we may hear God's Word, but we do not fully yield to it. In His patience, God continues to speak clearly through His Word. He does not adjust His truth to fit our comfort, but He faithfully leads us beyond it.

"But be doers of the word, and not hearers only, deceiving yourselves." (James 1:22 NKJV).

When listening is selective, renewal is limited. Growth slows because only the easier parts of truth are embraced. But as we allow God to remove these filters, trust deepens. We begin to receive His Word more fully, even when it stretches us. In relationships, selective listening often appears as partial attention. Words are heard, but assumptions shape understanding. Yet as God refines our listening, we begin to hear more clearly, both His truth and the hearts of others. Love matures where listening becomes whole.

3. Attentive Listening

Attentive listening reflects a heart that slows down and leans in. It is no longer reacting quickly but seeking to understand deeply. In this posture, the believer becomes willing to sit with God, to reflect, and to allow His truth to examine the inner life.

"Be swift to hear, slow to speak, slow to wrath." (James 1:19 NKJV).

Here, the mind begins to renew more deeply as everything is brought into the light of God's Word. Thoughts are no longer accepted without question but are tested in truth. Emotions are acknowledged, yet gently guided. Hidden assumptions are exposed, and truth begins to reshape the heart. This kind of listening is marked by humility and patience. It creates space for God's Word to speak more clearly. It also transforms relationships, as we begin to listen with greater care and compassion. Understanding grows, and love becomes more intentional and sincere.

4. Responsive Listening

Responsive listening reflects a heart that hears and follows. Trust has been established, and God's authority is settled in the heart, even when understanding is still growing.

"But be doers of the word, and not hearers only." (James 1:22 NKJV).

In this posture, truth moves from being heard to being lived. What God has spoken in His Word is not merely considered but obeyed. Obedience becomes a growing response, not driven by pressure, but shaped by love and reverence for God. As we respond with faithfulness, His truth becomes more deeply established in our lives.

Responsive listening is where transformation takes root, as what God has spoken is not only received, but faithfully lived out. What has been formed within begins to be expressed outwardly. Life increasingly reflects His work. In relationships, responses become more thoughtful, more patient, and more grounded in truth. This is the fruit of a life sustained by the U-Turn, a life that not only hears God's Word, but walks in it.

Listening Capacity and the Four Movements of the U-Turn

As the U-Turn becomes a way of life, God, in His kindness, continues to draw the heart deeper into alignment through one simple yet powerful posture, listening. This is not a strained effort to hear Him, but a gentle returning again and again to His voice as revealed through His Word and Spirit. In this journey back to the life we were created for, listening becomes the place where His truth meets us and leads us forward. Listening capacity shapes how deeply we receive and respond to what God is doing in each movement of the U-Turn. As we grow in attentiveness to Him, each movement becomes more steady, more anchored, and more life-giving.

Repentance requires a heart that is willing to release resistance and humbly receive truth. Receiving deepens as we let go of selective hearing and trust His Word fully. Renewal flourishes when we slow down and listen attentively, allowing His truth to reshape our thinking. Reproduction flows as we respond in obedience, allowing what God has done within us to be expressed through our lives.

"Today, if you will hear His voice, Do not harden your hearts." (Hebrews 3:15 NKJV).

The depth of our transformation is closely tied to our openness in receiving and responding to God's truth. As listening matures, alignment begins to stabilize. The spirit rests surrendered under His authority. The soul is continually renewed by truth rather than shaped by fear or distortion. The body follows with faithful, steady obedience. The mind remains anchored because it is continually hearing and responding to God through His Word. When listening weakens, drift quietly begins. But when listening remains open, transformation remains active and enduring. God does not call us to strive in our own strength, but to remain near to Him, listening and responding in faith. A heart that listens consistently will remain aligned, discerning, and fruitful over time. Listening is not simply how we hear, it is how we guard the mind, protect alignment, and walk in love with God and with others.

From Reaction to Governed Response: Emotional Stewardship in the U-Turn

As the U-Turn becomes a way of life, God's work reaches into the emotional life with great tenderness. He does not remove emotion; He redeems it. In His love, He teaches us not to be ruled by what we feel, but to be guided by His truth within what we feel. Emotion is not the problem in itself. It is often the doorway through which God reveals what is happening within the heart. Feelings can uncover fear, control, insecurity, or misplaced trust. Yet in His mercy, He does not leave us there. He gently leads us to bring every emotion under His truth, where it can be healed, reordered, and restored.

The goal is not emotional suppression, but faithful stewardship. We learn to recognize what we feel, bring it into His presence, and allow Him to reorder what is governing us. In each movement of the U-Turn, emotions surface because something is being surrendered, renewed, or entrusted to God.

Movement One

Repent — Surrendering to His Lordship

- Old Self — Reckoning the Flesh
- Fear — Rejecting the Spirit of Fear
- Control — Relinquishing Self-Reliance

Repentance often stirs deep emotion because authority is shifting within the heart. As the old self is confronted, feelings such as defensiveness, regret, or discomfort may arise. These are not signs of failure, but invitations to go deeper with God.

"For godly sorrow produces repentance *leading* to salvation, not to be regretted." (2 Corinthians 7:10 NKJV).

In His love, God meets us in these moments without condemnation. He gently reveals what needs to be surrendered, not to shame us, but to free us. Defensiveness can become a signal that pride may be being exposed. Fear reveals where trust is needed. Control uncovers areas where self-reliance must be released. Repentance is not emotional collapse; it is the loving realignment of the heart under God's authority.

As we respond to Him, even our emotions are brought into His redemptive work, no longer leading us away from Him, but drawing us closer as His truth restores the heart. Shame loses its hold, and humility takes root. What once felt heavy becomes a place of grace. Reaction begins to slow, and surrender becomes steadier. In this way, transformation reaches deeper, shaping not only what we do, but how we respond from within.

Movement Two

Receive — Hearing and Following God's Voice

- Identity — Who Am I in Christ?
- Calling — What Is My Calling?
- Gifts — What Has God Given Me?
- Direction — What Is My Next Step?

The movement of receiving often awakens vulnerability because identity, calling, gifts, and direction reach into the deepest places of the heart. As God reveals His truth through His Word and by His Spirit, emotions such as insecurity, hesitation, comparison, or fear of inadequacy may surface. These emotions are not signs that we are incapable. They reveal what has been shaping our understanding of ourselves apart from truth.

If insecurity leads, identity becomes uncertain. If comparison leads, gifts feel diminished. If fear leads, obedience is delayed. Emotional stewardship in this movement means allowing God's truth to define identity rather than past experiences or personal doubt. We receive what He has spoken without filtering it through fear, and we respond by trusting what He says about who we are and what He has entrusted to us.

"For God has not given us a spirit of fear, but of power and of love and of a sound mind." (2 Timothy 1:7 NKJV).

As fear is brought under truth and identity in Christ is embraced, the inner posture of the heart begins to shift from insecurity to confidence rooted in Him. Receiving becomes possible because truth, not emotion, is guiding the response. What God declares begins to settle more deeply, and the heart grows steady in who He is and who He has called us to be.

Movement Three

Renew — Living from a Transformed Mind

- Belief — Agreeing with God's Truth
- Mind — Renewing Thought Patterns
- Practice — Walking in the Spirit

Renewal is the ongoing work of aligning the mind with God's truth. What has been received must now be established. The patterns of thinking shaped by past experiences, fear, or worldly influence are not removed instantly, but they are steadily replaced as we bring them into the light of Scripture.

"Do not be conformed to this world, but be transformed by the renewing of your mind." (Romans 12:2 NKJV).

In this movement, emotional responses often reveal underlying beliefs. Anxiety may uncover misplaced trust. Frustration may expose unmet expectations. Confusion may point to areas where truth has not yet been fully established. These moments are not interruptions to growth. They are invitations to deeper renewal. As we bring our thoughts before God, we begin to test them against His Word. What is not true is surrendered. What is true is embraced. Over time, thinking becomes clearer, responses become steadier, and the inner life becomes more aligned with truth.

Renewal is not simply changing how we think but learning to live in agreement with what God has already declared as true. As the mind is renewed, walking in the Spirit becomes more consistent, not as an effort to perform, but as the natural outflow of a life shaped by truth.

Movement Four

Reproduce — From Personal Transformation to Kingdom Impact

- Abiding — Remaining in the Vine
- Modeling — Living What We Believe
- Discipleship — Walking Others Toward Christ
- Legacy — Leaving Kingdom Fruit That Remains

As the U-Turn becomes a way of life, transformation no longer remains within. What God has restored begins to extend into the lives of others. This movement is not about striving to influence, but about allowing His life within us to overflow naturally. The same grace that called us back now carries us forward into faithful participation in His work.

As this outward expression develops, new emotional tensions may arise. Responsibility, visibility, pressure, and even misunderstanding can stir feelings of insecurity or the subtle pull toward performance. Yet these emotions are not signs of failure. They are invitations to return again to abiding in Christ, where identity is secure and love remains constant. If approval begins to lead, the heart may become guarded. If comparison takes root, joy may quietly give way to competition. If insecurity rises, striving may attempt to replace surrender. But the way of the U-Turn always leads us back to abiding, not performing.

"He who abides in Me, and I in him, bears much fruit; for without Me you can do nothing." (John 15:5 NKJV).

Emotional stewardship in this movement means remaining near to Him. His presence steadies the heart, His truth defines identity, and His Spirit leads each step. From this place, what flows outward is not driven by pressure, but sustained by grace. Reproduction is not sustained by effort or emotion, but by abiding in Christ, where His life becomes the source of all lasting fruit. Leadership becomes steady, modeling becomes authentic, discipleship becomes life giving, and legacy reflects what God Himself has formed. The fruit that remains is not manufactured. It is the natural result of a life rooted deeply in Him.

The Sustained U-Turn

Across all four movements, emotion is normal and necessary. It often reveals what may be influencing the inner life at any given moment. When we learn to recognize emotion as a signal, bring it under God's truth, and allow Him to lovingly reestablish what governs the heart, the U-Turn becomes sustainable rather than situational. Repentance resets authority. Receiving restores identity. Renewal reshapes belief. Reproduction reorders influence.

From reaction to a response governed by God's truth, the heart begins to settle under His leadership. The spirit remains surrendered, the soul continues to be renewed, and the body expresses obedience with increasing consistency. Listening deepens because authority is secure. Obedience strengthens because identity is anchored. Peace stabilizes because governance is no longer divided. Transformation becomes more stable, no longer dependent on emotion, environment, or momentum. It is increasingly formed, aligned, and sustained under God's authority.

The U-Turn is sustained not by striving, but by a heart that continually returns to God's authority, truth, and presence. In this place, growth is not forced but faithfully formed over time as we walk with Him. The U-Turn does not end with personal alignment. What God restores within us is never meant to remain contained. As authority settles, alignment stabilizes, and listening matures, transformation begins to extend beyond the individual life. The same posture that shaped repentance, receiving, renewal, and reproduction now begins to shape relationships, leadership, and legacy. Personal transformation begins to be expressed in the lives of others. What has been governed internally begins to influence externally. The fruit of alignment multiplies not through striving, but through faithful stewardship of what God has already formed.

Part IV explores how the U-Turn expands without losing its heart. It examines how God takes what He has established in us and extends it into culture, community, discipleship, and enduring legacy. The journey continues, not by trying to become something new, but by faithfully walking in what has already been restored.

Reflection Questions

1. Where is the Lord gently inviting me to return to Him, not only in my actions, but in the posture of my heart and the way I listen?
2. In this season, which area of my life is the Holy Spirit drawing into deeper alignment under His loving authority, my spirit, my soul, or my body?
3. How attentive have I been to God's voice through His Word in my daily life, and how is that shaping the way I respond to Him and to others?
4. Are there any subtle filters such as fear, control, distraction, or familiarity that may be softening or dulling my sensitivity to His voice?
5. What is one clear, grace-filled step of obedience the Lord is inviting me to take, and how can I respond to Him with trust this week?

Prayer

Father God,

Teach me to listen with a yielded heart. Remove every filter that dulls my hearing, and align my spirit, soul, and body with

Your will. Give me the grace to respond in obedience and to walk in a true U-Turn that bears lasting fruit. Form in me a life that is steady, surrendered, and rooted in Your truth.

In Jesus' name, Amen.

Part IV — MULTIPLICATION

Practicing Transformation Without Losing the Heart

> "And the things that you have heard from me among many witnesses, commit these to faithful men who will be able to teach others also". — (2 Timothy 2:2 NKJV).

What God begins as personal transformation, He desires to multiply. What He restores in us, He also intends to express through us. As the U-Turn matures, God forms rhythms, relationships, and environments where transformation is not only sustained, but shared. What was once personal begins to take shape in community. What was once received is now lived and faithfully released through a life that remains yielded to Him.

Transformation is not meant to remain within us, but to be lived in such a way that others are drawn toward Christ through what He has done in us. In this way, a restored life becomes a witness, not through striving, but through faithful obedience and abiding in Him.

Here, transformation becomes a lived testimony that others can follow. Personal obedience strengthens the faith of others and builds up the community. As lives are restored, they begin to cultivate environments where others can encounter God's truth, grace, and transforming power. This is how God multiplies His work, through lives that remain aligned to Him and faithfully steward what He has formed within them.

Chapter 14 — The U-Turn Experience

> ***"As we stay connected to Him, His life shapes our thoughts, aligns our desires, and orders our steps according to His will."***

Living the Way of Jesus Together

The U-Turn is not merely a moment of decision but a lived experience that unfolds step by step as God faithfully leads His people back to the life they were created for. It is not produced by striving or human effort alone, but by His presence, His Word, and the quiet, steady work of His love. In this journey, we begin to see that God is not simply calling us to turn once, but to walk with Him daily, allowing Him to lead us with gentleness and truth.

Many begin by thinking transformation comes primarily through effort or understanding, yet the way of Jesus reveals that true change flows from abiding. It is in remaining with Him that our lives are formed. Jesus says,

> "Abide in Me, and I in you. As the branch cannot bear fruit of itself, unless it abides in the vine, neither can you, unless you abide in Me" (John 15:4 NKJV).

The U-Turn experience is rooted in this abiding life. As we stay connected to Him, His life shapes our thoughts, aligns our desires, and orders our steps according to His will. Transformation is not produced by pressure, but by the presence of God through His Spirit at work within us.

This journey is deeply personal, yet God, in His wisdom, leads us through relationships. He uses others to walk with us, to discern with us, and to gently guide us back to truth as revealed in His Word. In this, we reflect the way of Jesus, who formed His disciples through close and faithful relationships. Scripture reminds us, "*As* iron sharpens iron, So a man sharpens the countenance of his friend." (Proverbs 27:17 NKJV). Through these connections, we experience His care, His correction, and His encouragement in tangible ways. God is patient in the process, yet faithful to lead us forward in obedience, forming Christ within us according to His will. In one-to-one moments, He brings clarity and discernment, while in community He nurtures growth through encouragement, accountability, and love. Even in broader connections, He teaches us to trust Him as the One who leads each person uniquely and faithfully.

The beauty of the U-Turn experience is that it is not merely a system to follow, but a life to be lived with God. It is a life marked by abiding, shaped through relationship, and expressed through love. As this life is formed within us, it overflows into the lives of others, becoming both a witness and an invitation to encounter the restoring work of God. In this way, the U-Turn becomes not only something we experience, but something we carry with humility and faithfulness.

Formation Through Relationship, Not Information

When sin entered the world, the first fracture was not merely behavioral, but relational. Humanity turned away, yet God drew near, seeking to restore what was broken. From the beginning, His work of redemption has been rooted in relationship, where trust is renewed and fellowship with Him is restored.

For this reason, transformation does not come through information alone, but through truth received and lived in relationship. People are not changed simply by knowing more, but by encountering truth within love and walking it out in relationship. Scripture says, "speaking the truth in love, may grow up in all things into Him who is the head—Christ." (Ephesians 4:15 NKJV). Truth must be received in love to become formative in the heart. True transformation flows from relationship with God, not merely from information about Him.

Jesus Himself modeled this way. He formed His disciples through nearness, walking with them, teaching them, correcting them, and patiently leading them into truth. Even in their weakness, He remained faithful, and over time, they were transformed as they followed Him. As it is written,

> "that which we have seen and heard we declare to you, that you also may have fellowship with us; and truly our fellowship *is* with the Father and with His Son Jesus Christ" (1 John 1:3 NKJV).

This fellowship is the heart of formation.

The U-Turn Experience reflects this pattern. It creates space for people to walk in truth together, where growth is nurtured through presence, love, and faithful obedience rather than pressure or performance. God forms His people through His presence, not through pressure or performance, but through relationship that is anchored in His truth.

Abiding as the Foundation of All Growth

At the center of true transformation is abiding. Jesus said, "Abide in Me, and I in you... neither can you, unless you abide in Me." (John 15:4 NKJV). This is a call to remain close to Him, for apart from Him, we cannot bear lasting fruit.

The U-Turn Experience is sustained not by striving, but by abiding in Christ, expressed through faithful obedience. As His love is received, it renews the mind, aligns the heart, and strengthens us to walk in truth. When life becomes filled with noise, fear, or striving, abiding brings us back to stillness before Him and clarity rooted in His truth. "Be still, and know that I *am* God." (Psalm 46:10 NKJV). Every expression of the U-Turn flows from this foundation. Without abiding, activity becomes empty, but when we remain in Christ, growth becomes steady and enduring. Apart from abiding in Christ, there is no lasting fruit, but in Him, transformation becomes both sustained and fruitful. In His love, He faithfully leads us step by step back to the life we were created for.

The 14-Week U-Turn Discipleship Journey

The U-Turn is not merely a moment of decision, but a returning to God and a learning to walk with Him daily. Scripture reveals God's heart to restore and realign His people, "Return to Me, and I will return to you," Says the LORD of hosts (Malachi 3:7 NKJV). This invitation is one of grace, where God draws near and leads with faithfulness.

To help believers enter into this way of life, the U-Turn is experienced through a 14-week discipleship journey. This journey is not the destination, but a guided pathway that reflects a biblical pattern of transformation: awareness, alignment, response, and formation. Each week creates space for Scripture to lead as the final authority, along with prayer, reflection, and obedience, allowing truth to be received and lived out step by step. The journey is not about completing a process, but about walking in faithful response to God. This pathway is not built on striving, but on trusting the Lord.

> "Trust in the LORD with all your heart, And lean not on your own understanding; In all your ways acknowledge Him, and He shall direct your paths." (Proverbs 3:5–6 NKJV).

God leads patiently, bringing clarity and direction as each person yields to Him.

Transformation comes from God alone, by the work of the Holy Spirit, not from the structure itself.

"Being confident of this very thing, that He who has begun a good work in you will complete *it* until the day of Jesus Christ." (Philippians 1:6 NKJV).

The goal is not to complete fourteen weeks, but to learn how to walk daily with the Lord. This journey is often lived out within the context of a Life Group and under the spiritual care and oversight of the local church, providing care, accountability, and support as believers grow in truth and obedience.

The 14-Week U-Turn Discipleship Journey Overview

Phase	Week	Title	Focus
Foundation	Week 1	Introduction	Set expectations, create space, and prepare your heart for the journey
Awakening Your Present Awareness	Week 2	The Breaking That Became the Beginning	Recognize how God uses disruption to awaken alignment
	Week 3	Do Not Waste Your Pain	Learn how God uses pain to reveal what needs attention
Alignment Your Inner Life Restoration	Week 4	The Gap Between God's Design and Our Reality	Identify where your life is out of alignment
	Week 5	The Believer's Life Operating System	Understand how your inner life shapes your direction

	Week 6	When We Limit God	See where you have made God small
	Week 7	Awakening to Choice at Every Crossroad	Recognize the decisions shaping your direction
	Week 8	The U-Turn: God's Pathway to Lasting Transformation	Understand how realignment happens
	Week 9	The Reverse U-Turn: How We Lose Our Way	Identify patterns that lead to misalignment
Transformation Your Response	Week 10	Repent: Surrendering to His Lordship	Turn fully toward God
	Week 11	Receive: Hearing and Following God's Voice	Learn to recognize and follow His voice
	Week 12	Renew: Living from a Transformed Mind	Align your thinking with truth
	Week 13	Reproduce: From Personal Transformation to Kingdom Impact	Allow transformation to overflow into others
Multiplication Your Life Sustained Alignment	Week 14	When the U-Turn Becomes a Way of Life	Live a lifestyle of ongoing alignment and response

The 14-week schedule provides a clear and intentional pathway; however, based on specific needs, pace, and context, it may be prayerfully adjusted while maintaining the integrity of the journey. The 14-Week U-Turn Discipleship Journey serves as a beginning, helping establish a life of abiding in Christ. What God forms through this process continues beyond it, as each person is led forward in ongoing alignment, faithful obedience, and spiritual fruitfulness.

U-Turn One to One — Discernment in Personal Accompaniment

Throughout Scripture, God often brings guidance, wisdom, and growth through personal relationships. Moses received counsel from Jethro, Samuel was guided by Eli, and Timothy was strengthened through Paul. Jesus Himself, while ministering to many, gave intentional attention to individuals, calling them, teaching them, and walking with them in truth. This reflects a consistent biblical pattern in which God uses faithful relationships to strengthen, encourage, and guide His people.

U-Turn One to One creates space for this kind of intentional companionship. It is a place of listening, prayer, and seeking the Lord together. It is not about directing someone's life, but about helping one another discern and obey God's Word as guided by the Holy Spirit and grounded in Scripture. As it is written, "Therefore comfort each other and edify one another, just as you also are doing." (1 Thessalonians 5:11 NKJV). Discernment is strengthened as believers seek the Lord together in humility, remaining anchored in His Word.

In this relationship, the Holy Spirit, who works in agreement with Scripture, is the true Guide, and Scripture remains the foundation for all discernment. The one who walks alongside listens with care, prays with faith, and offers counsel that aligns with God's Word. "Where *there is* no counsel, the people fall; But in the multitude of counselors *there is* safety." (Proverbs 11:14 NKJV). Through wise and godly counsel that remains submitted to Scripture, clarity is strengthened and direction is guarded. At the same time, each believer is called to personally know and follow the Lord. Jesus said, "My sheep hear My voice, and I know them, and they follow Me." (John 10:27 NKJV). This reminds us that while others may encourage and support, each person is responsible, by God's grace, to walk in obedience to Christ. The goal is not dependence on people, but faithful dependence on God.

What U-Turn One to One Is

U-Turn One to One is a space of spiritual companionship where believers come alongside one another to seek the Lord through prayer, Scripture, and mutual encouragement. It reflects the heart of biblical fellowship, where truth is shared in love and lives are strengthened in Christ. In this space, growth is nurtured through presence, faith, and obedience as God leads each person step by step. It is a place where believers help one another remain attentive to God, anchored in His Word, and responsive to His leading.

What U-Turn One to One Is Not

U-Turn One to One is not a place for professional counseling, legal advice, medical guidance, or financial direction. It does not replace pastoral leadership, spiritual oversight, clinical care, or licensed support when such care is needed. Instead, it remains within its biblical purpose, offering encouragement and guidance rooted in Scripture while honoring the role of qualified professionals in their respective fields. U-Turn One to One provides spiritual encouragement and biblical guidance, and is not a substitute for professional counseling, legal, medical, or financial advice.

When a situation goes beyond the capacity or responsibility of a U-Turn One to One guide, it should be prayerfully and wisely brought to the attention of local church leadership or elders. In this way, care remains accountable, supported, and rightly ordered within the body of Christ. As it is written, "Obey those who rule over you, and be submissive, for they watch out for your souls." (Hebrews 13:17 NKJV).

U-Turn Life Group — Practicing Transformation in Community

Jesus formed His disciples in community. They did not grow through private instruction alone, but through shared life. They walked together, asked questions, misunderstood, learned, failed, and were restored together. In this way, transformation unfolded not only through what was taught, but through what was lived side by side in His presence, as Christ worked within them and shaped their lives. The early Church continued in this same rhythm, devoting themselves to teaching, fellowship, prayer, and daily life together. Scripture says, "And they continued steadfastly in the apostles' doctrine and fellowship, in the breaking of bread, and in prayers." (Acts 2:42 NKJV). Formation was not isolated, but relational, patient, and rooted in a shared life with God and one another. God's work in us is often strengthened through the life we share with others.

The U-Turn Life Group is designed to reflect this pattern. It creates a space where the movements of the U-Turn are practiced together in daily life. Through Scripture, reflection, prayer, and honest conversation, participants learn, by the grace of God and the work of the Holy Spirit, to walk in repentance, receive God's truth, renew their minds, and live in obedience. This growth remains rooted in God's Word, as Scripture renews the mind and directs the path. What is formed personally begins to take shape relationally, as faith is lived out in community. Transformation is not produced by community itself, but through Christ working in and among His people as they gather around His Word.

Community offers what isolation cannot. It brings encouragement when faith feels weak, loving and biblical accountability that calls one another back to truth, and grace when growth feels slow. As it is written, "And let us consider one another in order to stir up love and good works." (Hebrews 10:24 NKJV). In this shared journey, hearts are strengthened, and truth is reinforced through mutual care and encouragement. Transformation becomes a shared journey rather than a solitary burden. God often uses the presence of His people to strengthen the work He is doing within each heart.

What U-Turn Life Group Leaders Can Do

U-Turn Life Group leaders facilitate a space for spiritual growth through Scripture, prayer, and fellowship. They guide discussion, encourage participation, and help keep the group anchored in God's Word. Their role is to cultivate an environment marked by humility, trust, and love, where each person is encouraged to grow in their walk with the Lord.

Leaders also model a life of faith and obedience, offering encouragement and gentle accountability in alignment with Scripture. As it is written, "Shepherd the flock of God which is among you, serving as overseers... being examples to the flock." (1 Peter 5:2–3 NKJV). In this way, leadership is expressed through service and example, not control over personal decisions. Leaders create space for God to work through Scripture, prayer, and faithful guidance, but do not take the place of God in a person's life. At the same time, Life Group leaders are called to walk in alignment with the local church, faithfully following its guiding principles and any related requirements. This helps preserve unity, order, and wise spiritual care within the life of the church, allowing the group to remain anchored in the broader body of Christ.

What U-Turn Life Group Should Not Do

U-Turn Life Group is not designed to provide professional counseling, legal advice, medical guidance, or financial direction. It does not replace pastoral leadership, spiritual oversight, clinical care, or licensed services when such support is needed. While leaders may offer biblical encouragement, they do not give direction in areas that require professional or licensed expertise.

When a situation goes beyond the capacity or responsibility of the Life Group, it should be prayerfully and promptly brought to the attention of local church leadership or elders. In this way, care remains wise, accountable, and rightly ordered within the body of Christ. As Scripture reminds us, "Obey those who rule over you, and be submissive, for they watch out for your souls." (Hebrews 13:17 NKJV). This clarity protects both people and purpose. It allows the Life Group to remain focused on spiritual formation, fellowship, and encouragement, while honoring the role of qualified professionals and church leadership where appropriate. Clear boundaries help preserve a safe, healthy, and Christ-centered environment for growth.

In this way, the U-Turn Life Group becomes a place where what God is doing in individual lives is strengthened, sustained, and multiplied through community. As believers walk together in truth and love, they are gently led forward, step by step, into the life God has prepared for them to walk in. Over time, what is formed in community not only strengthens each life but becomes a testimony that can be shared with others.

U-Turn Alumni Fellowship

The U-Turn Alumni Fellowship is a relational gathering of believers who have completed the 14-Week U-Turn Discipleship Journey and desire to continue walking in alignment with Christ through His Word and in obedience to Him. It is a space for those who have been formed through the journey to remain connected, encouraged, and rooted in a shared life of abiding in Christ. The U-Turn journey does not end at the completion of fourteen weeks. What God begins in the heart by His grace, He is faithful to continue and bring to maturity as we walk with Him over time. The Alumni Fellowship provides a place where this ongoing work can be nurtured through relationship, prayer, and faithful encouragement.

Throughout Scripture, believers are called to continue together in faith, strengthening one another as they walk with the Lord. As it is written,

> "And let us consider one another in order to stir up love and good works, not forsaking the assembling of ourselves together." (Hebrews 10:24–25 NKJV).

This reflects the heart of fellowship, where lives are built up through encouragement, presence, and shared devotion to God. Transformation in Christ is not sustained in isolation but strengthened as believers walk together in truth and love.

The U-Turn Alumni Fellowship is not a program to maintain, but a continuation of a life that has been formed. It creates space for believers to share testimonies, pray, and encourage one another in truth. In this environment, what God has begun is strengthened through ongoing relationship. This fellowship is not about structure, but about continuing to walk with God together in faith and obedience. At the center of this fellowship is abiding in Christ. Jesus said,

> "Abide in Me, and I in you. As the branch cannot bear fruit of itself, unless it abides in the vine, neither can you, unless you abide in Me." (John 15:4 NKJV).

As believers remain in Him and walk in responsive obedience, growth continues and fruit is produced in its proper season. This fellowship also becomes a place where what has been received begins to overflow into others. As lives are strengthened, believers are able to encourage and walk alongside those beginning their own journey. In this way, multiplication flows from faithful living, not striving. The U-Turn Alumni Fellowship remains connected to and under the guidance of local church leadership, honoring biblical shepherding, accountability, and care within the body of Christ.

What God forms in us through abiding is never meant to remain contained, but to be faithfully lived out and shared for His glory. As believers continue together in truth, love, and obedience, this fellowship becomes a living expression of ongoing formation, where faith is sustained, relationships are strengthened, and the work of God continues to unfold.

Reflection Questions

1. Where have I depended on spiritual moments or breakthroughs rather than cultivating a steady, daily walk of formation with Jesus?
2. What internal noise, fear, or striving may be dulling my ability to hear and trust God's voice in this season?
3. Which area of my life is the Holy Spirit gently inviting into greater surrender and obedience under the lordship of Christ?
4. How willing am I to allow others to walk with me in this process of transformation rather than carrying it alone?
5. How might God be calling what He is forming within me to be shared as life, love, and witness to others?

Prayer

Jesus,

Thank You for calling me into a life of formation, not performance. Quiet my heart so I can hear You clearly. Help me yield every area of my life to Your loving leadership and walk faithfully with others as You shape me. Let what You are doing in me bear fruit for Your Kingdom, in Your time and Your way.

In the name of Jesus, Amen.

Chapter 15 — U-Turn Equipping

> ***"Equipping exists not to direct the Spirit, but to make room for His work to continue in health and freedom."***

Stewarding Transformation with Reverence and Love

God does not rush the work He does in the human heart, nor does He entrust that work casually. Throughout Scripture, restoration is often followed by a quiet and weighty invitation to walk with others in the same patience, mercy, and faithfulness one has first received. This invitation is never about elevation or recognition. It is a call to stewardship. It requires humility, spiritual discernment, and a settled confidence that God alone is the true agent of transformation. As Scripture reminds us, "I planted, Apollos watered, but God gave the increase." (1 Corinthians 3:6 NKJV). Any human participation is always secondary, supportive, and responsive to the leading of the Holy Spirit.

U-Turn Equip exists because transformation that is not carefully stewarded can become fragile, misdirected, or overly dependent on people rather than on God. While the Spirit brings conviction, healing, and renewal, Scripture reveals that God often uses faithful presence and mature guidance to guard and nurture what He is forming. Equipping, then, is not about producing leaders who know more or do more. It is about forming servants who listen more attentively, love more patiently, and consistently point others back to Jesus Christ as the one true Source of life and growth. U-Turn Equip is shaped by reverence for God's timing, deep respect for the human heart, and unwavering trust in the Spirit's faithful work.

Why Equipping Matters

Spiritual formation is holy ground. It touches the most tender places of the inner life where repentance, hope, obedience, and healing converge. Scripture repeatedly cautions against handling these sacred spaces carelessly. Teachers are warned to teach with humility. Shepherds are instructed to lead gently. Leaders are reminded that authority in the Kingdom of God is expressed through service rather than control. When Paul writes that leaders are given to equip the saints for the work of ministry, he is not describing a substitute for the Spirit's work, but a support for it. Equipping exists not to direct the Spirit, but to make room for His work to continue in health and freedom.

The goal is not to draw people toward ourselves, but to help them remain rooted in Christ, where true growth is sustained by Him alone. In its truest form, equipping protects the work of God within people. It guards against dependency on personalities, manipulation through pressure, and exhaustion born of striving. Wise equipping creates environments where growth can continue even when guidance steps back, because faith has been anchored in God rather than in human effort.

U-Turn Equip is designed for those who sense a call to walk alongside others with wisdom, patience, and care. It acknowledges that not everyone is called to accompany others in the same way, but those who are must be formed before they function. Spiritual maturity must precede spiritual responsibility. Reverence for God's work must come before activity done in God's name. Only then can equipping remain a gift rather than a burden, and a safeguard rather than a source of harm.

The U-Turn One to One Guide

The U-Turn One to One Guide reflects the biblical pattern of spiritual accompaniment. This role is not about providing answers, fixing problems, or directing outcomes. It is about helping another person become more attentive to God's presence and voice in their own life. Guides are trained to listen beneath words, to discern, in light of Scripture, where the Spirit may be leading toward repentance, trust, or obedience, and to remain present with patience without rushing the process. They resist the urge to rescue or advise prematurely, trusting that God reveals truth in His time and according to His wisdom.

This role requires deep inner formation. Guides must remain aware of their own inner responses, spiritual habits, and areas of growth. They learn to minister from humility rather than expertise, remembering that Jesus Himself often responded to questions with questions, inviting reflection rather than mere compliance. Like Philip walking alongside the Ethiopian official, the Guide helps another recognize what God is saying and then steps back in humility, continuing in prayer and support while trusting the Spirit to complete the work without control.

The U-Turn Life Group Leader

The U-Turn Life Group Leader serves as a steward of spiritual environment rather than a producer of outcomes. Transformation in community requires safety, consistency, and trust, and these conditions must be guarded with care. Leaders are equipped to foster these environments by guiding conversation with wisdom, honoring vulnerability, and anchoring the group in Scripture and prayer. They learn how to hold tension when questions arise, how to respond to pain without rushing to fix it, and how to encourage obedience without pressure or shame.

This role reflects the life of the early Church, where believers devoted themselves to shared life, teaching, prayer, and fellowship. Healthy leaders understand that they are not the center of the group. Christ is. Their task is to keep the group oriented toward Him through faithful presence, attentive listening, and quiet trust that the Spirit works powerfully through ordinary obedience and shared discernment.

The U-Turn Classes Facilitator

The U-Turn Classes Facilitator plays a vital role in helping believers move from understanding truth to embodying it. This role is not primarily about delivering information but about shepherding engagement with Scripture and guiding reflection that leads to lived obedience. Facilitators are trained to ask questions that open the heart rather than close it, helping participants explore how God's Word intersects with daily decisions, habits, and relationships.

Following the pattern of Jesus, facilitators allow space for wrestling, insight, and growth. They recognize that transformation is rarely immediate and often unfolds through repeated exposure to truth lived out in community. This role supports the integration of faith into everyday life, where obedience becomes visible, practiced, and enduring rather than theoretical.

A Shared Posture of Stewardship

U-Turn Equip is not an invitation to authority or visibility, but to responsibility. Those who step into this role do so as fellow pilgrims, not as those who have arrived. They continue to yield, to listen, and to be formed even as they walk alongside others. The work belongs to God. The timing belongs to God. The fruit belongs to God. Our role is faithfulness. As Jesus taught, the greatest in the Kingdom are those who serve with humility. U-Turn Equip forms a posture of stewardship marked by reverence, patience, and love.

True multiplication flows not from striving, but from abiding in Christ, where the life of God produces fruit that remains. Yet stewardship is not the destination. What God forms within us is meant to be expressed through us. When growth moves ahead of formation, it loses its foundation. But when lives remain rooted in Christ, fruit emerges in its proper time and endures.

Chapter 16 The Life That Multiplies turns our attention to this outward expression. It reveals how a life formed through surrender begins to multiply without losing its foundation. The work of the Kingdom is not driven by pressure, scale, or performance, but by obedience and alignment with God. As we step into multiplication, we are not called to build something for God, but to participate in what He is already doing. What He has formed through humility and faithfulness extends outward, carrying the same heart. In this, we do not simply multiply a pathway, but a life, one that remains yielded, grounded in truth, and led by the Spirit. This is how the Kingdom grows, quietly, faithfully, and in His perfect time.

Reflection Questions

1. How do I currently view my role in the spiritual growth of others: as a helper pointing to God, or as a problem-solver responsible for outcomes?
2. In what ways might God be inviting me to steward His work in others with greater patience, humility, and trust in the Holy Spirit?
3. Where do I sense a tension between activity for God and attentiveness to God, and how might equipping begin with deeper listening rather than doing?
4. Which posture do I need to grow in most as I walk alongside others: reverence, restraint, compassion, or discernment?

5. How is God forming me even now to serve others faithfully without losing my dependence on Him?

Prayer

Lord Jesus,

You are the One who brings true transformation. We release the need to control outcomes and trust the work You are doing in us and through us. Teach us to steward Your work with humility, patience, and love. Guard our hearts from striving or pride and keep us attentive to Your Spirit. As we walk alongside others, help us listen well, serve faithfully, and always point back to You as the true Source of life and growth. We place this calling in Your hands, trusting Your timing and Your ways.

In the name of Jesus, Amen.

Chapter 16 — The Life That Multiplies

"The life that multiplies is not measured by visibility or speed, but by faithfulness over time."

The U-Turn was never only about returning; it was about becoming. What begins as a turning back to God becomes a life rooted in Him, and a life rooted in Him will multiply. This is the fulfillment of the journey, not arrival, but overflow. The life you were created for is not only restored but also released. From the beginning, God's design has always been life that bears fruit and increases. Yet He never separates multiplication from intimacy or fruitfulness from formation. What He multiplies is first formed in the hidden place, shaped through surrender, obedience, and daily abiding. The life that multiplies is not built by striving but grows from staying connected to the Source.

The danger is not multiplication, but multiplication without formation. When growth moves ahead of abiding, it may expand outwardly for a time, but it cannot sustain what it produces. God is not moved by scale; He is attentive to the heart and to whether life flows from abiding in Him. The U-Turn brings us back again and again to where life truly flows, not from effort or ambition, but from communion with Him.

This is where the journey leads. Not to a finished place, but to a living one. A life aligned, surrendered, and continually returning to God becomes a life in which Christ lives and is made visible. And a life in which Christ is made visible will multiply.

Abiding Comes Before Multiplying

The life that multiplies is first a life that abides. Jesus makes this clear when He says,

> "Abide in Me, and I in you. As the branch cannot bear fruit of itself, unless it abides in the vine, neither can you, unless you abide in Me." (John 15:4 NKJV).

In the Kingdom of God, fruit is not produced through striving, speed, or effort. It flows from abiding in Christ and walking in responsive obedience to Him. When we remain in Him, His life moves through us. When that connection weakens, even subtly, activity may continue, but life begins to fade.

The U-Turn begins here. Before it becomes a pathway, a framework, or something shared with others, it is a return to the vine. It is a posture of the heart that chooses dependence over self-reliance and love over performance. Jesus does not ask us to produce fruit for Him. He calls us to remain with Him. From that place, fruit is not a demand, but a promise.

Abiding is not preparation for fruitfulness; it is the very place from which all true fruit is born. This is why the U-Turn has always led us toward slowness, listening, repentance, and attentiveness to the Spirit. These are not obstacles to growth; they are what sustain it. They guard the source of life within us. As this book comes to a close, the invitation remains simple and unchanging. Stay with Him. The life you were created for is found there, and the life that remains in Him will multiply.

Formation Protects the Heart of the Mission

The life that multiplies is first a life that has been formed. Jesus never rushed the shaping of His disciples. He walked with them through misunderstanding, failure, and growth, patiently forming their hearts before entrusting them with greater responsibility. In the Kingdom of God, formation always comes before multiplication. Without it, what increases is activity. With it, what multiplies is a Christlike life.

The U-Turn preserves this order. Transformation comes before transmission. Hearts are shaped before lives are sent. God's concern is not how much we accomplish, but who we become as we walk with Him. What He forms in us determines what will flow through us.

This is why practices such as prayer rooted in Scripture, attentive listening to God, discernment, repentance, and accountability remain central. They are not additions to the mission; they protect it. They keep the heart aligned so that what is multiplied carries His presence, not pressure, His peace, not performance. When formation remains at the center, multiplication stays true to its source. The life that multiplies does not drift into striving or ambition, but continues to reflect the patience, gentleness, and faithfulness of God.

Community Sustains Growth Over Time

The life that multiplies is not lived in isolation. From the beginning, God designed growth to flourish within relationship. As Scripture says, "As iron sharpens iron, So a man sharpens the countenance of his friend." (Proverbs 27:17 NKJV). Multiplication that endures is rooted in shared life, not just shared activity. Structured efforts may help initiate movement, but relationships sustain life.

The U-Turn was never meant to be walked alone. It is formed and strengthened in community, where there is space for honesty, encouragement, correction, and discernment. In these relationships, hearts remain soft, faith stays grounded, and alignment is continually restored.

When growth moves ahead of relationship, it often leads to exhaustion and fragmentation. But when community remains central, multiplication becomes steady and life-giving. It is no longer driven by pressure but sustained by grace. The life that multiplies is a life that walks with others. Together, we return, listen, and grow. In this, God forms not only individuals, but a people who reflect His heart, and through that shared life, His work continues to multiply over time.

Kingdom Legacy Over Personal Success

The life that multiplies is not measured by visibility or speed, but by faithfulness over time. Jesus pointed to seeds planted quietly, to obedience practiced in secret, and to fruit that comes in its proper season. As Paul writes,

> "And the things that you have heard from me among many witnesses, commit these to faithful men who will be able to teach others also." (2 Timothy 2:2 NKJV).

This is the pattern of Kingdom multiplication, life entrusted to life, generation to generation.

This kind of multiplication is not hurried or self-promoting. It is relational, intentional, and rooted in what God has formed within. The U-Turn leads us into this way of living, where what we have received is carried with humility into every place God sends us, into homes, churches, workplaces, and beyond.

The life that multiplies is not built on visibility, but on faithfulness to Christ over time. This is not about building something for us. It is about stewarding what belongs to God. When legacy becomes the focus, the heart remains guarded, the work stays humble, and love remains the motive. What is formed in abiding, strengthened in community, and entrusted through faithfulness will bear fruit that remains. The life that multiplies carries both fruitfulness and tenderness, because it flows from God's love and is sustained by His grace.

Reflection Questions

1. When you think about growth or multiplication, what emotions surface first, peace, pressure, excitement, or fear? What might those emotions reveal about your posture?
2. In what ways has God been forming your heart quietly, beneath the surface, during this season?
3. Where might you be tempted to move ahead of abiding, to act, teach, lead, or multiply before remaining fully anchored in Christ?
4. How do you discern the difference between Spirit-led multiplication and ambition-driven expansion in your own life?
5. What safeguards help you remain rooted in humility and dependence on God as your influence or responsibility increases?

Prayer

Lord,

We place everything we have become and everything You may do through us back into Your hands. Keep our hearts tender, our motives pure, and our roots deep in You. Teach us to abide before we act, to listen before we lead, and to trust You with the fruit. May what multiply through our lives carry Your heart, reflect Your love, and remain by Your grace. We choose faithfulness over visibility, surrender over control, and Your way over our own.

In Jesus' name, Amen.

Appendix A — Believer's Life Operating System Assessment Questions

Name: ____________________ ***Date:*** ______________

#	Category	Subcategory	Statement	Score (1-5)
1	**Holy Spirit**	Revelation	I am attentive and responsive as the Holy Spirit reveals truth throughout my day	
2		Guidance	I am learning to seek the Lord first in decisions, allowing His Spirit to direct my steps rather than relying on my own understanding	
3		Empowering	I actively depend on the Holy Spirit's power to live out what God calls me to do, rather than relying on my own strength	
4		Conviction	When the Holy Spirit brings correction, I respond with humility and realign my life to God's truth	
5	**Spirit**	Identity in Christ	I live from my identity in Christ rather than being shaped by performance, approval, or comparison	
6		Identity in Christ	When challenged or unsettled, I return to what God has established as true about me in Christ	
7		Righteousness by Grace	I relate to God from the righteousness given through Christ, not from	

			striving to earn His acceptance	
8		Indwelling Presence	I live with growing awareness that the Holy Spirit dwells within me, shaping how I think and respond	
9		Truth as Foundation	God's Word governs how I form beliefs, interpret situations, and make decisions	
10	**Soul**	Mind	I regularly examine my thoughts in light of God's truth rather than assumptions or past patterns	
11		Mind	My perspective is increasingly shaped by truth rather than by circumstances or emotional reactions	
12		Will	I choose obedience to God even when it is difficult or not fully understood	
13		Will	I follow through on what God leads me to do, not only what I intend to do	
14		Emotions	I acknowledge my emotions honestly without allowing them to govern my decisions	
15		Emotions	I bring my emotions under God's truth, allowing them to settle into peace over time	
16	**Body**	Surrender	I am learning to present my life to God, offering my actions and choices to Him	

17		Yielding	I yield my actions and decisions to God, allowing my life to reflect His direction	
18		Obedience	I consistently act on what God reveals, allowing truth to be expressed through what I do	
19		Walk	My daily life reflects a growing pattern shaped by the Spirit rather than by impulse or pressure	
20		Stewardship of Life	I steward my time, energy, and responsibilities in a way that reflects God's priorities and leading	

Rating Scale

Score	Description
1	Rarely true
2	Occasionally true
3	Sometimes true
4	Often true
5	Consistently true

Score Summary

Category	Max Score	Your Score
Holy Spirit (Source)	20	
Spirit (Foundation)	25	
Soul (Alignment)	30	
Body (Expression)	25	
Total	100	

Understanding Your Total Score

Score Range	Operating State	Summary	Next Step
80–100	**Steady Operating Alignment**	Your Believer's Life Operating System is functioning in a steady and aligned way, flowing from the Holy Spirit through to consistent daily expression.	Remain attentive and responsive, allowing God to deepen and strengthen this alignment.
60–79	**Forming Operating Alignment**	Your Believer's Life Operating System is functioning, but not consistently. Alignment is present, though sometimes shaped by pressure or habit.	Return intentionally to the Holy Spirit as your starting point and stand in what is established in Christ.
40–59	**Inconsistent Operating Flow**	Alignment is present, but the flow is often disrupted. Truth may be known but not consistently lived, leading to inner and outward inconsistency.	Restore order at the source by returning to the Holy Spirit and allowing truth to be reestablished within.

Appendix B — Pre–U-Turn Assessment Questions

Name: ______________________ **Date:** ______________

#	Category	Sub-category	Statement	Score
1	**Awareness**	Spiritual Awareness	I am aware when my thoughts, attitudes, or actions are not aligned with God's truth	
2		Spiritual Awareness	When I recognize misalignment, I turn to God rather than ignoring or justifying it	
3		Openness	I am willing to acknowledge areas where I need repentance and change	
4		Readiness	I am willing to submit every area of my life to God's authority	
5	**Repent**	Old Self	I recognize patterns of the old way of living that are not consistent with my life in Christ	
6		Old Self	When sin or misalignment is revealed, I confess it and turn from it before God	
7		Fear	I choose to trust God and do not allow fear to direct my decisions	
8		Control	I entrust my plans and outcomes to God rather than relying on my own control	

9	**Receive**	Identity	I understand that my identity is found in Christ and not in my performance or circumstances	
10		Purpose	I seek God's will in my decisions through His Word and prayer	
11		Gifts	I use the abilities and opportunities God has given me to serve others faithfully	
12		Direction	When I understand what God is leading me to do, I choose to obey	
13	**Renew**	Belief	I choose to believe what God's Word says even when it challenges my own thinking	
14		Mind	I allow my thinking to be shaped and renewed by God's truth	
15		Practice	I maintain regular practices such as prayer and Scripture that keep me grounded in God	
16		Practice	In difficult situations, I seek to respond in a way that honors God rather than reacting impulsively	
17	**Reproduce**	Abiding	I maintain a consistent relationship with God through prayer and His Word	
18		Modeling	My daily life reflects my faith in Christ in both words and actions	

19		Discipleship	I intentionally encourage and help others grow in their faith	
20		Legacy	I desire my life to bear lasting fruit that honors God and impacts others	

Rating Scale

Score	Description
1	Rarely true
2	Sometimes true
3	Often true
4	Consistently true
5	Established pattern

Score Summary

Add your responses and record your total: Total Score: ______ / 100. This score provides a general picture of how your life is currently functioning.

Understanding Your Total Score

Score Range	Condition	Description
80–100	Aligned	Your life is generally ordered by God's truth and expressed with consistency. Continue to remain faithful and attentive to Him.
60–79	Strengthening	There is evidence of alignment, though not yet consistent. Continue to return to God and walk in what you know to be true.
40–59	Unsettled	You understand truth but do not live it consistently. This is a call to return and allow God to restore order within.

20–39	Disordered	Your life is not functioning in its intended order. This is an invitation to turn back to God and begin again with Him.

About the Author

Sunny Wu Lawson is an author, biblical transformation coach, executive coach, and speaker who helps people break free from old patterns and live the life God created for them.

Her message was born from her own turning point. When Sunny returned to God, she discovered not condemnation, but the restoring grace of a faithful Father. That encounter became the foundation of the U-Turn Framework, a biblical pathway of Repent, Receive, Renew, and Reproduce that helps people rebuild trust in God and renew their minds from the inside out.

Sunny brings more than twenty years of corporate leadership experience across international organizations to equip individuals, leaders, and organizations for lasting change.

Sunny lives in the St. Louis area with her husband, Pastor Erik Lawson, Senior and Founding pastor at Element Church, and their golden retriever, Xiaobao.

Her passion is helping people return to God and live with purpose, freedom, and hope.

www.ingramcontent.com/pod-product-compliance
Lightning Source LLC
LaVergne TN
LVHW090312210926
848480LV00001B/222